MACMILLAN STUDIES IN TWENTIETH-CENTURY LITERATURE

Michael Black
D. H. LAWRENCE: THE EARLY FICTION

Carolyn Bliss
PATRICK WHITE'S FICTION

Laurie Clancy
THE NOVELS OF VLADIMIR NABOKOV

Peter J. Conradi
IRIS MURDOCH: THE SAINT AND THE ARTIST

Clare Hanson
SHORT STORIES AND SHORT FICTIONS, 1880–1980

Dominic Hibberd
OWEN THE POET

David Leon Higdon
SHADOWS OF THE PAST IN CONTEMPORARY BRITISH FICTION

Oddvar Holmesland
A CRITICAL INTRODUCTION TO HENRY GREEN'S NOVELS

Holger Klein with John Flower and Eric Homberger (*editors*)
THE SECOND WORLD WAR IN FICTION

Simon Loveday
THE ROMANCES OF JOHN FOWLES

Harold Orel
THE LITERARY ACHIEVEMENT OF REBECCA WEST

Tony Pinkney
WOMEN IN THE POETRY OF T. S. ELIOT

Alan Sandison
GEORGE ORWELL: AFTER 1984

Lars Ole Sauerberg
SECRET AGENTS IN FICTION

Linda M. Shires
BRITISH POETRY OF THE SECOND WORLD WAR

Patrick Swinden
THE ENGLISH NOVEL OF HISTORY AND SOCIETY,
1940–80

Eric Warner (*editor*)
VIRGINIA WOOLF: A CENTENARY PERSPECTIVE

Terry Whalen
PHILIP LARKIN AND ENGLISH POETRY

Anne Wright
LITERATURE OF CRISIS, 1910–22

Further titles in preparation

Series Standing Order

If you would like to receive future titles in this series as they are published, you can make use of our standing order facility. To place a standing order please contact your bookseller or, in case of difficulty, write to us at the address below with your name and address and the name of the series. Please state with which title you wish to begin your standing order. (If you live outside the UK we may not have the rights for your area, in which case we will forward your order to the publisher concerned.)

Standing Order Service, Macmillan Distribution Ltd, Houndmills, Basingstoke, Hampshire, RG21 2XS, England.

A CRITICAL INTRODUCTION TO HENRY GREEN'S NOVELS

The Living Vision

Oddvar Holmesland

M
MACMILLAN

First published 1986

Published by
THE MACMILLAN PRESS LTD
Houndmills, Basingstoke, Hampshire RG21 2XS
and London
Companies and representatives
throughout the world

Typeset by Wessex Typesetters
(Division of The Eastern Press Ltd)
Frome, Somerset

Printed in Hong Kong

British Library Cataloguing in Publication Data
Holmesland, Oddvar
A critical introduction to Henry Green's novels:
the living vision. – (Macmillan studies in twentieth-century literature)
1. Green, Henry *1905–1973* – Criticism and
interpretation
I. Title
823′.912   PR6013.R416Z/
ISBN 0–333–39093–8

Contents

Preface

This work was originally submitted as a doctoral thesis at the University of Edinburgh in 1983, but has been somewhat revised for adaptation to book form. Discussions of previous critical assessments of Green's novels are reduced to a minimum, but the main line of argument has been retained.

Henry Green, whose real name was Henry Vincent Yorke, was born near Tewkesbury in Gloucestershire in 1905 and lived to the age of sixty-eight. He was the third son of a Birmingham industrialist, was educated at Eton and Oxford, and later became the managing director of the family business. His sympathies for the proletarian characters in his novels grew from his experiences as a foundry worker, a kind of life he found more stimulating than bookish studies. During the Second World War he was an active member of the Auxiliary Fire Service.

Yet one looks in vain into his background for explanations of how he became such an intensely original writer. Little is revealed except that he was a businessman who wrote poetic fiction behind a pseudonym during the lunch-hour lest people should discover who he was. He was as private and mysterious as his novels; he carefully avoided photographers; when asked by an interviewer if he would consent to be photographed from the rear, he retorted, 'And a wag said: "I'd know that back anywhere"' (*Writers at Work: The Paris Review Interviews*, 5 (Harmondsworth, 1981) p.101).

What little information Green gave about his private thoughts makes an enticing background for a study of his art. The book opens with a comprehensive introductory chapter in which several complex issues are explored. It sets out to highlight the close relation between Green's fundamental ideas of life and his narrative technique. Considerable space is given to elaboration on the close connection between his dynamic visualization and the effect of film. The problem of 'tone' is shown to be clarified by a critical model based on montage theories which incorporate principles of film, poetry and painting. Five chapters (out of seven) are devoted to the examination of tone in Green's novels. They demonstrate that only a montage approach can provide the key to understanding his fiction. Perhaps the reader will find this analysis uncommonly detailed and exhaustive. But Green has gained a reputation as one of the most elusive and enigmatic novelists in contemporary literature, and I have found it necessary to try and refute such assumptions by looking into every obscure alley. I hope this book will convince the reader that Green's major fiction forms a coherent thematic and technical whole. *Blindness* and *Pack my Bag* are considered of minor importance and receive only cursory attention as part of the introductory chapter. In the chapter on *Living*, Green's use of symbolism and imagery is analysed and various types of montage conflicts thoroughly introduced and applied. Green's re-creation, in *Caught*, of the London of 1940 is not limited to the objective presentation of a representative atmosphere. The inability of ordinary prose to convey the emotional impact of an experience is the motivation behind Green's extensive use of visual montage in this novel. A brief examination of *Back* (in the same chapter) elucidates the close connection between form and content, especially the author's reasons for *not* employing montage. *Loving* is a comic novel, but one in which the reader's perception of values is reinforced through life's uncertainties and contrasts. Moments of poetic significance reflect the author's creative commitment to his world. *Concluding* is not a pessimistic comment on empirical reality, as most critics have assumed, but a world in which images of contradiction enact moments of human significance that provide hope of reintegration. The novel presents a vision that subordinates empiricism to the effect of wonder. *Party Going*, *Nothing* and *Doting* are examined in one chapter because of their thematic similarities. They are viewed as existentialist novels in which montage exposes ironically the characters' repression of their perceptual awareness and their estrangement from the reality of human beings. The Conclusion synthesizes the main issues of the argument and expands on the previous comparisons drawn between Green and various critics and writers, contemporary as well as non-contemporary.

My research was undertaken with the joint aid of an Edinburgh University Postgraduate Studentship and an award from the Committee of Vice-Chancellors and Principals of the Universities of the United Kingdom. I am extremely grateful for this support. My work at Edinburgh University was supervised by Professor W. W. Robson, and I should like to express my thanks to him for his advice and encouragement. My discussions with Mr Randall Stevenson have provided me with many new insights, and I am deeply indebted to him. I also wish to thank Dr Valerie Shaw for her helpful critical comments during the early stages of my writing.

O. H.

Acknowledgements

The author and publishers wish to thank Henry Green's Literary Estate and The Hogarth Press, and Viking Penguin Inc., for permission to quote from the works of Henry Green.

1 Introduction

The truth is, these times are an absolute gift to the writer. Everything is breaking up. A seed can lodge or sprout in any crack or fissure. (Henry Green, letter to Rosamond Lehmann, quoted in Lehmann, 'An Absolute Gift', *The Times Literary Supplement*, 6 Aug 1954)

In 1949, Mark Schorer wrote that as far as Britain is concerned, 'we must confess that, in the past fifty years, the distinguished novels have been written in the prose that risks'. Naming established writers – Conrad, Joyce, Lawrence, E. M. Forster, Virginia Woolf and Elizabeth Bowen – 'for whom there are no American counterparts', he concludes that 'to these we may now probably add the name of Henry Green'.[1]

Despite Henry Green's reputation as one of the most original and fascinating novelists of our time, he remains in the shadow of his contemporaries. He is probably one of the most neglected writers of our century. James Hall, in trying to answer why no one writes articles about Green, attributes this anonymity to a general 'modern embarrassment in writing about comedy'.[2] Green's style is, in Hall's words, 'witty, personal, symbolic, specific'. This observation seems to account for most of the interpretative difficulties which a student of Green's work confronts. As Hall says, the critic may find himself trying to explain 'the *how* of comedy'.

Critics commonly agree that Green's novels are too amorphous to define a moral preoccupation clearly. Each of his novels offers a wealth of percepts and phenomena with no apparent attachment to a coherent whole. Any conception of plot is disturbed by shifting points of view; alternations between past and present; triviality receiving disproportionate emphasis so as to look absurdly important; private obsessions gaining dominance over collective ones; unpredictable incidents, symbols and imagery chopping up the structure of the novels, apparently without

1

authorial control. Edward Stokes echoes the dominant critical attitude to Green when he says that he is 'one of the most elusive, tantalizing and enigmatic of novelists, whose work is extremely difficult to define or categorize'.[3]

To see Green's art as comic must not lead us into the fallacy of seeing it as merely amusing and inessential. Such an interpretation contradicts Green's belief that through an 'acute sense of the ridiculous' we are surprised into an awareness of ourselves and others; through this sense of surprise we 'learn the little we know about human nature'.[4] Green's belief points to his refusal to remain within the bounds of a traditional narrative structure. This refusal, however, does not prevent him from dealing seriously with life's complexities.

Green has never been inclined to explain his 'serious' themes. However, in 'A Novelist to his Readers', he presents some basic ideas of human life that account for his experimentation with style.[5] He attacks the 'know-all' novelist and the narrative technique whereby 'the writer, who has no business with the story he is writing, intrudes like a Greek chorus to underline his meaning'. That Green is not only thinking of the Thackerayan manner of stepping in front of the 'curtain' to speak directly to the reader is clear when he goes on to ask, 'And do we know, in life, what other people are really like? I very much doubt it. We certainly do not know what other people are thinking and feeling. How then can the novelist be so sure?'

Green's preoccupation with literary form reflects what he sees as basic facts about the world: the inability to communicate effectively and the impossibility of knowing the truth.

> For how do we, each one of us, find out anything in the lives we each lead? Very little by reading, still less by what we are told. We get experience, which is as much knowledge as we shall ever have, by watching the way people around us behave, after they have spoken. As to other people telling us about what they have found in life, about what they have said themselves upon occasion, it may be personal prejudice, but whenever I can check up, I find they are only giving their own version of whatever it might be.

The world Green describes here is one in which reality is determined by point of view, and truth depends on how we see.

Green's recognition of the subjective nature of all experience sets limitations for the author. Explanation is unreliable, because it is liable to perceptual distortions and incomprehension bred by the author's subjectivity. Correspondingly, it is inadequate to deal with an evasive reality in a rational and philosophical manner.

> Most people remember very little of when they were small and what small part of this time there is that stays is ... coloured and readjusted until the picture which was there, what does come back, has been over-painted and retouched enough to make it an unreliable account of what used to be.[6]

Life, according to Green, cannot be apprehended through a dependence on memory or recollections. The pictures to which he refers imply static, one-dimensional qualities which are incompatible with real life. His primary aim is to create a life which is *convincing*. He wishes to create 'pictures' that can absorb the flux to which the continuous present is subject. Green believes that only through direct confrontation with life's vicissitudes can one (in this case, the author) achieve an inclusive, yet ever-changing command of life's complexity.

Green's narrative method strives to grasp the multiplicity of existence. An artist, he says, must create that which is 'alive ... with an everlasting life of its own'.[7] This effect can only be achieved through the conveyance of vivid 'pictures'. He stipulates that these pictures should be 'as diffuse and variously interpretable as life itself'.[8] Autonomy in art, according to Green, is attained through minimal narrative intervention lest the author's subjectivity should 'colour', 'over-paint' or 'retouch' the presented reality: 'The writer must be disengaged or else he is writing politics.'[9] Authorial disengagement enables the reader to reassemble the narrative fragments and thus construct or determine meaning. According to Green, this technique 'induce[s] the reader to make an act of conscious imagination to fuse the narrative'.[10]

Green's theorizing about the indeterminate nature of his art raises a central problem: does his fiction produce any value statement beyond a mere portrayal of the multiplicity and complexity of life? This study takes the view that Green, in selecting the separate details of his fiction, subtly directs the imaginative participation of the reader. 'Even the most nearly neutral comment will reveal some sort of commitment', says Wayne Booth in *The Rhetoric of Fiction*. The author, he says, 'cannot choose whether or not to affect his readers' evaluation by his choice of narrative manner'.[11] Applied to Green, this argument is echoed by Frederick Karl: 'Characters have no substance and narratives no meaning without the novelist. Green theorizes as if the novel springs into being through a spontaneous creation and then lives on its own terms.'[12] There is an ambivalence in Green's view of art and the world which can only be resolved through systematic analysis of his novels. His aspiration to convey a realistic impression of life's contradictory quality indicates movement towards artistic objectivity and authorial detachment. On the other hand, his theory of 'non-representational' art cannot be fully interpreted in terms of Flaubert's idea of dispassionate description and his repudiation of thematic purpose. In 'A Novelist to his Readers', Green explains that

> I have tried to show that the purpose of the novelist is to create, in the mind of the reader, life which is not, and which is non-representational. This has nothing to do with the theme of his work. We are all individuals and each writer has something of his own to communicate. It is with communication that I have been dealing here.[13]

Green allows that 'the writer cannot dictate to himself the theme of his novel ... he has to write from his innermost beliefs'.[14] Green's temperamental affinity to certain themes seems to prevent him from writing a truly objective novel.

With regard to technique, Green's novels represent successive experiments in creating art which is oblique and visual in quality. If art is to be 'all things to all men', as is his stated objective, a certain degree of intentional ambiguity is required.

> What, after all, is one to do with oneself in print? Does the reader feel a dread of anything? Do they all feel a dread for different things? Do they all love differently? Surely the only way to cover all these readers is to use what is called symbolism.[15]

Narrative must be oblique, says Green, 'for how can one, as a novelist, cater for those estimable men who only admire girls with black hair and pale blue eyes? The answer is, of course, by not describing them.'[16] By avoiding specification, Green enables the reader to project his privately cherished images into the text. Essentially, Green's concern with the actual technique of communication does not preclude the implicit suggestion of thematic values. All his novels are non-representational, he says, in that they 'represent a *selection* of material', and so can appeal to the imaginations of varying kinds of readers.[17] Hence, dialogue should also be non-representational – that is, not a direct record of the way people talk. Green's justification for this is: 'To create life in the reader, it will be necessary for the dialogue to mean different things to different readers at one and the same time.'[18] For the same reason, Green's use of humour does not necessarily imply lack of value commitment. Humour functions as a device to enliven 'all men'; 'And if you *can* make the reader laugh, he is apt to get careless and go on reading. So you as the writer get a chance to get something into him.'[19] The mark of the true artist, for Green, is the degree to which he is able to create a 'life which does not eat, procreate, or drink, but which can live in people who are alive'.[20]

In 'The English Novel of the Future', Green writes that the reading public are only interested in the 'theme of people falling in and out of love', and that he is concerned with 'the way in which this theme can be presented'.[21] That love is his declared theme may be seen as indicative of a private value system. In order to be 'alive', this theme's manner of presentation cannot depart from the immediate present. This indicates that love, in Green's characters, can only live in the present, not through reliance on a sentimental past or rosy future. Green's statements, so far, suggest certain commitments that deflate the possibility of an objective novel. Themes, characters and technique are to form an artistic whole which can 'create life in the reader'. A major task of this study will be to find a method by which to interpret the degree and manner of Green's commitment to the characters and events he portrays.

A close investigation of some 'pictures' that compose Green's

novels is required to elucidate the relationship between his
narrative technique and certain thematic values. To render a
realistic impression of the variety and complexity of life, as is one
of his objectives, it is necessary for him to describe reality from
various angles and as perceived by the individual sensibility.
Since each character is a separate individual, each perceives
reality differently. But Green's beliefs that the work of art should
be 'all things to all men' and that the novelist should be
'disengaged', imply that direct description of his characters'
feelings must be regarded as authorial intervention. In order to
create the proper ambiguity and universality of expression, Green
often tries to visualize the subjective realities of his characters.
Two passages from *Concluding* illustrate his technique. In the first,
Green metamorphoses Mr Rock's sense impressions into imagery:
'he saw the beeches like frozen milk, and frozen swimming-bath
blue water, already motionless in a cascade, soundless from a
height, not sixty yards in front' (p.249). The next passage
describes Merode's knee, seen through Sebastian's eyes:

> he looked down on a girl stretched out.... A knee which,
> brilliantly polished over bone beneath, shone in this sort of
> pool she had made for herself in the fallen world of birds,
> burned there like a piece of tusk burnished by shifting sands,
> or else a wheel revolving at such speed that it had no edges
> and was white, thus communicating life to ivory, a heart to
> the still and the sensation of a crash to this girl who lay quiet,
> reposed ... she had mud on the white of leg below the knee,
> with enamelled toes in sandals caked with mud. Sun, through
> the bright leaves, lit all of this in violent dots, spotting the
> cotton with drips as of wet paint, and making small candle
> lamps of flesh.   (p.56)

Interpretation of the passages is made difficult because of the
surreal quality of the imagery. 'Beeches like frozen milk', 'tusk
burnished by shifting sands', 'candle lamps of flesh', or the image
of a revolving wheel, are not intellectual symbols in the sense
that they are in one-to-one correspondence with ulterior elements,
and thus help define more precisely what those ulterior elements
represent. Taken from our common fund of experience – from
nature, from daily life – their original meaning is informed with

an abstract quality by being placed in a context where they do
not naturally belong. The effect is what Green calls non-
representational. It is similar to that of a painting, he suggests:

> one tone or shade of colour lead[s] to another until this evolves
> into a harmonious whole which may have little direct relation
> to nature. Thereby painters produce something which isn't,
> that is to say, the result is non-representational, and yet if and
> when the painting is successful, it has a life of its own. This is
> also true of a good novel.[22]

A sensitive reading of the passages just referred to reveals a
difference in their composition. In the first passage, the images
are 'frozen', 'motionless', 'soundless', indicative of distance from
the scene which is observed 'sixty yards in front'. The reader's
impression is of authorial neutrality and a scenery coloured by
Mr Rock's subjective mind. The poetic intensity of the second
passage, on the other hand, far exceeds its presentational
function. Lifelessness and coldness, symbolized by 'white tusk',
collide and merge with the dazzling sun, which is reflected like
a revolving wheel, and so communicates 'life to ivory' and 'a
heart to the still' of this 'fallen world'. The image imprinted on
the reader's mind is one of powerful contrasts, between life and
lifelessness, an intense merging of opposites, time stopped, and
distance between scene, author and reader dissolved.

Beneath Green's attempt to objectify our subjective world,
there is an underlying commitment to forces that inform that
world with life. The dynamic depiction of Merode's knee 'creates
life in the reader' because it has 'a life of its own'. Like dots of
colour in a painting, the visual images fulfil their function only
as parts of a larger context. Full meaning only arises out of a
special arrangement of words and visual images in juxtaposition.
Both the quoted passages from *Concluding* represent an attempt
to render a sense of the moment, of time stopped. But Green
uses different classes of words and different methods of juxtaposition for this purpose. In the first example, the beeches, the
objects of perception, are described by similes, which again
are modified by adjectives. This particular syntax places the
emphasis on a pictorial description of the objects, and not on
the sensory quality of the impression. However, the surreal
nature of the images nevertheless indicates that they are not

directly observed, but created by an active, symbol-making
mind. As a result of this inner tension, the whole passage is
veiled with a sense of unreality, by a vague symbolism that gives
the immediacy of impression an air of detached contemplation.

A similar effect of emotional distance may be found in Virginia
Woolf's work. Her novels seem a series of attempts to fix the
moment of vision on paper, to hold still fleeting impressions in
the 'incessant shower of innumerable atoms' which is life. These
contexts of images are not so much objectifications of the actual
process of sensory interaction; the emphasis is on some latently
meaningful pattern. Thus it is that in *The Voyage Out*, Rachel
saw

> hot, red, quick sights which passed incessantly before her eyes.
> She knew that it was of enormous importance that she should
> attend to these sights and grasp their meaning, but she was
> always being just too late to hear or see something which
> would explain it all.[23]

Virginia Woolf's great concern is with the nature of reality, but
mainly in terms of a purely aesthetic visual pattern:

> Whatever the light touched became dowered with a fanatical
> existence. A plate was like a white lake. A knife looked like a
> dagger of ice. Suddenly tumblers revealed themselves upheld
> by streaks of light. Tables and chairs rose to the surface as if
> they had been sunk under water and rose, filmed with red,
> orange purple like the bloom on the skin of ripe fruit.[24]

This visual moment resembles Mr Rock's impression of the
beeches under the effect of moonlight. Both seem the visual
embodiment of a mood in the observer's mind, but rather as an
expression of the unconscious, separate from objective reality.
One does not get a strong impression of images directly inspired
by an external reality, or of sensual participation in that reality.

In Green's description of Merode's knee, on the other hand,
'tusk burnished by shifting sands' and 'candle lamps of flesh',
in themselves abstract, are placed in a context of swirling lines
and light where the images lose their substantiality and become
pure motion; the piece of 'tusk' is not 'burnished' – it *burns*.
Green here is more concerned to render a sense of the scene's

total presence than to describe and analyse its constituent parts. His stress is not, as is Virginia Woolf's, on the aesthetic beauty of the scene, but on a natural dynamism that is beauty. Its apprehension calls for sensual involvement. It is not a straightforward celebration of natural order, but a visualization of the affective and experiential interchange between observer (whether reader or author) and scene.

One also finds visual passages of deeper involvement in Virginia Woolf's novels. Sometimes the very act of aesthetic contemplation evokes associations so vivid that the reader reaches a sensuous level of identification with both the character and his experience. From an initial attempt to determine the special quality of sound impressions, Septimus Warren Smith loses himself in the physical movement of the trees and clouds:

Happily Rezia put her hand with a tremendous weight on his knee so that he was weighted down, transfixed, or the excitement of the elm trees rising and falling, rising and falling with all their leaves alight and the colour thinning and thickening ... would have sent him mad.... they beckoned; leaves were alive; trees were alive. And the leaves being connected by millions of fibres with his own body, there on the seat, fanned it up and down; when the branch stretched he, too, made that statement.[25]

What these quoted passages from Henry Green's and Virginia Woolf's fiction have in common is technique. The attempt to define a state of consciousness is rendered in a language that is rather abstract, symbolic and statically descriptive. Sensual communion with life, on the other hand, they reveal by the opposite technique. Language no longer becomes an obstacle between object and reader; the sensuous characteristics of the scene arise before him; in their own purity they make a dynamic appeal to which the creative artist must respond. If one were to use terms from cinematography, one might say that the description gives the sense of a sudden zoom-lens close-up which makes identification with projected values acute.

These selected passages from Virginia Woolf's novels indicate that she is interested in two aspects of man's relationship with nature. On one level, she strives consciously to assimilate fleeting impressions into some meaningful, aesthetic pattern. On a different plane, she reveals the strong impulse of characters towards sensual reconciliation with the natural world. Whether these two concerns are conflicting in Green's fiction is a central question in this book. In Virginia Woolf's novels, they can hardly be distinguished as opposites, for the sensuousness intermingles with, even grows out of, a character's search for aesthetic coherence. Green's characters, however, are not introspective, intellectual people as are Virginia Woolf's. They are ordinary characters, occupied with more earthy problems, such as finding some measure of happiness which can make their days more fulfilling. Thus Lily, in *Living*, wants a child she can love and to whom she can devote her life.

I have tried to demonstrate ways in which Green modulates his language in order to vary the sensuous immediacy between scene and reader. Green's choice of different techniques indicates certain values, but it is necessary to look more deeply into the nature of his value commitments. The circular recurrence of various symbols and images throughout his novels may cause ambiguities in interpretation. Revolving 'wheels' of sunlight, the turning lathes in the factory, and the ever-returning pigeons create a harmonious pattern of regularity; the cyclic structure of his world may reflect the promise of patterned renewal. Since Green is so acutely aware of life's tragic aspects and the transience of everything living, does he perhaps really seek an aesthetic form to counterbalance the lack of human order and permanence? Such motives might incline him towards T. S. Eliot, for whom repetition approximates static perfection:

> Only by the form, the pattern,
> Can words or music reach
> The stillness, as a Chinese jar still
> Moves perpetually in its stillness . . .
> The detail of the pattern is movement.

A comparison of Eliot's and Lawrence's visions and methods will clarify Green's. Eliot engages in the kind of abstract contemplation that leads to the disclosure of form. This attitude makes Eliot the direct opposite of Lawrence. Lawrence disparages abstract contemplation and celebrates the sense of fulfilment derived from sensual and physical submission in the natural rhythms of life. He writes in his preface to the American edition of his *New Poems* (1920),

Let me feel the mud and the heavens
in my lotus.
Let me feel the heavy, silting, sucking
mud, the spinning of sky winds.[26]

Lawrence's vision, in fact, is similar to Green's as Green portrays, in sensual terms, the reclining Merode who has mud on her white leg and sandals 'caked with mud'. Lawrence's 'spinning of sky winds' corresponds to Green's 'revolving wheel' of reflected light. This is not to say that Green's and Lawrence's visions are altogether identical. Green is acutely aware of the irreversible march of time towards decay. Hence, he cannot make the same confident commitment to the continuum of nature as does Lawrence. They nevertheless reveal their kinship. Both writers strive to unite heaven and earth through sensual experience of the moment.

The analysis and comparison of selected passages indicate that the nature of Green's attitude towards the moment is quite complex and must be treated with subtlety. To Green, the value of sensual communion with natural rhythms comprises the value of love. Commitment to the moment represents a way to channel the constructive impulses of the heart. 'Moons' – circles of reflected light – are visualizations of Jim Dale's love for Lily. He sits watching her on one occasion as she

swilled water over the plates and electric light caught in shining waves of water which rushed off plates as she held them, and then light caught on wet plates in moons. She dried these. One by one then she put them up into the rack on wall above her, and as she stretched up so her movements pulled all ways at his heart, so beautiful she seemed to him.

(*Living*, p.311)

Similarly, if we return once more to the sensual presentation of Merode, the forces that make 'candle lamps of flesh' at the same time communicate 'a heart to the still'. This suggests that love, in Green's work, is a value which cannot easily be distinguished from sensuality. They both demand involvement and commitment to the living present.

The comparison of T. S. Eliot's preoccupation with abstract contemplation and Lawrence's insistence on dynamic participation provides a framework in which to analyse Green's attitudes. I have indicated how the circling motions in passages from Lawrence and Green are bound up with sensual involvement with life. Depending on the context, therefore, rotation, in Green, may express hope in the human potential and not an aesthetic substitute for lack of human pattern. This aspect of Green's technique is highly significant for a full understanding of his novels. *Living* contains recurrent images of movement in circles and spirals. The lathes and wheels in the factory form a monotonous pattern of repetition approaching stasis. But as a counteracting organic force, there is the more irregular motion of the sparrows which distract the factory workers by circling among the belts and the lathes. At one moment, fluttering pigeons gather around a baby's pram; in the next they soar in ascending circles above a gardener who is digging in barren soil. They are constantly on their wings, their free flight transcending the circular stasis and the symmetric pattern of the machinery. Only when life itself has become stagnant do the birds stop flying, as in Hannah Glossop's sentimental, escapist dreams of the tropics: 'And always the boat was circling round that land. Then ... tropical birds came out and rested on this ship' (p.316). Circles do not always represent a consolatory promise of patterned renewal. The turning of the world leads nowhere but towards death, of which Dick Dupret in *Living* is only too aware. 'He thought you made a little circle and yours reflects other circles. Death, death, sackcloth and ashes' (p.256). Dick Dupret reminds one of T. S. Eliot's 'detached observer'; he is unable to find hope in the message given by a fluttering bird.

It is not only in the nature of their commitment to the present moment that Eliot and Lawrence are opposites; they also differ in their response to the time before and after. 'There is no rhythm which returns upon itself', says Lawrence, 'no serpent of eternity with its tail in its own mouth. There is no static perfection, none of that finality which we find so satisfying because we are so frightened.' For Lawrence, 'it is obvious that the poetry of the instant present cannot have the same body or the same motion as the poetry of the before and after'. In contrast to Lawrence's

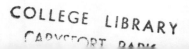

accepting attitude, Eliot's rather uniform metre, as well as his frequent literary allusions to the ordered experience of ancient times, reveal his fear of the temporal; he finds 'Ridiculous the waste sad time / Stretching before and after'. Like Green's prose, the free form of Lawrence's writing is devised to capture the birds' flight at each single moment.

The bird is on the wing in the winds, flexible to every breath, a living spark in the storm, its very flickering depending upon its supreme mutability and power of change. Whence such a bird came: whither it goes: from what solid earth it rose up, and upon what solid earth it will close its wings and settle, this is not the question. This is a question of before and after. Now, now, the bird is on the wing in the winds.

Lawrence has confidence in the time after, for the spirit of the instant moment may be infinitely recaptured. Green, perhaps, cannot share the same strength of convictions that makes Lawrence's poetry, like Whitman's, 'a wind that is for ever in passage and unchainable' and which is thus 'without beginning and without end'.[27] Green's tragic conception of life makes the sheer appreciation of the present moment vulnerable to time. His epigraph to *Living*, however, implies confidence that the better moments will recur: 'As these birds would go where so where would this child go?' The line suggests an acceptance of life's transience, as does the optimistic inconclusiveness of Green's plots.

Despite Green's strong awareness of life's inherent emptiness and separateness, the sensuous appreciation of the instant moment – the fluttering of birds – has a unifying impact on the intent observer. Such experience is a source of joy as well as of reconciliation in the time after. The following scene from *Concluding* is a particularly good example of this. Mr Rock and his granddaughter, Liz, are out walking one night, and both are worrying. Mr Rock is anticipating his loneliness if Liz marries Sebastian, whom he mistrusts, and Liz is thinking of the insecurity of the future for them all.

Then, as they came to where the trees ended, and blackbirds, before roosting, began to give the alarm in earnest, some first starlings flew out of the sky. Over against the old man and his granddaughter the vast mansion reflected a vast red; sky above paled while to the left it outshone the house, and more starlings crossed. After which these birds came in hundreds, then suddenly by legion, black and blunt against faint rose. They swarmed above the lonely elm, they circled a hundred feet above, until the leader, followed by ever greater numbers, in one broad spiral led the way down and so, as they descended through falling dusk in a soft roar, they made, as they had at dawn, a huge sea shell that stood proud to a moon which, flat sovereign red gold, was already poised full faced to a dying world.

Once the starlings had settled in that tree they one and all burst out singing.

Then there were more, even higher, dots against paler pink, and these, in their turn, began to circle up above, scything the air, and to swoop down through a thickening curve, in the enormous echo of blood, or of the sea, until all was black about that black elm, as the first mass of starlings left while these others settled, and there was a huge volume of singing.   (pp.176–7)

The entire scene is filled up with starlings. First a few, then hundreds, and finally by legion they swarm and circle around the lonely black elm which is suggestive of man's separateness. 'The old man wondered, as often before, if this were not the greatest sound on earth.'

When it is all over, it has had a healing effect on the two spectators. '"I'm glad I had that once more", Mr Rock said aloud.' For Liz, there is new hope of reintegration:

'We're to have the most lovely night', Elizabeth told her grandfather.... 'I want you to know', she said, from the heart, 'in spite of everything, whatever happens, absolutely, if Seb asks me to marry him even, there'd be nothing could alter the way I love you, Gapa. I wouldn't let it.' 'Don't allow yourself to grow sentimental, child', he answered. She gave a soft laugh.   (pp.177–8)

Green's method for communicating the conciliatory quality of the previous scene is essentially what I will call 'montage'. 'Montage' is the French term for editing shots in film: a shot *A* is placed next to shot *B*, etc. I am using it here in the sense defined by the Russian film director, Sergei Eisenstein. This means that the relation of shot A to shot B is characterized by dynamism and conflict so that the two shots collide to generate a synthesis *C*. Eisenstein explains that the combination of two separate representations

> is to be regarded not as their sum, but as their product, i.e. as a value of another dimension, another degree; each separately, corresponds to an *object*, to a fact, but their combination corresponds to a *concept* ... by the consideration of two 'depictables' is achieved the representation of something that is graphically undepictable.[28]

The dynamic conflict of depictable images in Green's sunset scene is basically composed of contrasting colours. 'Black and blunt' the starlings appear against 'faint rose' in an 'enormous echo of blood'. What symbolic message the blackness of the starlings might otherwise carry – the tendency to associate black with death – is de-emphasized through the montage trope. It is in the graphic totality of the picture, in the basic clash of opposites, and in the increasing domination of swarming birds that lies the meaning.[29] The fluctuation of the starlings, reflected in the very structure of the sentences, transcends the clash of opposites and visualizes emotions too subjective and too profound to be expressed in a straightforward narrative. Out of the depicted scene arises a new 'concept', as it were, a value of a different dimension, a diffuse sense of reconciliation. The effectiveness of Green's technique depends on his ability to make the reader refrain from interpretation while the scene moves on. What is demanded of the reader if he is to grasp its depths is not an intellectual identification with particular characters or images and what they may seem to represent, but rather imaginative participation in the life which is portrayed. Green accounts for this process in *Pack my Bag*: 'Prose is not to be read aloud to oneself alone at night, and it is not quick as poetry but rather a gathering web of insinuations.' Prose, according to this idea, should be a 'long intimacy between strangers' and should 'in the end draw tears out of the stone'.[30]

Eisenstein formulates what Green has just dramatized: montage of images is to stir the spectator so that he is 'being drawn into the process as it occurs'.[31] A characteristic feature of Green's method is the manner in which he suffuses separate forms and antagonistic colours with a dynamic force that draws the spectator into the 'life' of things. Thus, the expanding fluctuation of starlings in Green's sunset scene has, on one plane, the same function as the dynamics of colour in his portrayal of Merode's knee: the sun covers the entire scene with 'violent dots ... as of wet paint' and so merges contradictory forces into an artistic harmony.

The visual impression of the sunset scene is 'non-representational'. This is a term closely connected with the effect of film, the reason why Eisenstein's ideas apply to Green's dynamic visualization. Consequently, the analysis of Green's method in relation to film form will clarify his artistic vision and intent. With regard to technique, Green's presentations subserve the immediate present. Impressions stored in memory, he says, are 'inaccurate and so can no longer be called a movie, or a set of stills'.[32] The technique of the cinema captures the visual vividness and perceptual immediacy Green seeks in fiction. Richard Roe, in *Caught*, attempts to apprehend the reality of the London blitz:

> 'The extraordinary thing is', he said, 'that one's imagination is so literary. What will go on up there to-night in London, every night, is more like a film, or that's what it seems like at the time. Then afterwards, when you go over it, everything seems unreal.' (*Caught*, p.174)

It is significant that the accuracy and immediacy Green attributes to movies (as in the preceding scene) do not depend on the movies' transcription of actuality. Richard Roe's experience is formed of images imprinted in his subjective mind. Green states that his non-representational method 'was meant to represent a picture which was not a photograph, nor a painting on a photograph, nor, in dialogue, a tape recording'.[33] Consequently, it should not be the object of the critic to discover correspondences between Green's language and empirical reality. The positivist schools of criticism are inapplicable. According to Roland Barthes, 'critical activity must take two kinds of relationships into account: the relationship between the critical language and the language of the author under consideration and the relationship between the latter (language-as-object) and the world'. 'Criticism', Barthes argues, 'is defined by the interaction of these two languages.' Since Green himself stresses the point that his fiction is an artifact, his concept of non-representational art is clarified by Barthes's ideas of criticism. Language is a system of relationships that does not represent reality directly, but is a form, 'a very special semantic system, the aim of which is to put "meaning" into the world, but not "a meaning" '. The work of literature presents itself to the reader 'as a declared system of significance, but as a signified object it eludes his grasp'. Consequently, 'the critic is not called upon to reconstitute the message [i.e. the definite meaning] of the work, but only its system'; 'meaning' is contained within the system of 'signs'.[34]

Thus, the cinema does not equip Green with a model of mimetic representation, but with principles for creating verisimilitude of expression, or what Structuralists would term 'vraisemblance'.[35] Green's visual images function as metaphor to create meaning and a semblance of reality. Green explains that his aim is to awaken the reader 'to a new reality beyond his experience, thereby creating something which, however abstract, has a life of its own, if it succeeds in being what is called "convincing" '.[36] For this reason, the cinema serves as an important model precisely because it is not 'real'.

Green's conception of 'vraisemblance' denies objectivity in the novel; it implies a value commitment. He compares the role of fiction to that of the plastic arts, stating that 'the function ... of a good painting or piece of sculpture is to appeal by or through the eye to the memory of things seen ... which is after all appreciation'.[37] Far from merely presenting fleeting impressions of a non-coherent world, Green's art appeals to vital human sensibilities. The following scene in the cinema reinforces the distinction between mimetic realism and Green's idea of vraisemblance.

Later they got in and found seats. Light rain had been falling, so when these two acting on screen walked by summer night down leafy lane, hair over her ears left wet on his cheek as she leant head, when they on screen stopped and looked at each other. Boys at school had been singing outside schoolroom on screen, had been singing at stars, and these two heard them and kissed in boskage deep low in this lane and band

played softly, women in audience crooning. Lily Gates sank
lower over arm of her seat. Mr Dale did not move.

(*Living*, p.216)

Life on screen is not a recognizable transcription of the life of
individuals among the audience. The film is 'all things to all
men' in the sense that it represents 'a *selection* of material' with
which all the spectators can identify in their individual ways.
The film serves as a metaphorical reflection of the spectators'
emotional needs. Green's alternate focusing on Lily and Bert,
the lovers on the screen, the audience, and then again on Lily
and Bert, unites subjects and objects into an evocative sense of
emotional reciprocity. These juxtapositions together with the
dynamic rhythm of the sentences give the scene 'a life of its own'.
It is an impetus to the reader to participate in the kind of 'life'
created in the juxtaposition of images.

The capacity of film form to incite life in the spectator, and
reader, is compellingly dramatized in the following scene from
Living:

She hummed tune band was now playing whey widdle o . . .
'Why they're playin' it again' she said. She looked at screen.
She saw heroine's knickers again were coming down, now in
young man's bedroom.

ooeee she screamed.

EEEEE the audience.

The band played that tune. Tum tum ti tumpy tum. Dum
dum di dumpy dum. She jumped her knees to time. Da da
DID DEE – (it wasn't her knickers after all) – did dee dee
tum ta.   (pp.224–5)

The passage enacts Barthes's distinction between language as
object and language as referential instrument. It produces
'meaning' but not 'a meaning' (not a transcription of Lily's
experience in the cinema). 'Meaning' is created through a
cinematic editing of visual and auditory images. Rapid transitions
between succinct, disconnected phrases (analogous to shifts in
focus between disparate glimpses in film) combined with the
preponderance of active verbs within the sentences (similar in
function to the verbal force effected by the depiction of actual

movement and action in film)[38] create a kinetic unit stimulating the reader's response.

The animating medley of filmic flashes and enticing tunes, resounding in Green's cinematic narrative style, contains an implicit value statement. Green's manner of conveying to the reader the impact of the movie on Lily and the audience resembles the film director's technique of channelling the audience's emotional participation.

> A great number were in cinema, many standing, battalions were in cinemas over all the country, young Mr Dupret was in a cinema, over above up into the sky their feeling panted up supported by each other's feeling, away away, Europe and America, mass on mass their feeling united supporting, renewed their sky. (p.245)

Audiences everywhere experience a sense of 'renewal' and spiritual community in the cinema. The principle of the cinema's appeal resides in the camera's ability to fuse disparate fragments in space and time into a sense of simultaneity.[39] Concentrated units of visual impulses possess a potential to stimulate the spectator's projection of private needs and longings into a contrived semblance of life. By selecting and arranging his visual images according to cinematographic principles, Green applies the film-maker's technique in inciting the reader's commitment to latent human values:

> Later her head was leaning on his shoulder again, like hanging clouds against hills every head in his theatre tumbled without hats against another, leaning everywhere.

> Eight o'clock of morning. Thousands came up the road to work and few turned in to Mr Dupret's factory. Sirens were sounded, very sad. (p.217)

Green's juxtaposition of two contrasting realities, both experienced by the same masses of people, produces meaning on two levels. From the point of view of social realism, the Friday-night cinema offers little but illusions to the working people of Birmingham. Lily finds nourishment for her dreams about warm, tropical countries, ironically incompatible with her reality. However, two different realities are juxtaposed on the level of 'language-as-object'. Pressing human needs and longings are enacted against mechanical routines presided over by the machine. In the conflict of images there is an appeal for sympathetic understanding and an awareness of organic human values.

As a form of art, the cinema serves the same purpose that Green ascribes to literature: to 'create life, of a kind, in the reader', 'to quicken [his] unconscious imagination into life while reading'.[40] For the same effect, Sergei Eisenstein bases his work on the montage principle. He stresses the unique capacity of filmic montage to instigate 'that great power of inner creative excitement in the spectator'. Eisenstein realizes that 'a work of art, understood dynamically, is just this process of arranging images in the feelings and mind of the spectator'.[41]

There is sufficient biographical information about Green's career to affirm his strong interest in this kind of visual effect. At Eton, Green and other members of the Society of Arts set up a play, 'a strange amalgam based on the story of *Hansel and Gretel*, put into verse by Alan Clutton-Brock, the scenery designed and created by myself, the actors created by Mark Ogilvie-Grant, the music by Tchaikovsky (*The Nutcracker Suite*) and electric lighting effects by Henry Yorke'.[42] Film form also has great attraction for Green. In his first term at Oxford, he recalls, 'I felt extremely ill and every day went alone to a cinema after which I tried to write.' It seems that in the cinema Green found inspiration to write. The nature of the cinema's influence on his writing is not difficult to discern. Film, although an illusion, creates a semblance of truth due to its potential for arousing response in the spectator. Green recalls occasions of strong emotional impact, 'as when on the news films one sees any scene of parting between strangers and however much one may not want to, is caught into an inevitable experience'.[43]

Previous examples have indicated that Green uses filmic devices to stress the emotive quality of a context. This method requires an adequate critical approach to its significance. The precise quality of the cinema's evocative power is not translatable. Green's experience of it is transmitted in the undefined communication between text and reader, in the 'life' created through the juxtaposition of diverse images.

For me the darkness, that is the light subdued, the snivelling and soft laughs, those heads more intent on each other's breath as in the oldest gesture they inclined one to the other against the lighted screen the orchestra played low to, here was the place in which to work out the sense of guilt, to conquer that nausea of lunch after the night before's drinking.[44]

The images in the scene – such as the 'darkness' of the cinema – possess no precise denotative qualities. Consequently, meaning will have to be sought through isolated images' interaction within a larger context. The Russian film producer Pudovkin contends that

> To the poet or writer separate words are as raw material. They have the widest and most variable meanings which only begin to become precise through their position in the composed phrase, to that extent is its effect and meaning variable until it is fixed in position, in the arranged artistic form.... To the film director each shot of the finished film subserves the same purpose as the word to the poet.[45]

From this point of view, the making of film and poetry involves the transmutation of fragments of reality into a non-representational artistic form. Accordingly, meaning must be determined only through comprehension or recognition of form.

Meaning varies with genre: there is a distinction between the meaning of prose and the suggestion, through nuance, of poetry. Jonathan Culler stresses the importance of this kind of context. He argues that a text achieves different meanings when read as prose and as poetry, 'because we approach the poem with different expectations and interpretative operations'. Read as poetry, Green's passage no longer serves as a record of particular visits to the cinema; it 'takes on a different force' by creating a tension between past and present. According to Culler, 'this is due to our conventions about the relationship of poems to the moment of utterance'. 'Secondly,' Culler says, 'we expect the lyric to capture a moment of some significance, to be thematically viable' and, 'thirdly, we expect a poem to be a unified whole'. Thus, 'the conventions of the lyric create the possibility of new and supplementary meanings'.[46] This idea corresponds with Green's desire to awaken the reader 'to a new reality beyond his experience'.

Culler's statement pertains to the arbitrary nature of language in Green's account of his experience in the cinema. Green defines the 'darkness' in the cinema as 'the light subdued'. His specification lacks expressive power; there is no frame of reference as to whether it is to be read as a dispassionate description of factual conditions, or as an element in a scene of poetic evocation. Only within a context of other images does the darkness become meaningful. Not only the light is 'subdued', but also sounds ('soft laughs' and 'snivelling', the 'soft' music from the orchestra) and gestures (heads inclining towards each other's 'breath'). All these low-toned impressions are given dynamic force through contrast with the 'lighted screen' and the 'intent' audience in a poetic visual moment, the experience of which Green finds highly cathartic.

The preceding examination of Green's term 'non-representational' reveals crucial aspects of his artistic vision and technique. It suggests that assessment of the manner of his commitment to the characters and events he portrays is best approached through analysis of 'tone'. Green himself makes a statement to this effect: 'The fascination in words is that by themselves they can mean almost anything; dictionaries get longer every day. It is the context in which they lie that alone gives them life. They should be used as painters use colour, to give tone.'[47] Tone is an ambiguous literary term, which implies the writer's sense of the particular situation he portrays. Wayne Booth defines 'tone' in literature as 'the implicit evaluation which the author manages to convey behind his explicit presentation'.[48] For I. A. Richards, tone denotes 'the perfect recognition of the writer's relation to the reader in view of what is being said and their joint feelings about it'.[49] Together, these two definitions serve to identify one major concern of this book. The term 'tone' suggests a tendency to think of a literary work as a mode of speech. In an indirect manner, the author expresses his attitudes towards the characters and events within his work, as well as towards the audience to whom the work is addressed.

As no direct narrative technique fully reveals Green's attitudes, the comprehension of form represents the greatest obstacle to the analysis of tone. Green's ambition to grasp the multiplicity of existence requires a high degree of artistic objectivity. This

complexity implies various obstacles to an evaluative interpretation of individual characters. Green's susceptibility to some
general values needs to be seen alongside his Modernist conception of the world. There is all the time an underlying sense that
true communication and order are beyond the realm of social
intercourse. This impression is strengthened by Green's progress-
ive attempts to view life and characters from without. Similarities
between Green and T. S. Eliot can be found in their art, as well
as in their theories about art. Just as Green tries to create a 'life
which does not eat, procreate or drink', so Eliot argues in
'Tradition and the Individual Talent' that the artist's task is to
create universality of experience through depersonalization, by
abstracting reality from the larger world outside the work of art
itself. The work of art must, in return, be re-created in the
creative imagination of the reader. Mario Praz argues that

> the very atmosphere of Green's novels, the substitution of a
> much subtler arabesque of conversations and inconclusive
> episodes ... for a plot in the current sense of the word, the
> flattening of personal traits in the characters, so that they
> may be molded upon the arabesque and become almost
> indistinguishable from the pattern itself, the placing of the
> story almost outside a definite time and space (as in *Concluding*,
> and, in some cases, in *Nothing*, for instance) the nearly total
> absence of descriptive passages – all these features contribute
> to the impression of abstract art.[50]

Despite the abstract aspects of Green's art, his portrayals are
still sufficiently intricate to include individuality. A comparison
of two passages from *Living* will indicate ways in which Green
incorporates a moral tone in his depiction of individuals. Young
Mr Dupret, the callow, new factory manager, stands in the
foundry shop contemplating the ornamental beauty of the hand-
made iron castings, reaching out his fingers to touch their reality.
He pompously 'declaimed to himself that this was the life to
lead, making useful things which were beautiful, and the gladness
to make them, which you could touch' (p.211). What Dick is
prophesying is a fusion of the poetic and the prosaic, beauty and
drabness. The statement produced by this interaction is deeply
ironic. Green juxtaposes the 'incidental beauty' which Dick finds
in the castings with his idea that these would 'last and would

be working in great factories' (ibid.). Dick postulates an external order where beauty and material necessity are in a permanent state of harmony. Despite his desire to 'touch' the idealized castings, he is, ironically, out of touch with their reality. His alienation is revealed by the fact that the order he experiences can only be found in a detached state of contemplation. Green emphasizes this point by focusing on Dick and his ideas rather than on a scene which generates a sense of identification. The inefficacy of the intellect as a guide to man on his way through life, is ironically present in Dick's sudden realization that it had all been said before: 'Ruskin built a road which went nowhere with the help of undergraduates and in so doing said the last word on that' (ibid.). Standing in the dirty factory in his fine clothes, Dick Dupret senses the incongruity of his own position. Green lets the works manager add the final ironic comment as he leads young Dupret out of the iron foundry: 'It's all beautiful work we do Mr Dupret, beautiful work. And we *turn it out*' (ibid., emphasis added).

In contrast to the irony surrounding Dick Dupret, the next passage reveals the author's sincere commitment to a poignant moment in the factory:

Then, one morning in iron foundry, Arthur Jones began singing. He did not often sing. When he began the men looked up from work and at each other and stayed quiet. In machine shop, which was next iron foundry, they said it was Arthur singing and stayed quiet also. He sang all morning.

He was Welsh and sang in Welsh. His voice had a great soft yell in it. It rose and rose and fell then rose again and, when the crane was quiet for a moment, then his voice came out from behind noise of the crane in passionate singing. Everything in iron foundries is black with the burnt sand and here was his silver voice yelling like bells. The black grimed men bent over their black boxes.

When he came to end of a song or something in his work kept him from singing, men would call out to him with names of English songs but he would not sing these. . . .

Every one looked forward to Arthur's singing, each one was glad when he sang, only, this morning, Jim Dale had bitterness inside him like girders and when Arthur began singing his music was like acid to that man and it was like that girder

was being melted and bitterness and anger crystallized, up
rising up in him till he was full and would have broken out –
when he put on coat and walked out and went into town and
drank. Mr Craigan did not know he was gone till he saw he
did not come back.

Still Arthur sang and it might be months before he sang
again.... That night son had been born to him.   (pp.265–6)

Arthur Jones's voice rings like silver bells in the midst of noise
and blackness, and makes the 'grimed men' forget the drabness
and monotony of the factory. In this scene there is no contemplation of an ideal order, separated from reality. Almost like the
fluctuating birds in the sunset scene, the voice rises and falls,
circulates around the lathes, filling the whole foundry. Arthur
Jones's singing is a spontaneous outlet for the joy he feels for
having been given a son. The sense of natural fulfilment conquers
the darkness around him, makes him free from the mechanized
order of the factory; when he sings, he is his own master, he declines to sing the songs the other men suggest to him. No obvious
criticism characterizes the contrasting portrayal of Jim Dale,
although he appears, throughout the novel, as an unimaginative
and moody fellow. By juxtaposition, however, Green's emphasis
is on his life-denying attitude which makes him unresponsive to
the serenity of the present moment, and an outsider.

These two passages from *Living* give some indication of the
manner in which Green reveals his attitude to various characters,
even though he attaches no moral labels. His stated intention –
to create art which can 'live in people who are alive' – involves
not only his non-representational technique whereby the reader
must participate actively to recreate the meaning of the work.
Green's statement must be seen against the background of
existential barrenness that marks his fiction. To revitalize man
through his art seems to be his underlying concern. Consequently, tone can only be detected if his art is approached
like a poem, as a medium for direct communication with the
reader. The reader confronts a fragmented, contradictory world
contrived in accordance with a Modernist conception of reality.
To the poetic sensibility, however, a sense of unification and
purpose can be found in the midst of darkness and fragmentation.
As Green points out, 'The truth is, these times are an absolute
gift to the writer. Everything is breaking up. A seed can lodge

or sprout in any crack or fissure.'[51] Green's convictions 'lodge' and 'sprout' in his arrangement of scenes and images. They are not fully transmitted in terms of a traditional narrative line or plot. Meaning arises through the reader's response to the 'life' of the entire novel.

By observing the world from different angles, Green juxtaposes scenes and images so as to expose the contrasts and conflicts of life. I have indicated that it is primarily by this method of juxtaposing incongruous elements that one is able to discern an evaluative authorial tone. I will try to show that the conflicts that operate in Green's fiction – between social classes; between generations; between men and women – are conflicts of individual attitudes rather than of social or biological determinants. The large world of 'living' is continually brought down to the microcosmic personal level. In this way, Green not only transmits the multiplicity of reality into a formal order of abstracted scenes; by juxtaposing different attitudes to life in relation to changing scenes, he tests their viability. Green's own statements encourage this approach: 'just as the composition of a painting gives it meaning, so the way in which the writer places his characters in the shifting scenes of his book will give the work significance'.[52]

I have indicated that tone is a highly elusive term which derives, not from separate images, but from a wider context. Green compares tone to the effect achieved by the composition of colour in a painting. Consequently, tone can be explored only through recognition of his method of juxtaposing different elements. I have attempted to show how the dynamic quality of his fiction is closely connected with the visual impact of film. Green himself states that, as the 'composition of a painting gives it meaning', 'the superimposing of one scene on another, or the telescoping of two scenes into one', gives the novel 'substance and depth'.[53] It is interesting that Green uses terms taken from film production to suggest analogies between his own narrative method and painting, as well as filmic art. This statement is comparable to Eisenstein's idea that the juxtaposition of two filmic images creates a third image which is qualitatively different from the content of either independent image or their sum. In order to be incorporated into a useful methodology for the examination of Green's fiction, however, Eisenstein's ideas require further investigation.

Eisenstein founds his theory of film on the premise that all art forms have basic principles in common. First, 'photo-fragments of nature are recorded'. 'The musician uses a scale of sounds; the painter, a scale of tones; the writer, a row of sounds and words – and these are all taken to an equal degree from nature.' But, as previously argued, Green's method is not basically an arrangement of naturalistic 'shots' or denotative words. Eisenstein goes on to explain that these 'reproductions' may be combined in various ways to form 'montage'.

> Both as reflections and in the manner of their combination, they permit any degree of distortion – either technically unavoidable or deliberately calculated. The results fluctuate from exact naturalistic combinations of visual, interrelated experiences to complete alterations, arrangements unforeseen by nature, and even to abstract formalism, with remnants of reality.[54]

Such arrangements of words and visual images explain how Praz and Melchiori can find in Green's work elements of Mannerism, Futurism, Cubism and Funambulism.[55]

Since Green, however, is a novelist and not a painter, the idea of comparing the structure and style of his work with particular schools of painting has its natural limitations. To seek for correspondence based on what Praz calls 'air de famille ... between the expressions of the arts in any given epoch of the past' seems a dubious approach.[56] René Wellek argues that most methods for the comparisons of the arts 'are based either on vague similarities of emotional effects or on a community of intentions, theories, and slogans which may not be very concretely related to the actual works of arts'.[57] Jean Hagstrum writes that, if a description or image is to be called 'pictorial', 'its leading details and their manner and order of presentation must be imaginable as a painting or sculpture'. In other words, visual detail is not necessarily pictorial. 'Such detail must be ordered in a picturable way.'[58] Much of Green's abstract imagery cannot be directly translated into painting. Also, Green often renders a sense of process – the rhythm of visual perception – which is essentially not pictorial.

This study builds on the premise that comparisons of Green's novels with Cubism, Futurism, and so forth, tend to overemphasize his cognitive perspective on man's predicament. The affective aspect, the author's attitude towards characters and events, can only be fully analysed if Green's fiction is approached on a more microcosmic level. It is necessary to investigate the ways in which descriptions and individual images are composed, as well as how they interact.

The reservations previously expressed concerning the comparison of different art forms also apply to the relationship between literature and film. The analysis of Green's fiction, then, needs a unifying approach that can clarify abstract, pictorial and dynamic aspects. For dealing with such complexities, Eisenstein's principles prove extremely useful. Discussing how a synthesis may arise from the interaction of two contradictory elements, Eisenstein claims that

> a dynamic comprehension of things is ... basic ... for a correct understanding of art and of all art-forms. In the realm of art this dialectic principle of dynamics is embodied in
>
> CONFLICT
>
> as the fundamental principle for the existence of every art-work and every art-form.[59]

Applied to the relationship between the visual arts and literature, one may ask why artistic creation need necessarily be based on conflict.

Eisenstein explains that the 'fundamental principle' of art is always conflict:

1. according to its social mission,
2. according to its nature,
3. according to its methodology.[60]

Art is conflict according to its social mission (1), says Eisenstein, because 'It is art's task to make manifest the contradictions of Being.' Eisenstein's intention is to confront the spectator with life in all its complexity, to create a 'dynamic clash of opposing passions' in his mind, and thereby stir him to form 'equitable views' (what Eisenstein calls 'intellectual concepts'). Green's preference is for a novel which can induce the reader to fuse presented fragments of life in his own imagination. However, Green points out, 'this is not to say that the depersonalization . . . has anything to do with a writer keeping himself out of his novel. He has, of course, to be extremely personal in narrative. He has to create or inspire a conscious act of imagination in the reader.'[61] Similarly, Eisenstein's emphasis is on the way in which the spectator's creative participation enters into a 'process of fusion with the author's intention'. The artist, he says, has before his perception 'a given image, emotionally embodying his themes'.

> The task that confronts him is to transform this image into a few basic *partial representations* which, in their combination and juxtaposition, shall evoke in the consciousness and feelings of the spectator, reader, or auditor, that same initial general image which originally hovered before the creative artist.[62]

The similarities between the theories and practice of Eisenstein and Green point to a method by which tone can be detected. Eisenstein's work on his montage theories was motivated by a desire to resolve 'one of the most difficult problems in constructing works of art . . .: *the problem of portraying an attitude towards the thing portrayed*'. What Eisenstein calls 'attitude' in film resembles I. A. Richards's definition of tone in literature; the attempt to answer

> with what methods and means must the filmically portrayed fact be handled so that it simultaneously shows not only *what* the fact is, and the character's attitude towards it, but also *how* the author relates to it, and how the author wishes the spectator to receive, sense, and react to the portrayed fact.[63]

Eisenstein actually suggests that the cinematographic concept of montage may provide a discriminative method for the interpretation of tone in literature. He argues that 'Literature *per se* has as many means and circuitous expositions as there are ways of perception. But without our premises these mingled forms remain closed to us.'[64]

Art, for Eisenstein, is also conflict according to its 'nature' (2),

because 'Its nature is a conflict between natural existence
and creative tendency.' This statement can best be understood
as meaning a conflict between form (or art as an artifact) and
the formlessness of organic life, of Being. '*The interaction of the
two*', Eisenstein argues, '*produces and determines Dynamism.*' As an
underlying principle of every art form, this tension between
form and formlessness also extends into the relations between
'customary   conception   and   particular   representation   as
dynamic – as a dynamization of the inertia of perception – as
dynamization of the "traditional view" into a new one'.[65] This
consideration justifies my intention of examining the interaction
between particular images in Green's fiction rather than relating
them to the traditional concepts of various schools of painting.
Out of this conflict, new viewpoints and values are seen to arise.
Eisenstein's ideas link him with the Modernist developments in
literary criticism, especially with Cleanth Brooks's view of poetic
language as the language of 'paradox'. 'The poet', Brooks says,
'must work by analogies, but the metaphors do not lie in the
same plane or fit neatly edge to edge. There is a continual
tilting of the planes; necessary overlappings, discrepancies,
contradictions.' In this way, 'the terms are continually modifying
each other, and thus violating their dictionary meanings'.[66]

The interaction of form and formlessness takes place not only
between juxtaposed concepts and images, but also between
words that compose individual images and descriptions. It can
therefore be studied through a common approach in painting,
in poetry and prose, as well as in music. '*The quantity of interval
determines the pressure of the tension*', Eisenstein explains. 'There can
be cases where the distance of separation [notably distortion in
rhythm or metre] is so wide that it leads to a break – to a
collapse of the homogeneous concept of art.' Due to the formal
tension that is created, one may be able to discern some attendant
thematic conflict to which the author invites the reader's or
spectator's response. Or perhaps the values are found precisely
in the intersection of form and formlessness, as in speech where,
according to Eisenstein, 'all its sap, vitality, and dynamism arise
from the irregularity of the part in relation to the laws of the
system as a whole'.[67]

The creation of tension and of tonal qualities, due to a change
in rhythm, can be studied in *Living*:

Evening. Was spring. Heavy blue clouds stayed over above. In small back garden of villa small tree with yellow buds. On table in back room daffodils, faded, were between ferns in a vase. Later she spoke of these saying she must buy new ones and how nice were first spring flowers.   (pp.213–14)

Melchiori compares this passage with an Impressionist painting and the way in which the Impressionist painters heighten 'the emotional quality of the picture by concentrating on the really significant features'. But in this case, he thinks, Green's 'Impressionism' is 'cheap', lacking a 'genuine lyrical . . . power'.[68] Melchiori's interpretation shows how traditional concepts of artistic intention (notably Impressionist) can obscure more than clarify. Green's aim here is not to create a poignant moment of lyrical intensity. The passage must be seen in context, for it occurs immediately after the works manager, in front of his wife, has poured out all his frustration over conditions in the factory. It depicts a natural beauty which cannot be thoroughly appreciated because of an intervening mood. This condition accounts for the pictorial rather than dynamic quality of the passage. Yet the omission of articles together with short, broken sentences give most words a heavy stress, like filmic close-ups, thereby intensifying the vitality of spring and the values of the moment. In contrast, the last sentence runs on monotonously. It suggests the fading away of sense impressions and the inability of the spectator to respond emotionally.

This sentence structure of short, broken phrases and the elimination of articles dramatizes an aspect of the term 'tone' which has been touched on briefly: the tendency to think of 'tone' as a mode of speech. Eisenstein broadens this connection when he argues that 'the very principle of montage, as is the entire individuality of its formation, is the substance of *an exact copy of the language of excited emotional speech*'. His citation from Joseph Vendryes's book *Language* has direct relevance to Green's fiction. Tone is dealt with as an objectified quality, not produced by an interfering author, but arising out of the compositional structure.

The main difference between affective and logical language lies in the construction of the sentence. This difference stands out clearly when we compare the written with the spoken tongue. . . . The elements that the written tongue endeavours to combine into a coherent whole seem to be divided up and disjointed in the spoken tongue: even the order is entirely different. It is no longer the logical order of present-day grammar. It has its logic, but this logic is primarily affective, and the ideas are arranged in accordance with the subjective importance the speaker gives to them or wishes to suggest to his listener, rather than with the objective rules of an orthodox process of reasoning.

According to Vendryes, spoken language 'is cut up into short sections whose number and intensity correspond to the speaker's impressions, or to the necessity he feels for vividly communicating them to others'. Whereas spoken language may have the sensory impact of filmic close-ups, Eisenstein associates the typical 'written' language with a 'long shot'.[69]

By alternating between intense and less intense images and descriptions, or between 'spoken' and 'written' language, Green invites the reader to confront and to watch constructively. His idea that a situation should enact itself dramatically on the reader's mind implies that there is no basic break in method between scenes of dialogue and of description. Eisenstein lists a series of filmic montage conflicts that will be dealt with throughout the following chapters. Of dynamic conflicts both within and between shots, applicable to Green's fiction, can be mentioned conflict of graphic directions, conflict of scales, conflict of volumes, conflict of masses, conflict of depths, conflict of planes, close shots and long shots, conflict between matter and viewpoint, conflict between an event and its duration, and audio-visual counterpoint.[70] These visual conflicts can be either temporarily conceived (the second shot acts as an 'impulse of intensification'), or they arise spatially as in a painting. 'What comprises the dynamic effect of a painting?' Eisenstein asks. As far as conflict of graphic directions is concerned, he suggests,

the eye follows the direction of an element in the painting. It retains a visual impression, which then collides with the impression derived from following the direction of a second element. The conflict of these directions forms the dynamic effect in apprehending the whole.[71]

The dynamic interaction of elements in a painting, as Eisenstein sees it, can be translated into prose, as in *Concluding*:

> The panelling was remarkable in that it boasted a dado designed to continue the black and white tiled floor in perspective, as though to lower the ceiling. But Miss Edge had found marble tiles too cold to her toes, had had the stone covered in parquet blocks, on which were spread State imitation Chinese Kidderminster rugs. As a result, this receding vista of white and black lozenges set from the rugs to four feet up the walls, in precise and radiating perspective, seemed altogether out of place next British dragons in green and yellow; while the gay panelling above, shallow carved, was genuine, the work of a master, giving Cupid over and over in a thousand poses, a shock, a sad surprise in such a room.   (pp.11–12)

This description demonstrates how Green, by juxtaposing contradictory details, is able to objectify an unfavourable attitude towards Miss Edge, the straitlaced headmistress of a girls' boarding-school. The onward progress of the 'precise' black and white pattern is opposed by a tasteless collision of green and yellow dragons. Only in the 'gay' panelling is there a 'genuine' artistic quality, a lively flexibility of Cupid in 'a thousand poses'. It is significant that, whereas the Cupids are described in what Eisenstein refers to as 'excited emotional speech', the rest of the scene is rendered in a sober 'written' style. The overall impression of the room is of discord. In its right context, the passage serves as an indirect comment on how Miss Edge, by her rigorous ways, subdues a harmonious rhythm.

The 'dramatic' principle underlying the 'methodology of art' (3) is accounted for in Eisenstein's discussion of the montage cell:

> The shot is by no means an *element* of montage. The shot is a montage *cell*.

> Just as cells in their division form a phenomenon of another order, the organism or embryo, so, on the other side of the dialectic leap from the shot, there is montage.

Eisenstein goes on to explain that 'Conflict within the shot is potential montage, in the development of its intensity shattering the quadrilateral cage of the shot and exploding its conflict into montage impulses *between* the montage pieces.'[72]

Montage and 'potential' montage have much in common with Imagism. Ezra Pound's idea of an image is that it 'presents an intellectual and emotional complex in an instant of time'. Eisenstein actually suggests such a connection himself when he says that the idea of art as conflict is 'an "imagist" transformation of the dialectical principle'.[73] Characteristic of Imagist poems is their rendering of the writer's response to a visual object or scene, often by means of metaphor or juxtaposition of very concrete details. Images together with an essentially irregular rhythm form a highly energetic unit intended to stimulate the reader's imaginative involvement. A telling example is Ezra Pound's celebrated 'In a Station of the Metro':

> The apparition of these faces in the crowd,
> Petals on a wet, black bough.

Naturally, descriptions in prose cannot reach the same degree of concentration as in poetry. Green, therefore, relies on energizing the connections between images by active, verbal phrases and by creating an energetic rhythm. Among several other obvious examples, the previously cited cinema scenes illustrate these qualities.

Two important conclusions may be drawn from Eisenstein's ideas, and applied to the pursuit of tone in Green's fiction. First, Eisenstein believes that tone arises through the juxtaposition of images and events that act against one another in a spatial framework. The depicted scenes are not elements along a traditional story line, so that their meaning may be inferred through a logical development of the plot. Secondly, the 'montage of attractions' stresses that the position of the separate representations in a frame becomes more important than the specific denotations of the separate representations. Eisenstein states that montage in film achieves its effect by 'combining shots that are depictive, single in meaning, neutral in content'.[74] Whether this principle of filmic montage is directly translatable to literature is more uncertain. Eisenstein realizes that 'the frame is much less independently workable than the word or sound' and that 'the shot's tendency toward complete factual immutability is rooted in its nature'.[75] Due to the more connotative or symbolic quality of words, one can hardly speak of singleness of meaning or neutrality of content in a strict sense. However, Eisenstein's principles are useful, for Green does not embody tone in the separate images that form the montage trope. As in an Imagist poem, various shades of meaning are attached to a metaphor, but real meaning is produced only when the metaphor is juxtaposed with other elements. Thus, Green chooses a bouquet of tulips as the proper image to express Bert's and Lily's celebration of their love, for the sake of which they undertake their runaway trip (*Living*). At the railway station, however, the metaphorical meaning changes quality. By an arrangement similar to what Eisenstein calls association montage,[76] Lily's and Bert's situation becomes deeply ironic.

> Trembling, breathing deeply, she peered round his shoulder at those who were to travel with them. She stood by shoulder of the arm below which hung the tulips, his head bent over hers as she peered round and this movement repeated in her knee which was bent over heads of the tulips as they hung. She had on silk stockings today.   (p.345)

The irony is achieved by a careful closing in of juxtaposed details. First, we follow the direction of Lily's eyes as she turns around to peer at the other travellers. Her movement draws attention to her prospective role as traveller, seen from her own point of view. A sudden shift of focus brings Lily's and Bert's predicament into perspective before the reader; a conflict of matter and viewpoint is created, because what Lily sees differs from what the reader sees from his angle. Lily's and Bert's heads are identified with the drooping heads of the tulips, suggesting the tragic outcome of their love relationship (the tulips have been bought at the cemetery). The repetition of this movement in Lily's knee suggests her inability to carry out her plan of escape. It is significant that all the details taken in by the second shot are tightly knit together in one long sentence without natural breaks. Its structure renders a sense of contraction, enhances the simultaneity of the impressions, and produces a sense of latent conflict. Tension is increased by the succinctness of the last line. Lily's silk stockings point to the ironic delusion of her dream,

because they are worn for this special occasion, she having worn
woollen stockings for a long time to save money for the trip. The
fact that Lily takes her eyes away from the travellers and fixes
them on the drooping flowers confirms the meaning just laid
out. 'She gave up looking at the travellers. She looked now at
the tulips.' Their confusion over where to put the flowers –
'Where'll you put them?' 'Where will I put them?' – reveals the
hopelessness of their dream of settling down in the 'Promised
Land'. 'He raised them up till they were upright as they grew.
"Do not!" she said and snatched at his wrist and turned them
upside down.'

In the final analysis, the whole idea of montage builds on a
view that takes life's contradictory nature into account. Eisenstein
rejects a 'dualistic picture of the world' in which two 'lines' of
conflict run 'towards some hypothetical "reconciliation" where
... the parallel lines would cross, that is, in that infinity, just as
inaccessible as that "reconciliation"'. Eisenstein claims that 'the
microcosm of montage' should 'be understood as a unity, which
in the inner stress of contradictions is halved, in order to be re-
assembled in a new unity on a new plane, qualitatively higher,
its imagery newly perceived'.[77] Although Eisenstein's outlook is
coloured by Marxist dialectics, it suggests interesting similarities
with Green's. It corresponds basically with Green's view that it
is through perception, not ratiocination, that we come to know
life's meaning. The montage trope accommodates the fusion of
conflicting images and events. Selected examples have shown
how the situations of Green's characters are marked by contrasts
and conflicts. By a conventional reading, the depicted complexity
of life may seem to be merely presentational. This study proposes
that the concept of montage will aid the identification of conflicts
that give rise to the tone of Green's fiction.

BLINDNESS (1926) AND *PACK MY BAG* (1940)

Blindness and *Pack my Bag* will receive only cursory attention.
They are mainly autobiographical accounts of adolescent
impressions and experiences.[78] *Blindness* is an introspective portrait of the growth of an artistic consciousness. Green's interest
in the protagonist's consciousness rather than in a reality viewed
from shifting angles reduces the value of a critical montage

approach. Although *Pack my Bag* adopts a more disengaged point
of view, the book still attains the quality of a narrated story
rather than of a dramatized reality.

Despite the minimal use of montage in *Blindness* and *Pack my
Bag*, these works evince themes that illuminate the vision behind
Green's montage technique in other novels. John Haye, a
schoolboy at Noat, encounters tragedy when blinded by a stone
thrown through a train window. The accident is a confrontation
with utter darkness and isolation. The boy's blindness has its
symbolic counterpart in the darkness and confinement of the
factory in *Living*, in the impenetrable fog in *Party Going*, and in
the threat of impending war and death in *Caught* and *Pack my
Bag*. *Pack my Bag* opens with forebodings of catastrophe caused
by 'the war which seems to be coming upon us now and that is
the reason to put down what comes to mind before one is killed,
and surely it would be asking much to pretend one had a chance
to live'.

The poetry of the visual moment, however, counteracts death:
'there must be a threat to one's skin to wake what is left of things
remembered into things to die with. The crime is to forget.'
Green recreates vivid images in his mind: 'we might as well turn
back to when we stumbled home through the dark, our faces
still burning with the day's sun'. These images, Green says, we
should 'take with us like a bar of gold'.[79] The polarity of sunlight
and dark is an essential component in Green's montage of reality's
contradictory facets. The image of contradiction enhances the
acute vitality of perception.

Like *Back*, *Blindness* records the protagonist's struggle towards
a sensuous reintegration with reality. 'There were so many things
to do, all the senses to develop, old acquaintances of childhood
to make friends with again. To sit still and be stifled by the
blackness was wrong.'[80] The acquaintance with childhood does
not imply escape to memory, but the development of a childlike
sensibility: 'they looked back into a past that lived only in their
memories, they did not see the present, the birth of a new life,
of a new art'.[81] Above all, Haye recognizes the necessity of
accepting fate: 'I cannot understand how you endure your life if
you don't see the fineness in its being as it is.'[82]

Haye sees that 'the man who chased tulips on a bicycle was
silly as well as being an idiot, but the piano-tuner might make a
story'.[83] Communion with Life is crucial in order to conquer

alienation in Green's world. Green believes that 'we grow up by
sharing situations, what we share of another person's increases
us'.[84] Nevertheless, he does not explore the vital importance of
these values caused by a contradictory world. The narrators'
reflections and evaluations are more central than the
objectification of life's complexity. Consequently, the use of
montage is not as essential here as in other works of Green. Most
of his fiction contains an intricate fabric of disparate scenes and
points of view. Montage highlights values and tone in relation
to characters' interaction with a contradictory reality.

2 *Living* (1929)

As pointed out in the Introduction, Green's idea of 'non-representational' fiction entails the conveyance of life's complexity. This effect is achieved through authorial 'disengagement' (although not consistently maintained in Green's early novels), through visualization and the use of metaphor. Hence, it is natural that an examination of tone in Green's second novel, *Living*, should begin with a discussion of its most central motif: birds. The pervasive prominence of the birds obviously attaches more to them than mere literal significance. Suggesting freedom and escape, they serve as metaphorical objectification of the characters' subjective feelings. In some symbolic way, they also are connected with the main conflict in the novel: that between freedom and confinement. Prior to an examination of montage conflicts, therefore, one should try to determine to what extent birds symbolize the tone of *Living*'s plot.

Green makes extensive use of a scenic method in *Living* in order to depict the lives of the Birmingham foundry workers and their families. Disparate, fragmented and rapidly shifting scenes reveal different aspects of the predominant monotony, blackness and petty foundry rivalries. The communal aspiration among the workers towards illumination and freedom is suggested by the invasion of sunbeams and birds through the stained factory windows. 'We pay them [the workers] while they bet on these sparrows', Mr Bridges, the works manager, complains to the new director, Dick Dupret, 'and you can't stop it. You can't keep the sparrows out. I've had a man on the roof three weeks now patching holes they come in by. But they find a way' (p.208).

In a similar manner, pigeons provide a symbolic equivalent for Lily's flight from home. Lily is a young woman who keeps house for Mr Craigan, a taciturn, aging moulder who governs his domicile with authority. Joe Gates, the irascible, discontented father of Lily, and the young Jim Dale, Craigan's assistant, also inhabit the house. For Mr Craigan, the maintenance of domestic order is paramount. 'In this 'ouse', he tells Lily, 'the wage earners must 'ave hot meals every night bar Fridays, if they don't come back midday for it. And on Saturdays, there is to be two 'ot meals, and one on Sunday' (pp.342–3). In order to secure the continuity of the household, Mr Craigan has even picked a potential husband for Lily, the dependable Jim Dale, to whom Lily is indifferent. The basic conflict between Lily and the other members of the Craigan household emanates from her anxiety to escape her domestic entrapment towards some kind of freedom she has difficulties defining. Conflicting with Lily's need for freedom are the obstacles to self-assertion represented by the attractions of security and her attachment to old Craigan. The complex symbolic quality of the pigeons is analysed by Keith Odom in his observation of their connection with Lily: 'The principal objects that she assimilates with her obsessions are pigeons, symbolic of escape and freedom as well as of home and security.'[1] Like the pigeons, Lily travels far away but eventually returns home. Green comments upon the direction of Lily's flight: 'For as racing pigeons fly in the sky, always they go round above house which provides for them ... so her thoughts would not point away long from house which had provided for her' (p.348).

A central question is whether Green's symbolic equation of Lily and the pigeons signals the tone of the plot. The correlation between Lily's movement and that of the pigeons suggests Lily as the central character of *Living*. It is her movement that holds the central focus in the second half of the novel. Like the pigeons, Lily returns to Craigan's house after disappointment in love. This fact might suggest a reconciliation with her former role as housekeeper, and a submission to Mr Craigan's mandates.

Although the pigeons are representative in many ways of characters, they are nevertheless insufficient for the clarity and consistency necessary if symbols are to define the tone of intricate conflicts. Green's correlation of Lily and the pigeons represents his cognitive perspective on man's predicament in an irreconcilable world. It expresses a sense of generic inevitability: 'With us it is not only food, as possibly it is for pigeon, but if we are for any length of time among those who love us and whom we love too, then those people become part of ourselves' (p.348). By equating Lily's dependence with that of the pigeons, Green

relates Lily to all the other characters in the novel, most of whom
dream of freedom but are unable to escape. A sense of destiny
hovers over Lily's instinctual return home, suggesting man's
need for attachment.

The pigeons' inevitable return places the characters' escapist
dreams in an ironic perspective. However, since Lily's escape is
merely a symptom of her lack of fulfilment, the same pigeon
symbolism does not evaluate deeper personal needs and motives.
Accordingly, the pigeons' symbolic homeward flight cannot
affirm the resolution of conflict for Lily. Continuing conflict,
rather, seems to be her subjective experience. This view finds
support in the image of the cinema, a reflection of Lily's emotional
needs. Prior to her elopement, she regularly goes to the cinema
to seek vicarious fulfilment in tropical settings. After her return
home, she still goes to the movies, as if little has changed.
Significantly, standing by the kitchen window, 'she thought in
feeling of that band, which was playing now in her heart, in the
cinema, and even without a pang now she thought of band in
that railway train. And at the cinema last night, what a good
band that was' (p.379). Suddenly, at the cry of her neighbour's
baby, she runs out of Mr Craigan's house and round to Mrs
Eames's. The last scene in the novel shows Lily in a moment of
bliss, pushing Mrs Eames's baby in the pram. Pigeons are
fluttering above her head.

The meaning of the fluttering pigeons in the last scene is a
complex one. There is no evidence that the scene symbolizes
Lily's change of heart and her submission to Craigan's values.
It depicts a *moment* of delight, which is applauded by the pigeons.
The pigeons' celebration of the poetic moment points to their
related function in other contexts: birds' freedom and vivacity
under the sky, or as they flutter among the machinery in the
factory, contrast positively with the unfulfilled lives of most of
the characters. Lily's joy gives the novel a hopeful ending, but
her still unfulfilled needs are revealed by her preoccupation with
the Eameses' baby. The window, by which she stands dreaming
before the final scene, is a recurrent motif in *Living*. It suggests
a sense of disparity between Craigan's kitchen and an envisaged
world outside, filled with pigeon flocks. In the same mode, it is
important that the Eameses live next door to Mr Craigan. In
several contexts, shifts of focus between the adjoining houses
produce contrasts that objectify Lily's unfulfilled needs. It is

crucial to note that this opposition induces a central value statement in *Living*. Accordingly, only a montage approach can fully reveal Green's message. In the following passage, different montage conflicts combine to accentuate this discordance, and thereby convey the appropriate tone. The first shot provides a glimpse into the Craigan household:

> Weather was hot. They lived back of a street and kitchen which they ate in was on to their garden. Range made kitchen hotter. A man next door to them kept racing pigeon and these were in slow air. They ate in shirt sleeves. Plump she was. They did not say much.
>
> Baby howled till mother there lifted him from bed to breast and sighed most parts asleep in darkness. Gluttonously baby sucked....
>
> Later woke Mr Eames. Sun shone in room and Mrs woke.
> 'Oh dear' he cried. He sneezed.
> 'What makes you always sneeze at the sun I don't know' she said most parts asleep and he said 'another day'. She now was not quite woke up and said you wouldn't believe, she was so happy now.
> 'Dear me' he murmured sliding back into sleep. They slept.
> Later alarm clock sounded next door.
> They woke.   (p.215)

Green's picture of racing pigeons under the sky heightens, through a conflict of *scales*, the sense of a stuffy, narrow 'range' in Craigan's kitchen. The montage serves to accent its subdued atmosphere. A sudden *audio-visual counterpoint*, produced by the Eameses's baby, collides with the subdued silence in the Craigan household, enhancing the conflict of *planes* between the two houses. In this context, moreover, the baby, through *association montage*, points directly to Lily's unfulfilled needs. The contrasting image of the Eameses, lying in bed, half asleep, happily greeting the sun coming in through the window, represents the kind of fulfilling relationship for which Lily is yearning. This idyllic picture is soon distorted, through an *audio-visual counterpoint*, by Craigan's alarm clock next door. Mrs Eames emphasizes the tone of the passage and its allusion to Lily's situation:

She said was one thing to these houses with narrow walls it
saved buying alarm clocks. . . . Rod of iron he [Mr Craigan]
ruled with in that house she said . . . 'or more likely a huge
great poker. That poor girl' she said, 'and not even his
daughter but 'e won't let 'er go out to work, nor out of the
House Hardly.' (pp.215–16)

As demonstrated in this scene, montage enhances the sensory
immediacy of the content. Thus, montage produces tone by
intensifying the emotive quality of the opposition.

A discussion of how the montage of incongruous images
fashions the tone of *Living* demands a close consideration of the
Eameses. The minor role played by them in the active formation
of the plot, and their less prominent existences as compared with
the Craigan household, might imply that the essential balance
is too unequal to connote a major conflict. However, almost like
the spirit of Mrs Ramsay in *To the Lighthouse*, the example of the
Eameses suffuses the novel and brings characters and events
into relief. Various episodes in *Living* develop depth through
comparison and association with the Eameses' values. They are
by no means an ordinary and average pair, although they, like
most others, are connected with the factory, comply with its
routines, and lead an outwardly unadventurous life. The Eameses
appear as the only thoroughly satisfied couple in the whole of
Green's canon. Seen against the sordid background Green
depicts, this is a consideration of great importance. They also
seem to be the only characters in *Living* who do not dream of
escape. This aspect adds to the almost unreal quality of their
existence, and sets them up as an ideal which others can only
approximate.

Some characters suffer from a sense of futility at the limited
opportunities for escape. In the mind of Dick Dupret, the flux
of time is felt as a continuous, disintegrating force.

And what was in all this, he said as he was feeling now, or in
any walk of life – you were born, you went to school, you
worked, you married, you worked harder, you had children,
you went on working, with a good deal of trouble your children
grew up, then they married. What had you before you died?
Grandchildren? The satisfaction of breeding the glorious
Anglo-Saxon breed? (p.328)

Mrs Eames's words to her child stand in sharp contrast to Dick's:

> Why do we bring kids into the world, they leave you so soon
> as they're grown, eh? But you don't know one of these things
> yet. But sure as anything you'll leave us when you're a man,
> and who'll we 'ave then, eh cruel? Sons and daughters, why
> do we bring them into the world? She was laughing. Because,
> because she said laughing and then lay smiling and then
> yawned.   (pp.222–3)

Mrs Eames's laughter stems from the pleasure she finds in
breeding the 'Anglo-Saxon breed'. John Russell, however, is not
entirely right when suggesting that her contentment at knowing
that her son will become a turner like his father signifies 'her
allegiance to the continuum, that promises fruition'.[2] Green deals
with more than one level of reality. It seems that her acceptance
of the monotony which most of the characters want to escape has
to do with her recognition of the material necessity represented by
the factory. 'Yes,' she says, 'and so long as 'is lathe goes round
he'll be there, earning 'is money like 'is dad.... We shan't be
up to much work not when you've been a man for long so you'll
look to our comfort' (p.222). The thought of her son becoming
a factory worker like all the others is burdensome to Mrs Eames:
'She sighed. She fed him. She felt cold but he was warm.' And
Mr Eames, listening to his wife's monologue, then remarks that
'it always did rain in this town though garden would benefit'.
The Eameses have a private world (i.e. garden) not envisaged as
drab and monotonous. Despite the blackness of the surroundings,
they are able to perceive and cultivate organic values. Mr Eames
stresses the positive aspect of bad weather; the rain is a
prerequisite for growth in the garden.

Rather than committing themselves to the 'continuum', the
Eameses are divided between the need to find some compatibility
with life in the factory and in the private world where the garden
is seen as a vital force. Mr Eames is a conscientious and
industrious working man, a turner at the factory and a gardener
at home. But his devotion to the values associated with the
garden is enhanced by the fact that one never sees him at
the factory. The following scene effectively accentuates basic
conflicts, lending tonal affirmation to Mr Eames's attitude
to life. He is working in his garden when Mr Bentley, a

fellow worker, comes up to him and starts to criticize conditions in the factory. However, Mr Eames refuses to let intrigues interfere with his gardening. When Mr Bentley tells him that he had seen Bert Jones back at work that morning, after having been dismissed for some offence against the management, Eames answers rather casually that he had not noticed. Bert's leaving without a fight annoys Bentley while Mr Eames is diplomatic: ''E didn't 'ave any choice.' When Bentley goes on to denounce the unfairness of it all, Mr Eames is just as impartial: 'Well they 'aven't trespassed against the law.' Bentley's resentment for their treatment of another worker, Alfred Parker, cannot arouse Eames's indignation: 'I ain't got nothing to say for that.' Another fellow, Whitacre, had, according to himself and Bentley, been unfairly dismissed, but Eames cannot accept one-sided criticism: 'Well I don't know anything about what you just said there – it ain't anything but 'is story is it?' Mr Eames's reasons for attempting to avoid conversation about negative experience are similar to Bentley's reasons for not telling his wife about his problems: 'she 'as 'ardships enough keeping her and me alive on our money without me telling 'er the pinpricks you get all the time at our place' (pp.238–9).

A shift of focus suddenly interrupts Bentley's tirade of abuse, as if thinking of his wife has put him in a more appreciative mood. The reader's attention is drawn to the smoke from Bentley's pipe which 'went slowly up through bars of sunlight here and there which came between leaves of apple tree' (p.239). The smoke, in its association with the factory and with Bentley's discontentment, merges with the life-giving sun and the apple tree of Mr Eames's garden. Bentley's obsession with injustice, with working conditions he considers 'contrary to nature', has diverted him from natural values. The smoke's movement, however, is a metaphorical visualization of the way in which his mind is suddenly transported towards the sun: '"Ah it's a fine crop" Mr Bentley said, changing tone, "and it's a good thing for a man to get away in the evenings out into the air"' (ibid.). Significantly, the fusion of disparate images provides the appropriate tone of the passage. Smoke and sunlight merge in a conflict of *masses* to create a moment of natural beauty. The juxtaposition of different intensities of light deepens the conflict between the smoke and the sunlight. By their contiguity, however, the former also heightens the value of the latter. The resultant image is an

intensification of Mr Eames's garden and of his attitude to
life.

It should be pointed out that Mr Eames's reluctance to
criticize or take sides does not mean that he is out of touch with
actuality, or that his domestic contentment is the result of his
inability to penetrate the orderings of his illusions. That the
problems in the factory are just as real to Mr Eames as to Bentley
is clear from the way Mr Eames speaks to his wife when he
comes into the house.

> 'I'm not saying a lot of what 'e touched on 'e wasn't justified
> in saying. To my way of thinking they didn't ought to keep
> the tackle in the way they do. The crane in our shop ain't safe
> now and Aaron Connolly driving it don't make it safer.'
>
> The lathes he said were all anyhow and any time now he
> said glass roof might fall in if gale of wind came.
>
> 'You'll give me fits' she said.
>
> 'And the government inspector's meant to look to all that
> but there's a woman comes to our place mostly and what can
> she know about it. And there ain't a girl in the whole factory.
> Old Bentley didn't mention that nor did I for I thought 'e
> might never stop if I went on suggesting things to 'im.'
>
> 'That's right' she said 'don't get into argument with that
> sort ...
>
> It ain't going to do no good to your wife or child.'　(p.248)

The Eameses' self-sufficiency is a conscious attitude which they
adopt to make possible the growth of the garden.

Even if the Eameses' values answer to the ideal communicated
in *Living*, this does not imply that Green advocates escape into
private seclusion and avoidance of social responsibility. It
suggests first of all that his preoccupation is with the importance
of cultivating the human spirit as a prerequisite to growth. The
fact that the Eameses are not actively involved in political issues
or with the concerns of society does not distinguish them from
most of Green's other characters. Their largely apolitical attitude
reflects Green's statement that his novels are about love, and his
belief that people are not interested in 'political, religious, or
sociological' ideas.[3] The values communicated through the
Eameses do not so much enjoin the extrusion of society at large
as the necessity of filtering out negative influence which may

infect the creative powers associated with the garden. It is significant, for example, that Mrs Eames thinks it unreasonable that Craigan denies Lily the right to go out to work. For the same reason, it is not from the factory itself that Mrs Eames wants to dissociate herself when, referring to Bentley, she asks her husband not to 'get into argument with that sort'. Nor does she express opinions against improvement of conditions for the factory workers. She is primarily anxious about the contagious influence that may spread from people (Bentley is a member of a revolutionary group) who are generally dissatisfied with their lot.

Green's message is that, against the disintegrating forces in society, man must try to respond with the best in himself: love. Mrs Eames resembles Mrs Ramsay in *To the Lighthouse*, who knits, tends her garden, mediates and creates in face of disorder. Mrs Eames's convictions point to some sort of existentialist value system in the author. Obsession with injustice is self-denying, and therefore life-denying, because disorder is permanent, and the attempt to abolish it can only bring bitterness and frustration. This is the wisdom behind the Eameses' struggle to build love and meaning upon flux: 'love', Mrs Eames says to her baby, 'they might come in the night and steal you away. And what would we do then, and what would we do then?' (pp.248–9).

The values insisted upon by the Eameses are recurrently contrasted with less reverent attitudes. Mr Bridges and Mr Walters are complaining about the workers and how they escape from work all the time by going into the latrines. 'Then I go into the latrines, what do I run into, more trouble, two robbers sitting on the seat, without even their trousers off, smoking. I said to them "You might as well go straight to the chief's back pocket and take the money from it"' (p.231). Problems are redoubled by the fact that old Mr Dupret, the elderly owner of the factory, has become bed-ridden and has handed over the management to his son, Dick, who is a disturbing influence in the foundry. Problems and intrigues are paramount in the consciousnesses of Bridges and Walters.

'And I've served 'im faithfully for fifteen years. It's a nightmare. Where am I, eh? Where do I stand then, tell me that.'

Mrs Eames put cold new potato into her mouth.
'Ain't they good' said she.
'They are' he said.
'Better'n what you could get up the road or if you took a tram up into town.'
'There's none like your own.'   (pp.231–2)

A sudden shift of focus from the factory to the placid domesticity of the Eameses, who are savouring crops from their garden, creates a conflict of *planes*. The incongruity of atmosphere accentuates the life-denying quality of Bridges's and Walters's states of mind. This conflict of planes draws attention to other montage conflicts. In context, they serve to exalt the Eameses' attempt to build a microcosm of private serenity by eschewing the disturbing forces around them. 'So for a time they ate supper. She sat on then looking out of window. When she turned and put hands on table to get up and clear away supper she noticed those flowers.'

The window, through which Mrs Eames sits in her kitchen, observing the macrocosm of the distant town, fashions a conflict of *scales* between two spatial dimensions, suggesting her separation from what she sees. A conflict between *close and long shots* intensifies this impression. It is created when Mrs Eames shifts her attention from the outer world to the inner. There is a shift of focus from what can be observed to what can be touched, connoting closeness and concord. The moment she puts her hands on the table, she notices the flowers. '"Why look" said she "you brought 'em back from the garden only yesterday and I put them in that pot, and now all their faces 've turned to the sun"' (p.232). The bright infinity of the sun creates a conflict of *masses* and *scales* in contrast with the pot which, by juxtaposition, connotes a sense of confinement. Green's personification of the flowers in the pot indicates his symbolic equation of the pot and the finiteness of the Eameses' world. However, the fruition of the Eameses' attitude to life is affirmed by the fact that the flowers' 'faces' have turned to the life-giving sun.

Significantly, the values of the previous scenes are communicated by the series of montage conflicts just referred to; montage accents vital aspects of the context. Green intensifies the tone of the preceding passage by a conflict of *planes*, through which impressions from the Eameses' household collide with impressions from the Craigan household.

> Water dripped from tap on wall into basin and into water there. Sun. Water drops made rings in clear coloured water. Sun in there shook on the walls and ceiling. As rings went out round trembling over the water shadows of light from sun in these trembled on walls. On the ceiling.
>
> They came back from work. Mr Joe Gates was speaking.
>
> 'Ah and didn't I tell that foreman only a month or two back it would go, silly cow keeping on using it till it went.'   (Ibid.)

Due to their central role in related contexts, the basin in Craigan's kitchen and the pot in the Eameses' form symbolic counterparts. The idea that the basin symbolizes the Craigan household is affirmed by Green's equation of the trembling water rings and the sun which 'shakes' on Craigan's walls and ceiling. This image, however, does not suggest hope or fruition, but repression of life-giving forces. The collision (conflict of *graphic directions*) of the trembling sun with the walls and ceiling effects a sense of entrapment. It serves as an ironic comment upon the life-denying atmosphere in Craigan's house.

Green adds precision to his use of the montage technique by immediately focusing on Joe Gates, who, together with Craigan, has just come home from work. Gates is vehemently blaming the foreman at the foundry for an accident in which a wire rope parted and missed Craigan by inches. Green, however, is not primarily concerned with social or institutional amendment. As previously suggested, the lack of a consistent point of view in his novels hinders effective satire or criticism of society. The central issue in this scene is Gates's obsession with injustice and his readiness to blame his surroundings for any ill fortune. This interpretation is supported by certain systematic parallels between the two patriarchs in *Living*, Craigan and Dupret.[4] The most significant parallel in this connection is the way in which both are finally faced with life's capriciousness. Whereas Craigan is nearly killed by the whip of a wire rope, Dupret is bed-ridden after slipping on excrement in the street. These two accidents, if viewed together, reflect the incidental nature of life which no one is really able to control.

Montage of visual images is the most important device by

which Green deepens the meaning of the scene in Craigan's kitchen. By varying the distance between the 'camera' and the object, and by focusing on different details, Green manipulates the point of view of the narrative so that meaning is put in an unexpected perspective. Gates is raging over the stupidity of the foreman and over all the injustice he encounters in the factory. Suddenly, his tirade of abuse is interrupted by other details: 'Mr Craigan washed first in basin. Lily Gates came in then' (p.232). Green's association of the basin with a sense of conflict and confinement has already been suggested in the preceding scene. Here he links the basin with the disturbing effects of Gates's resentment. They are all burdened by notions of life's precariousness in the factory, reinforced by Gates.

Green uses various grammatical devices to stress the function and significance of the basin image. His omission of the definite article to modify 'basin' accents the noun, increasing thereby the immediacy of its visual impact.[5] Craigan's and Lily's movement, described in two brief, succinct statements, collide with the sentence structure of Gates's colloquial flow of words. These features contribute to the dynamic quality of the two shots in that they generate a sudden visual *close-up*. The effect is intensified by recurrent repetitions of the basin image, interrupting Gates's continuing monologue: 'Lily Gates went to basin and stood there by Mr Craigan.... Joe Gates put head under water in basin' (pp.232–3). The fact that Gates puts his head into the basin stresses his separation from the Eameses, whose flowers (symbolic of their 'faces') in the pot stretch towards the sun. Gates's act suggests his mental confinement, and his alienation from the sun.

Such connected images as the basin, the pot and the sink possess referential qualities only when viewed in relation to other images, such as the sun. Their indefinable meaning in isolation probably explains why critics seem to have completely overlooked them. Even more recognizable images – pigeons and sparrows – lack the precision of reference and consistency commonly characterizing symbols.

The question whether Green's arrangement of images really corresponds to themes of the intellect requires further elucidation. It is correct that most of his images are not of the kind which W. B. Yeats names 'intellectual symbols', as opposed to 'emotional symbols'. Yeats gives examples of these two categories of symbols:

If I say 'white' or 'purple' in an ordinary line of poetry, they evoke emotions so exclusively that I cannot say why they move me; but if I bring them into the same sentence with such obvious intellectual symbols as a cross or a crown of thorns, I think of purity and sovereignty.[6]

The tone of the scenes in which these symbols combine is immediately clear; one knows how the author relates to them, because 'purity' and 'sovereignty' are commonly associated with these symbols through cultural conditioning. Images of birds, on the other hand, have no fixed symbolic meaning, even when combined with colours such as blood red, red gold, and black, as in the sunset scene in *Concluding*. Yet Green's birds – whether pigeons, sparrows, or starlings – do not completely lack an intellectual content; they are not a strictly subjective expression. Birds, as cultural phenomena, are generally associated with values of freedom and vivacity, and so they are in Green's work. What makes their metaphorical value difficult to determine is that Green's fiction can be read on different levels of meaning; the reader must try to discriminate between the birds' purely presentational functions and their significance in the creation of tone. The latter function, as has been suggested, is discernible through Green's intensification of the dynamic quality of his narrative, notably by rapid transitions from one visual detail to another, by a distortion of sentence rhythm, or by a spatial collision of lines, forms and colours.

The possible reservation that Green's images lack meaning because lacking a definite reference to known facts or persons also requires attention. The 'cross' and the 'crown of thorns' in Yeats's example, combined with 'white' and 'purple', gain symbolic power in light of events that link these images to one specific person. It is difficult to see how the pot, the sun or the birds, combined with certain colours, can express personal qualities in a similar way. Green, however, has no intention of evaluating characters' motives or integrity through their representation by definable symbols. His images contribute to the creation of tone in concrete situations, and their function depends on the particular context. This technique implies that the same image used in different scenes does not necessarily give identical tonal qualities to these scenes. Tone is created by the 'camera angle', the distance of the camera from the photographed object, the scope of the screen, or the special sequence of shots. In this manner, the image of the pot or the basin may be used with different tonal effect in situations involving the Eameses, Joe Gates or Mr Craigan.

Sometimes montage of several images and scenes is required to evolve the tone of one particular situation. An illustrative example is provided by the scene in which Lily expresses her desire to have a job. The job represents a certain measure of freedom to her. Most of the time, she is isolated from normal contact with people her own age. As she tells Bert Jones, 'Oh yes, and how would you like to stay in all day by yourself and keep a place tidy ... and then when they give you the 'ouse-keeping money Friday night to have nothing but black looks' (p.257). Lily's father compounds the difficulties of her situation through indifference and insult. Jim Dale increases Lily's sense of confinement by sulking whenever he feels rejected. His role is to conform to Craigan's orderings: 'Lil ... we ought to be going 'ome or the old man won't like it' (p.236). When Lily asks permission to have a job, Craigan denies her this right on the grounds that 'None o' the womenfolk go to work from the house I inhabit' (p.215). Lily 'carried dirty plates to the sink then'.

In isolation, Lily's act and the *close-up* of the sink convey no precise meaning, except that the sink is suggestive of Lily's sense of confinement. However, Green's use of the time adverbial 'then', combined with the sudden determination of Lily's action, suggest that the 'shot' is, on one level, meant as an objectification of Lily's private emotional response to Craigan's rigidity. It is impossible to determine the nature of the author's response on the basis of this single 'shot' alone. Previous examples have shown, however, how clues to the determination of tone may be found in the choice of words and syntax, as well as in the selection of visual details. In the passage immediately preceding the clash between Lily and Craigan, Green looks into Craigan's kitchen at dinner time:

> Craigan sat at head of table in his house. His mate Mr Gates sat with him to supper and his mate's daughter brought over shepherd's pie from range and the young fellow also was at table who worked with him also in the foundry, Jim Dale.
> She laid dish on the table. She wiped red, wet hands on dishcloth.   (pp.214–15)

The different members of the group are focused on consecutively. However, by means of various syntactic devices, Green brings them all (except Craigan) together in one single photographed frame. This effect is achieved by an elision of commas, which makes the different clauses (which are linked with 'and') run into one another, and which increases the flow and speed of reading. A distortion of a normal syntax is also noticeable in his presentation of Jim Dale. By this device, Green avoids interjectional clauses to introduce Jim Dale, and concentrates first on placing him as a member of the group. The summary impression of Green's technique creates a sense of detachment or distance from the people around the table – a group of people who as separate individuals do not deserve special focus. The relevance of this analysis becomes clear in the next 'shot': a *close-up* of Lily's hands as she puts the dish on the table. Eisenstein's definition of a close-up has direct applicability here. As opposed to the American film producer Griffith, who attaches the term 'close-up' to 'viewpoint', to what is 'near', Eisenstein associates the term with 'large scale', because what is important is the 'qualitative side of the phenomenon', 'the value of what is seen'. The 'principal function of the close-up', therefore, is 'not only and not so much to show or to present, as to signify, to give meaning, to designate'.[7] The curt, paratactic style of the two sentences centring on Lily (both begin with 'She', and all connectives are omitted) sets them off from the smooth flow of the preceding sentence. By giving each word in 'red, wet hands' heavy stress, Green creates a 'large-scale' moment of intensified perception. The associations of hard labour and servitude evoked by Lily's 'red, wet hands' signal the author's warm support for her needs.

In order further to heighten the tone of the previous scene, Green shifts his focus from the conversation in the kitchen to the racing pigeons in the background. The pigeons are mainly a device used by Green to enhance the sense of confinement in the kitchen, by juxtaposing the kitchen with the freedom of the sky. This incongruity between foreground and background provides a detached, ironic comment on Craigan's life-negating insistence on domestic discipline.

Birds are commonly used for the purpose of commenting on various events, rather than for representing tone in relation to individual characters' motives. They serve this latter function, however, in the scene in which a bird is caught between the window frames in Craigan's kitchen. After unsuccessful attempts by Craigan, Dale and Gates to free it, they fetch Mrs Eames next door, who, with a gentle manoeuvre, releases the bird. 'She said, "Where's Lily then?" ' (p.220). The bird, which throughout *Living* has been linked with freedom and the organic, is here associated with Lily, due to the sudden juxtaposition of the two. Just like the bird, Lily is trapped in Craigan's kitchen, and none of the men in the house can give her what she needs. Joe Gates, who does not recognize the symbolic reference between Lily and the bird, has been put into a jocular mood by the incident and starts telling coarse stories (in fact, he has just been telling dirty jokes about 'tarts and birds'). When Mrs Eames leaves, offended, Gates explains to the others that 'he wanted to wake her up'. The discrepancy between Gates's remark and Mrs Eames's previously revealed attitudes produces tone through irony. Mrs Eames certainly is wide awake to the less innocent sides of life, as well as to the lack of reverence for life as exhibited by some people.

Green's attitude towards the conflict between Craigan and Lily is amplified through a conflict of *close and long shots*. The focus shifts from the group of people to Craigan, who has suddenly left the small, stuffy kitchen: 'He sat outside in the last light of sun which had shone all day' (ibid.). Due to the ambiguous relation between image and context, this 'shot' offers two possible interpretations. However, this deliberately cultivated ambiguity only heightens the richness of the passage in that the two possible meanings together contribute towards the creation of a basic tone. When Mrs Eames, after freeing the bird, asks for Lily, her question is addressed to Craigan, 'but Craigan was saying no more'. Craigan's muteness indicates his recognition of the symbolic connection between Lily and the trapped bird. He seems to feel guilt because of his restrictive treatment of her, for, while sitting outside, he 'looked troubled in his mind'. The fact that he is sitting under a fading sun may thus be read as a reflection of his troubled conscience. Craigan's sudden impulse to seek the last rays of sun also emphasizes another possible interpretation: namely, that he wants to dissociate himself from Gates and his lack of respect for Mrs Eames, and indirectly for Lily. Either interpretation puts the happening in the kitchen in perspective before the reader. Green praises

Mrs Eames's reverence for life and disapproves of the conditions which make Lily's situation burdensome: Gates's lack of sensitivity to fellow beings, and Craigan's restraining domination. At the same time, there is some suggestion that Craigan attempts to eschew the cynicism which radiates from Gates, and which Lily finds so intolerable.

Craigan's deprecation of ill feeling in his surroundings is drawn attention to several times throughout *Living*. When Gates loses his temper with the foreman who stands watching him and Craigan in the foundry and mutters, 'Dirty bleeder', Craigan cuts him off: ' "You talk more'n is natural in a man" ... and then no word was said between them' (p.228). When another time one of the boys in the foundry denigrates Gates, Craigan snaps at him, 'Clear off my lad and don't tell tales' (p.222). One night in the pub Gates begins making derogatory remarks about Mr Bridges in a most humiliating way. 'And Joe was about to draw attention of all the world to Mr Bridges, and bartender was already saying with appeal Joe, Joe when Craigan got up and butted him in the stomach with his head' (p.376). Although Craigan's desire to avoid intrigue and ill feeling takes a cruder and more authoritarian form than does Mr Eames's, their basic motives are similar. Both, in their individual ways, recognize that resentment is infectious and may degrade life.

Craigan may in some respects, then, be said to share attitudes with the Eameses, attitudes which represent basic values in *Living*. Craigan's situation, however, is different and more complicated, for, whereas the Eameses' home is an oasis in a world of conflict, it is in his own home that Craigan's mediatory powers are tried. He has to contend with crossing ambitions and needs that exist on a larger scale in the factory and in society at large. The question Green indirectly asks is how life is best served in such a situation. It is on this level that a consistent pattern of visual devices emerges, contributing to the revelation of tone.

Craigan's basic humanism notwithstanding, he distrusts the deeper motives behind Lily's romantic longings. He especially questions her unwillingness to settle down with Jim Dale. Seeing that she is really indifferent to Jim Dale's courtship, Craigan believes it is only because she wants to 'fly higher':

Suddenly he broke out into loud voice: 'I wouldn't educate

my son above the station 'e was born in', he said and then
whispering 'what is there in it, old Dupret 'ad to work twelve
hours a day to keep 'is money I'll be bound 'e did. . . . An' a
motor-car, aint we better on the feet our mothers bore
us.'   (p.312)

In an attempt to discourage Lily from ever leaving the household,
Craigan tells her about her Aunt Ellie, who, as a young woman,
had married a drover. But, he says, Ellie had not found him
good enough and had run away, for which she had bitterly learnt
her lesson. 'Her [Lily] blubbered when I told 'er of her Aunt
Ellie', Craigan chuckles to himself. '"Ah" he said "but as the
tree leans so the branches is inclined"' (p.311). Craigan interprets
Lily's restless yearning to be only a wish for self-betterment and
a sign of vain pretentiousness. At times, he thinks 'it was
selfishness that was all of Miss Gates' (ibid.). Craigan emphasizes
the painful limitations of his own adolescent dream of making
his way up in the world: '"But I'm no more'n a moulder, a sand
rat, and will be till they think I'm too old for work. . . . No that
sort never do" he said, and smoked pipe and did not watch her
crying.' His own lack of fulfilment in his present situation is
stressed by the fact that he then 'got up and went inside and
listened to the wireless' (pp.269–70). The wireless is the habitual
means by which Craigan finds escape.
   Craigan's admonition to Lily foreshadows the failure of her
attempted escape. With his dominant awareness of life's limitations, however, Craigan is himself a victim of self-deception.
He fails to see Lily's human potential for what it is, and misjudges
the force behind its need for realization. Green makes sure that
the reader sees a more complete picture of Lily than what can
be attributed to mere selfishness and vanity. Her bewildered cry
in bed is the expression of her fundamental need to serve and to
fulfil her female nature:

   Why may I not have children, feed them with my milk.
   Why may I not kiss their eyes, lick their skin, softness to
   softness, why not I? I have no man, my work is for others, not
   for mine.
   Why may I not work for mine?
   Why mayn't they laugh at my coming in to them. Why is
   there nothing that lives by me. And I would do everything by

my child in the morning and at evening, why haven't I one? I
would work for him who made child with me, oh day and
night I'd be working for them, and get up in the night to feed
him and in the morning to get father's tea. I would be his
mother, he his father, why have I no child?   (p.278)

What Lily wants most is to live in the kind of fulfilling relationship
that Mr and Mrs Eames have created. Green's sympathy for
Lily's motives suffuses his dramatization of the conflict between
her and Craigan. Even though her dreams of escape are, to a
large extent, based on romantic illusions, there is no inconsistency
in tone, whether Green is dealing with the Eameses or with the
relationship between Lily and Craigan. If life's natural limitations
prevent her from finding absolute fulfilment, Green does not
treat ironically her need to be 'I, I am I.' Returning pigeons
may symbolize man's inability to break out of a predestined
pattern or circle, but Lily is also identified with the bird
entrapped in Craigan's window, which only Mrs Eames is able
to set free. Mrs Eames is the only one to appreciate that Lily's
efforts are directed towards the sun. She is the only one that sees
how unfair it is to restrict Lily's freedom, and her opportunity
to find the man she likes. Furthermore, by the image of the
trapped bird, Lily is also linked with the birds that are impossible
to keep out of the factory, and thus with the needs of the
thousands of people who are streaming in and out of Dupret's
factory every day. The suggestion that their needs are natural
and indomitable gives them universal validity. Craigan's effort
to pin Lily down is against nature, and his desire to make the
order of his house permanent is therefore doomed to failure.

Green's manner of selecting and emphasizing details of his
narrative delineates two clashing sets of values in the Craigan
household. Whereas Lily is reaching out for the sun, Craigan's
preoccupation is with material necessity, including his own
security and comfort, which he thinks only Lily can provide:
'Love's all right for them that 'as Rolls Royces', he says to her,
'but for the wives of working men it's the money that comes in
regular at the end of the week that tells' (p.320). Green's attitude
towards the conflicts connected with these two attitudes is
stressed by montage throughout the novel.

The predominance of work, in *Living*, bears witness to the
necessity of material concerns. Lily admits that 'where we'd've

been without 'im I don't know at all. We all live by Mr Craigan' (p.235). Security, however, is not an alternative to 'loving' and 'living'. The confinement of Craigan's domicile has its counterpart in the staleness of the factory. In the iron foundry, 'Black sand made the floor. Men knelt in it' (p.208). Human values, in these surroundings, can only be sustained by a symbolic feeding of the sparrows. The precise meaning of this motif is not clarified by Green, because it concerns attitudes that are strictly subjective. However, it broadly refers to the imaginative capacity to turn plain existence into 'living'. Green demonstrates man's potential to perceive a poetic beauty in the midst of drabness. For a moment, the motion of Bert Jones's lathe takes on a beautiful stillness:

> Now the job, revolving so many turns a second, now it had a stillness more beautiful than when actually it had been still. On the small surface of it was sheen of light still and quiet. . . . And pace of events bearing on his life quickened so that for two moments their speed had appearance of stillness.   (p.334)

Or joy may occur through a sense of togetherness:

> They talked. John and Mr Bridges's faces grew red with companionship and Bridges waved cigar and John got smoke once in lungs and coughed; – they shouted together and held each other by the arm.   (p.218)

The factory workers can only find meaning by nourishing their own human selves in face of the drabness that threatens to mould them into stereotypes.

Living begins with a passage of visual montage that anticipates the tone of the whole novel.

> Bridesley, Birmingham.
> Two o'clock. Thousands came back from dinner along streets.
> 'What we want is go, push', said works manager to son of Mr Dupret. 'What I say to them is – let's get on with it, let's get the stuff out.'
> Thousands came back to factories they worked in from their dinners.

'I'm always at them but they know me. They know I'm a
father and mother to them. If they're in trouble they've but
to come to me. And they turn out beautiful work, beautiful
work. I'd do anything for 'em and they know it.'

Noise of lathes working began again in this factory. Hundreds went along road outside, men and girls. Some turned
in to Dupret factory.   (p.207)

Green repeatedly widens and narrows the range in front of the
'camera' so that various details interpenetrate in the mind of the
reader. The dynamic effects produced by this technique give rise
to tone. Green's survey of the scene is recurrently interrupted
by sudden acoustic close-ups of Bridges's resounding voice. The
tension between visual and acoustic experiences created by
these *audio-visual counterpoints* sensitizes the reader to underlying
thematic conflicts, which are more fully conveyed in terms of a
conflict of *matter and viewpoint*. Crowds of men and women
returning to work are pictured in repeated glimpses from the
point of view of the author. The monotony of his style mimes
the collective movement of workers, which suggests the stifling,
mechanical pattern of factory routine. Viewed against this
impersonal background, Bridges's reassuring remark, that all
human needs are being looked after, becomes deeply ironic.
Green, instead, stresses the incompatibility of the management's
ambition to 'go, push' and man's need for beauty and human
understanding. At times, Green's sympathy for the individual
worker is revealed through exposure of their subjective feelings:

That day Mr Bert Jones had one of his spells on him. Were
days when he could not work, his mind was not in it. It was
not that he couldn't concentrate because he was thinking of
something else, but rather as if his mind was satiated by the
trade he worked at, as if he had reached saturation point as
day by day, year by year he did very much the same things
with almost identical movements of arms and legs.   (p.304)

It is against this background of satiety and frustration that
Green presents Dick Dupret's ambition to rationalize the factory.
Part of his plan is to suspend those workers who cannot keep up
production. 'What we want in the place is some go and push',
he tells his mother, echoing Bridges, and betraying thereby a

similar lack of understanding for the human aspect (p.230). Dick Dupret's character is exposed in the scene where old Tupe stops Dick and Bridges during their excursion round the foundry. When Tupe, appealing for attention and sympathy, wants to tell Bridges how he fell that morning, Dick Dupret is deaf to his needs. Instead, he focuses his attention on a person signalling in the distance, and interrupts old Tupe: 'Mr Bridges I think there's someone wants to see you ... that man behind that thing over there' (p.211). Dick's use of demonstratives, 'that' and 'there' (at the expense of 'this' and 'here') indicates his mental aloofness; and his inability to name 'that thing' (i.e. a machined cylinder) by its proper name is a symptom of his detachment from his immediate surroundings. The fact that Green also stresses each word in that demonstrative clause heightens the active insistence of Dick's utterance, and increases the tension between the *close* and the *long* shot. Green's montage technique highlights meanings which might otherwise have escaped the reader as merely minor details in a larger context.

Bridges's attempts to engage Dick's interest in the life of the foundry are futile. On entering the foundry, Dick fails to notice the grimed men who are kneeling in black sand on the floor. What catches his attention is the fleeting image of a young man passing by: 'What a beautiful face' (p.208). Dick's preoccupation with beauty, however, is merely an abstracted aestheticism devoid of deeper values. His fascination with his girlfriend, Hannah Glossop, is nourished by her good looks. '"It was because, all of it, because she was so beautiful", he repeated to himself, "so beautiful"' (p.245). Montage effectively sharpens the emotional aloofness of the two, and their lack of commitment to the living present. Leaning on his arm, Dick thinks it is because of him that Hannah looks so happy. In fact, she is thinking of somebody else. The dance band is singing:

Your eyes are my eyes
My heart looks through ...

'Oh' she whispered, 'Oh' and he felt quite transported.

Just then, Mr Dupret in sleep, died, in sleep.   (pp.287–8)

Green treats ironically the lack of communication between the two superficial lovers. The sudden juxtaposition of Mr Dupret who dies in 'sleep' ('sleep' is emphasized through repetition) reflects their sleep-like illusion. This juxtaposition furthermore ties in with the immediately preceding exposé of Hannah, who is so afraid of death. She had cried bitterly when a doctor's chauffeur, a man she barely knew, got caught in a flywheel and was killed. The image of the turning wheel again symbolizes the mechanical rotation of life towards death. Hannah's, as well as Dick's, sense of futility accounts for their lack of response to the present moment. Instead, they go to London to be 'distracted' from it. As Hannah thinks to herself, 'but for that useless feeling she would not have cried when chauffeur was killed' (p.286). Isolated and bored, Dick resorts to contemplation of a satisfying order severed from the world human beings inhabit. When real human beings interfere with his polished visions, he defies those people. 'How horrible they all were and everyone too for that matter, loathsome the people in buses, worse in trams, of course' (p.247).

Many critics have noted the contrast there is in *Living* between the busy, down-to-earth lives of the workers and the idleness and boredom of the upper classes. In various contexts, the latter are ironically portrayed through a conflict of *planes*. Against the picture of Craigan and his work mates, toiling towards the end of a hard working day, is set that of Mrs Dupret complaining about the boredom of discussing engagements and how tiring and uncomfortable are trains (p.229). Her lack of involvement with her surroundings is revealed by her preoccupation with trivialities. When Dick attempts to tell his mother about how he would like to manage the family business and even reveals some little enthusiasm about his plans, she is not listening. Instead, she is worrying about what has happened to James, the footman, who has been sent upstairs to fetch her handkerchief. The repeated elision of articles in the following passage, combined with its heavy, staccato rhythm, functions as filmic *close-ups* of cold stone and metal – a reflection of Mrs Dupret's personality (this connection is suggested through *association montage*).

She pushed button of bell; this was in onyx. She laid hand by it on table and diamonds on her rings glittered together with white metal round onyx button under the electric light. Electric

light was like stone. He was cut short by her. He was hurt at
it. He kept silence then.   (p.230)

This scene between Dick and Mrs Dupret highlights other
aspects than those indicative of a major structural conflict
between the idle rich and the workers. The fact that Green
emphasizes the way in which Dick is offended by his mother's
interruption indicates conflicts within the Dupret family. Dick's
need for self-realization is suggested by the interest he shows for
the management of the factory. What little enthusiasm he
expresses about his plans, however, is quenched by the metallic
coldness of his mother's preoccupations. The mechanical rituals
and routines which determine Mrs Dupret's life petrify vital
human needs.

The thematic conflicts in *Living* extend beyond class barriers.
They are revealed mainly in terms of montage, not primarily
along the structural dividing line between the workers and the
upper classes. Human needs suffer under the pressure of factory
routines and greater productivity. Repression of human needs,
however, also takes place in the Craigan and Dupret households
under the enforcement of the established order. Mrs Dupret has
been dominated all her life by her husband, to such an extent
that she has lost all power to influence her own life. Like a train
that must follow its predestined track, she can but feel the
boredom and monotony of being possessed by security and
institutionalized purpose. Only when her husband falls ill and
becomes entirely dependent on her care does Mrs Dupret recover
from her emotional lethargy. 'Mrs Dupret though she had never
been very fond of him, was now thinking how very fond of him
she was' (p.268). Similarly, Dick's freedom to mature and
develop is restrained by his father's dominance. As a result,
aggression and hate have suppressed what might have been love
and understanding. 'Young Mr Dupret sat in their country house
picking his nose. "Why", he said in his mind, "why could not
the old man die? Of course was gratitude and all that of sons to
fathers but, old mummy, why couldn't he die"' (pp.278–9).

The conflict between Dick Dupret and his father cannot be
reduced to a mere generational conflict. Edward Stokes finds
that *Living* 'reflects the breakdown of the old paternalistic
industrial organization and the substitution of a system less
human and personal'.[8] This may be so, except that Green does

not contrast these two systems to suggest improvements in the actual organization of the factory. He reveals his sympathy for the factory workers, but he does not question the necessity of keeping the lathes and wheels going in the way they do. By his montage technique, however, Green brings the conflicts down to the level of personal intercourse. His portrayals centre on the vital human needs that suffer due to some people's lack of understanding and tolerance. The tone of *Living* is in praise of individuals who defend their human qualities and are guided by an openness before life's possibilities. Lily follows her heart despite attempts to mould her into conformity. As Mrs Eames says, 'what I like about Lily is she's got the spirit to do what's in 'er mind' (p.323). Whereas Lily fervently reaches out to life, Dick Dupret is reduced to an impotent contemplator, driven by his obsession with life's limitations and lack of possibilities for fulfilment.

Green pictures the pathetic figure of Dick Dupret sitting in a garden by the River Thames. Autumn leaves fall into the river, and as the river carries the dead leaves away towards the sea, Dick drifts into sleep.

Sunshine was pale. So drifted into sleep. Yet came party from Maidenhead in launch up the river, men and women, a silver launch. Laughter came like birds from women in it. It came on slowly and he opened eyes and it went by, this laughter reaching ... back to him and then in wide circle launch turned leisurely and came back past him and he thought why did they turn it there. Why did they turn it there he thought and then man on launch played dance tune from the wireless they had on it and it went on down with stream till he could see them no more but still hear them, then he could not hear them any more....

Still flowed river Thames and still the leaves were disturbed, then were loosed, and came down on to water and went by London where he was going, by there and out into the sea. (pp.281–2)

Green's river scene in *Living*, says Melchiori, is taken from T. S. Eliot's *The Waste Land*.[9] The following lines are an excerpt from 'The Fire Sermon':

The river's tent is broken: the last fingers of leaf
Clutch and sink into the wet bank. The wind
Crosses the brown land, unheard. The nymphs are departed,
Sweet Thames, run softly, till I end my song . . .
The river bears no empty bottles, sandwich papers,
Silk handkerchiefs, cardboard boxes, cigarette ends
Or other testimony of summer nights. The nymphs are
    departed . . .
By the waters of Leman I sat down and wept . . .
Sweet Thames, run softly till I end my song.

Like Green, Eliot makes extensive use of incongruous juxtaposed images in order to convey his message. The repeated line, 'Sweet Thames, run softly till I end my song', alludes to the refrain of Spenser's 'bridal song' in 'Prothalamion', a poem of unsurpassed innocence, depicting a wedding party of nymphs on the Thames. In *The Waste Land*, these literary allusions are placed in an inconsonant context producing an atmosphere of vulgarity and desolation. The nymphs have been replaced by rubbish. The Thames itself symbolizes the life of humanity, drifting, like the barges, helplessly towards death and entropy, the sea. The mechanical sound of a gramophone increases the sense of spiritual cheapness.

> The river sweats
> Oil and tar
> The barges drift
> With the turning tide

Melchiori argues that images from *The Waste Land* also fuse in Green's river scene to form a picture of 'lassitude and emptiness'. This statement needs amplification. Eliot's images possess the precision of reference and consistency generally characterizing symbols. Through consistent allusions to an idyllic and innocent past, Eliot informs his river images with a clear referential meaning. The result is the creation of a cultural landscape which the spectator, through ironic detachment, defies altogether. In terms of graphic conflicts in the picture, the main dividing line is between the solitary contemplator on the one hand, and the entire river scene on the other.

It is interesting to see how Green avoids giving his images

a specific intellectual, referential quality, and thereby freely manipulates the lines of conflict in his river scene. He does not pass value judgement on the scene itself, but instead deprecates Dick's lack of an affirmative response to life. The lonely figure of Dick Dupret is fused with the dead autumn leaves and the floating river as he drifts into sleep, lulled by the flowing river. Even the sunshine fades away as if drifting into sleep. 'Yet', laughter from women in a silver launch, and then dance music from a wireless, create an *audio-visual counterpoint* and break up a visually depicted stillness. The fact that the laughter is associated with birds strengthens its symbolic value as a substitute for the absent sun. Simultaneously, a conflict of *graphic directions* is produced as the launch is moving against the single direction of the river, thereby placing itself in opposition to the river, the dead leaves, the faded sun and Dick Dupret. (It is significant that the barges in Eliot's poem are drifting passively along the river towards the sea.) Green also presents a more immutable reality in a picture of the river itself: 'Still flowed river Thames'. It stresses the temporal nature of the intermezzo *on* the river. The fact that the launch turns in a circle and goes downstream again may suggest the direction of flux, but the launch still does not represent an image of 'lassitude and emptiness'. Green holds the focus on Dick's subjective experience of the happening, his puzzlement over 'why ... they turn it there', and the gradual fading away of the launch out of his range of vision and hearing. There is finally no opposition of values between the launch on the river and Dick's experience of it; in fact, the interest which Dick takes in this event signals that he would have liked to hold on to it. The main significance of the scene is stressed by the series of montage conflicts. Montage animates the picture, intensifies its sensory immediacy, creating a tension between dynamism and stagnation. It is essentially Dick's detachment from the vividness created by juxtaposed images that produces the irony.

Meaning and fulfilment, Green suggests, can only be created in the process of opposing the downward stream of the 'river' and of imposing oneself positively on life. This is Green's indirect message to the reader as he lets the experience by the river have a regenerative, though short-lived, influence on Dick's reticent personality. He would seek the company of women, he says to himself, 'like on that silver launch' (p.282). And he would bring

his mother with him to London; 'Also mother needed rest.'
Besides, he would go back to work and not mind all the conflicts;
'he thought was no use in struggling against that one defeat with
Bridges' (notably his humiliation at his father's and Bridges's
countermand of his order to remove the guard controlling workers
at the lavatories). For a short moment, Dick thinks thoughts
that might have resulted in a more fulfilling involvement with
life, and with his own human potential for sympathy and
tolerance.

Living encourages an affirmative participation in present
reality. Failure at this means letting life be undermined by the
predestined flow of the 'river' towards the 'sea'. Green's ideal
entails 'living', from moment to moment, in the flow of one's
creative response to natural human impulses. What is more,
Green sees hope in the human potential to love and care for
other people. Lily makes a mistake when, in her eagerness to
commit herself to an ideal love union with Bert Jones, she fails
to realize that she is suppressing other vital commitments, such
as her love and sense of responsibility for the care of old Craigan.
Lily's attachment to home, therefore, is one major reason why
her romantic ideals prove an illusion. She cannot escape from
her own self, and her own self eventually turns out the stronger
and healthier.

Lily's and Bert's abortive runaway trip to Liverpool involves
incidents that stress the delusion of the couple. Their elopement
is charged with irony through Green's creation of montage
conflicts. The following passage depicts the moment before Lily's
flight from home:

Lily stood in hat and coat by kitchen window quickly cutting
stairs of bread. When she had stack of these by her she reached
to tin of beef that was by the loaf and in stretching she raised
head and saw man in garden next theirs digging in his garden.
Behind him was line of chimney pots, for next street to theirs
in that direction was beneath, hidden by swell of gardens back
of their street. This man, then, leant on his spade and was
like another chimney pot, dark against dark low clouds in the
sky. There pigeon quickly turned rising in spirals, grey, when
clock in the church tower struck the quarter and away, away
the pigeon fell from this noise in a diagonal from where church
was built and that man who leant on his spade. Like hatchets

they came towards Lily, down at her till when they were close to window they stopped, each clapped his wings then flew away slowly all of them, to the left. She had drawn back at full height. Then again she looked at that man and he also had been watching the pigeon. He again began to dig but the clock striking had told her she had time yet and she wondered at him digging in that unfruitful earth and that he was out of work and most likely would be for most of the rest of his days. There he was digging land which was worn out.   (p.336)

It is significant that whenever flying pigeons are observed by one of the characters in *Living* (except in the last scene) they are seen through a window. The window is a favoured technical device used by Green for creating a sense of distance and separation from the observed object. A comparable effect of this motif may be found in the first section (named 'The Window') of *To the Lighthouse*: the image of Mrs Ramsay by her drawing-room window contemplating life's 'myriad impressions' and gazing at the distant lighthouse. The scene just quoted is like a painting or photo in which 'grey' pigeons and the man in the garden, the chimney pots, and the 'dark low clouds in the sky' are arranged behind one another in the background. Between these elements there is no conflict of *depths*; to Lily they can hardly be distinguished from one another in their greyness. The main graphic conflict is thus between Lily in the foreground and the complete depicted scene which constitutes the background. This graphic conflict is filled with dynamic intensity by the quickly circling pigeons and the toll of the church clock (*audio-visual counterpoint*). When the pigeons suddenly dash towards Lily and turn short but inches from her window, they create a conflict of *graphic directions* which deepens Lily's withdrawal from the scene she is observing. At the same time, the pigeons draw an imaginary link between the man in the garden and Lily, giving the conflict between them a precise reference.

The main conflict in the scene is linked with basic human values. Both Lily and the man in the garden have been intently watching the sloping flight of the pigeons, which, combined with the sound of the church clock, produce some never fully revealed meaning. Green, however, stresses the fact that Lily and the man in the garden interpret the symbolic meaning of the pigeons differently, and that they respond differently to the sight of them.

The man, after watching the pigeons' flight, goes on imposing his creative powers on the unfruitful land; Lily only sees the futility of his activity, and becomes even more intent on escape. When viewed in relation to significant contexts of montage and visual imagery in *Living* (the gardener is obviously Mr Eames), Lily's decision is put into an ironic perspective.

The window image attracts great attention during Lily's and Bert's escapist train journey to Liverpool. When Bert detrains for a moment at Derby station, Lily leans out of the compartment window as if to reach for him. Her act suggests that initially their journey is directed towards oneness and harmony. 'So their heads inclined one to the other, so their breathing fell in one with the other, so they took breath together in one breath' (p.350). Later, however, the window signals a conflict of *scales* which heightens the sense of confinement within their compartment, and their separation from the outside world. This montage conflict mirrors Lily's increasing scepticism of their undertaking, and her growing self-awareness. 'Now she had drawn back from him.' Bert 'let down the window to let country air in onto air they had brought with them from Birmingham, but Lily asked him to close it' (p.352). When a band of musicians board the train and start playing their instruments in the next carriage, Bert 'opened window to listen better to them and hung head out. "Bert" screamed Miss Gates. She jumped up and pulled at his shoulders ... "a bridge might 'ave come and cut your head off and where would I be then?"' (p.354). Lily's fears show her growing distrust of the distant music (of sunbathed tropical countries) which has for so long tingled in her ears. Her exclamation, 'and where would I be then', echoes Mrs Eames's words to her child, and her fear that someone might come and steal it away (p.249). Mrs Eames recognizes that some measure of security in life is necessary as a condition for growth. Lily's reorientation signals that love does not exist as a permanent state of being; it must be continuously struggled for.

Even if Lily's abortive escape confirms Craigan's warnings that life has its limitations, Green never questions the rightness of Lily's wilful assertion of her own personality against Craigan's restrictions. This is a crucial point in understanding *Living*. Craigan should have known Lily well enough to realize that her attachments would bring her home to him. He should have been more tolerant and given her the freedom she needed. Craigan seems to have learnt his lesson by the end of the story; 'his old authority was gone', and he has become more attentive to Lily's needs. 'Mr Craigan mumbled she didn't want to sit moping indoors, nor nobody wanted her to' (pp.369, 379). Lily herself, though dejected after her return, does not question the basic rightness of her motives, only her singlemindedness: ' "that's what it was", she said, "yes, I 'ad too much heart" ' (p.363).

The basic conflict between Craigan's and Lily's attitudes to life is still the central issue at the novel's end. Craigan believes that Lily has learnt the same lesson about life that he has been experiencing for years. ' "Nothin' dain't ever come of dreams, I could 'ave told yer but that wouldn't be of no use, you 'ad to find out of yourselves and so you 'ave", he said' (p.366). If Lily has learnt about life's limitations, she does not allow material necessity to determine the future course of her life. Here lies the difference between Craigan and Lily.

> He thought what had he got out of fifty-seven years' work? Nothing. . . . He thought what was there now for him? Nothing, nothing. He lay. But Miss Gates was not that way inclined. Everything, so she felt, was beginning for her again.   (p.380)

> Sitting at window-sill of her grandad's window she overlooked Birmingham and the sky over it. This was filled with pigeon flocks. Thousands of pigeons wavered there in the sky, and that baby's raucous cry would come to her now and again.   (p.377)

The latter picture resembles the scene that anticipates Lily's flight, where she stands by the window observing the man digging in the garden, below the circling pigeons. Like the toll of the church clock in the previous scene, the *audio-visual counterpoint* created by the baby's cry heightens dynamic tension. Here, however, the counterpoint serves to dramatize the strength of Lily's longings, which are unchanged. Tension is also created by the conflict of *scales* between the kitchen and the sky of Birmingham. This montage technique emphasizes the basic thematic conflict in *Living*. It expresses Lily's urge towards reconciliation with the world she perceives outside the window. That world does not represent an objective 'continuum'. The world of Lily's perception – thousands of swarming pigeons in the sky, and the baby's cry – is a metaphorical reflection of Lily's needs. Characters' attribution of metaphorical meaning to different images reflects subjective values. Prior to her escape, Lily, through the kitchen window, only sees the 'unfruitful' picture of the gardener and the circling pigeons. In the final scene, she affirms her affinity with Mrs Eames, to whom the baby, the pigeons and the garden signify fruition.

In *Living*, juxtapositions of incongruous images and scenes stress disparities in the characters' lives. The emotive quality of these contexts are intensified through the visual immediacy of the montage trope. By this technique, tone is not determined by individual symbols; images function as elements in a larger context. This is the reason why the equation of the predictable pattern of the pigeons' flight and a resolution of conflict in the novel is an inadequate approach. Birds may serve a symbolic function, but just as often they are metaphors for characters' subjective feelings, or they deepen conflicts in the novel through their contrast with the plight of certain characters. Montage enhances vital aspects of different contexts. The image of contradiction heightens the vividness of a scene and the immediacy of perception. For this reason, only a montage approach can fully convey the tone of *Living*. The tone of various scenes gains depth in relation to the Eameses' world of 'loving'. By his montage technique, Green applauds Lily's natural capacity for 'living'.

Pushing Mrs Eames's baby in the pram at the end of the book, Lily has pigeons fluttering directly above her head, out in the open, for the first time. The image exudes fertility, procreation and fulfilment. The pigeon fancier is present and puts a grain onto the apron of the pram in front of the baby. 'Soon all were laughing at way this one pigeon, which alone dared to come onto apron dodged the baby which laughed and crowed and grabbed at it' (p.382). Lily stands fascinated at the sight of this one pigeon which, like herself, possesses the spirit to go its own way, and at the sight of Mrs Eames's baby, which confidently reaches out for the pigeon. 'Suddenly with loud raucous cry ... she rushed at baby to kiss it' (ibid.). Lily's human integrity is as strong as ever. She can still dream, because her longings are unchanged, but she is wiser; fecund tropical settings no longer pull her away from herself. 'She cruised across that well charted ocean towards that land from which birds landed on her decks', but 'that land round which she steamed was every inch of it her own, her case still enchanted her as she kept watch on it' (p.373).

3   *Caught* (1943) and *Back* (1946)

CAUGHT (1943)

Caught is composed of a variety of scenes, shifts in location, juxtapositions of present and past, and shifting points of view. Not all these transitions produce tonal effects and not all may be labelled montage as utilized by Eisenstein, a basic technique for the creation of tone in *Caught*. Rather, they are often what Eisenstein calls 'parallel montage' (a technique extensively used by the American film director Griffith), invoked primarily for the purpose of realistic representation. Green's use of 'parallel montage' in *Caught* may be accounted for by citing Eisenstein's comment on Griffith's achievement:

> His close-ups create atmosphere, outline traits of the charac-
> ters, alternate in dialogues of the leading characters.... But
> Griffith at all times remains on a level of representation and
> objectivity and nowhere does he try through juxtaposition of
> shots to shape import and image.[1]

This technique pertains to Green's stated aim in his foreword to *Caught*: to re-create the London of 1940 and to construct his characters 'on the reality of that time'.

From the point of view of 'representation and objectivity', Green's scenic method serves two purposes. Glimpses into the various characters' private worlds, or flashbacks into a character's past, suggest hopes, fears, ambitions and experiences that are and have been determinants in the shaping of a character's life. Green also observes these different personalities, shaped by different circumstances, as they are 'caught' in wartime London. At a time of chaotic disruption of conventional standards and ways of life, separation from families, and uncer-

71

tainty about the future, these characters confront the challenge of filling the empty gaps in their existences. Being 'caught' by the war thus becomes for them the test of coping with life's new exigencies. Green's twofold objective, to suggest the nature of conditioning circumstances and to examine his characters' behaviour in these trials of life, induces a scenic structure.

Albert Pye, a sub-officer in the London fire brigade, and Richard Roe, an auxiliary, are the two principal characters in _Caught_. The suggestive meanings of their names (Weatherhead notes that, in combination, they produce 'pyro', the Greek term for fire[2]) indicate analogies in their situations. Both are 'caught' by the impending war, and by the past. Roe, a widower, is nostalgically entrapped in memories of an idealized garden. Pye is neurotically preoccupied with memories involving his mentally deranged sister. Furthermore, their nondescript names (John Doe and Richard Roe is a term for 'Mr Anybody') link them with the commonalty, suggesting Green's intention to portray a representative reality.

Pye is primarily presented as an unhappy victim of circumstances that are beyond his control. He gradually loses his ability to withstand external as well as internal pressures and finally seeks escape in suicide. Since Green does not really clarify what Pye should have done differently in order to avoid failure, his life does not clearly specify a moral to the reader. All the montage conflicts and themes in _Caught_, however, are in some way directly or indirectly related to Roe's and Pye's lives. For this reason, their stories need close attention. They constitute the essential background which indicates Green's major concerns and so delineates the tone.

Pye's tragedy is bound up with his sister's abuction of Richard's five-year-old son from a London toy shop, for which she is detained in an asylum. Pye finds abhorrent the injustice done to his sister by her imprisonment, and Richard's presence in his brigade becomes a constant reminder of her plight. Pye is also obsessed by the possibility that he may have committed incest with his own sister 'in the blind moonlight' several years ago, and if so may be responsible for her mental derangement. 'Caught' by his past, his command of the present gradually deteriorates, his ego compulsively subordinated by the haunting shadow of fate. He is ultimately pictured one moonlit night as he prowls the streets 'to try once more to find how much he

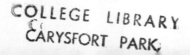

could recognize by this light in the bright river of the street'
(p.162).

Another important aspect of Pye's tragedy is the extent to
which his needs are misunderstood and his motives deprecated,
a factor which makes him an outsider and a loser. Having been
an ordinary fireman, he suddenly finds himself promoted to the
position of sub-officer without having the qualifications of a
leader. Anxious to meet the demands for efficiency from his
superiors without sacrificing the favour of his subordinates, he
fluctuates nervously between authoritarian discipline and effusive
paternalism. 'With remarkable tenderness', knowing that it may
'cost him his pension', he tells one of the cooks, Mary Howells,
that he is willing to cover up her absence for a few days to help
her solve family problems, but she misunderstands his intentions
and declines his offer. 'Pye was discouraged. He knew now, for
the first time, the sense of impotence which goes with authority,
the feeling that those he commanded did not care' (p.82). Pye's
strong sense of being misunderstood promotes his insecurity and
his feeling of inferiority, which in turn causes aggression and so
increases his subordinates' resentment and dislike of him. Due
to some very bad decisions as a result of his inadequacy as a
leader, Pye also arouses his superiors' disapproval. His most
humiliating mistake occurs when the firemen, under his direction,
enter a house adjacent to the house where the fire actually is.
After that incident, 'Pye was never the same' (p.80). Walking
the dark streets alone shortly before his suicide, he makes one
last gesture that will later be misunderstood. He finds a little
boy in the dark, takes him to the fire station, although visitors
are not allowed, feeds him and gives him a bed. Pye justifies
himself, 'You could not send him away hungry. After all, there
was a war on' (pp.170–1).

Pye's disastrous failure to cope with life is fomented by the
atmosphere of disruption prevalent in phoney-war London. The
mood is one of suspended boredom, of people 'caught' in routine
and petty triviality which appears all the more trivial since
overshadowed by the urgency and enormity of the war. 'We
come here ready for at least death', Richard complains, 'and
then we get into trouble for not doing under our beds' (p.94).
Excitement, romance and self-abandonment are self-consciously
sought by people who become submerged in the desperation of
the times. Richard observes the women

hungrily seeking another man, oh they were sorry for men and they pitied themselves, for yet another man with whom they could spend last hours, to whom they could murmur darling, darling, darling it will be you always; the phrase till death do us part being, for them, the short ride next morning to a railway station; the active death, for them, to be left alone on a platform; the I-have-given-all-before-we-die, their dying breath.   (p.63)

Pye becomes a victim of the new conditions effected by the war. When Prudence, with whom he has had 'nothing but bed in common', soon gets bored, Pye loses more than he had cynically bargained for. 'I realize I owe more than life to you, my dear, all the trouble I've been through these last few weeks, yes more than life' (p.152). Prudence, however, thinks 'this is awful, I shall never manage to get rid of him'. She refuses to see him, 'no, not till she felt quite different about firemen' (pp.151–2).

Despite analogies in their situations, Pye and Roe also serve distinctly different functions in the novel's plot. Richard, partly because of the tragic example of Pye, emerges as a wiser man, and reveals inchoate emotional growth. However, precisely in what way his experiences converge into a new revelation about life Richard can only partially explain. It is only in retrospect one learns that the war has had such a profound effect on him. At the end of the novel, Dy, Richard's sister-in-law, tries to comprehend the story Richard has been telling her:

> 'I wonder what's the meaning of it all?' she asked.
> He felt a flash of anger. It spread.
> 'I know this', he announced in what, to him, was direct answer, 'you've always been most unfair to Pye'.
> She was astounded.
> 'Pye?' she asked.
> 'Yes, to Pye', he said. He stopped, turned away from her.
> 'That's the tragedy.'   (p.194)

In some obscure way, Richard's new sympathy for Pye is linked with the recognition of his own essential loneliness in comparison to the meaningful experience of belonging to a group of men, fighting together against immense fires. Richard's own story, however, fails to convey the real emotional impact of the war.

'"I don't know", he said, "only the point about a blitz is this, there's always something you can't describe, and it's not the blitz alone that's true of. Ever since it happened I feel I've been trying to express all sorts of things."' Dy thinks she understands. '"No", he said, exasperated suddenly, "there's an old fault of yours, you're always trying to explain difficult things prosaically"' (pp.179–80).

The inability of ordinary narrative prose to convey the emotional impact of an experience is the motivation behind Green's extensive use of visual montage in *Caught*. Green's, and Richard's, desire to explain personal feelings stresses a crucial aspect of *Caught*: Green's recreation of the London of 1940 is not limited to the objective presentation of a representative atmosphere. Like Coleridge, Green emphasizes the process of authorship as counterpointed to objectivity. Richard's experience of the blitz is more fabulous than what he can express. Green's attempt to re-create its vivid personal significance thus implies a synthesis between objective details and the artist's projected emotional response.

It is typical of Green's narrative technique that tone is communicated not so much in terms of a character's or narrator's personal account, but is presented directly to the reader by visual devices. It arises in the interaction of juxtaposed scenes and images. Similarly, tonal qualities are not confined to a protagonist's direct experience or point of view (the subjective views of a protagonist are unreliable and may differ from the tone arising from the overall montage structure in the novel), but may be derived from all the different aspects of reality presented in the novel. Montage enhances the affective interchange between text and reader and is thus an appropriate technique for creating tone. It stimulates the reader's active participation in the life of the novel. In accordance with Green's use of montage in *Caught*, his thematic concerns and the tone of the novel are defined by the consistency with which he stresses certain emotive aspects of selected scenes.

Richard's new sympathy for Pye is awakened by the total atmosphere of wartime London. Consequently, Green wants to evoke the whole situation in scenic glimpses in order to incite the reader's own capacity for understanding, and sympathy. The nature of basic emotional needs becomes more obvious in the disruptive conditions under which the characters in *Caught* live.

It is precisely the many confrontations between basic human needs and conditions or attitudes obstructing their fulfilment that shape the tone of the novel. 'Human' values are recurrently emphasized by the way in which montage enhances the affective impact of certain scenes. The inhumanity of the war is echoed in the sterility of the local saloon bar, in itself a naked appeal for a human response.

> Those who would have a part to play, who were to have fires to put out, could strike attitudes in this saloon bar into which no outside air penetrated, so that ferns, hanging stiff in wire baskets from false beams, seemed carved out of painted iron plate. And the stray women, who looked older, with hats tilted this way and that, black and brown, their lips sealing wax, the skin of their faces the stop press, were unnaturally quiet, murmuring oh dear to the beer.
> 'It brings everyone together, there's that much to a war', Richard said to Chopper.
> 'It does, Dick', he said.

With great subtlety, Green shifts the focus from the suffocating room and the abandoned women whose only friend is the beer, to Richard's incongruous statement about human companionship.

> One of these women spoke.
> 'When it doesn't put blue water between', she said, but Richard did not notice. He had begun to eat again.   (p.48)

Green's careful juxtaposition of details (similar to the kind of juxtaposition Eisenstein terms 'cross-montage'[3]) ironically accentuates Richard's disengagement. At the same time, the nature of the juxtaposition suggests a close connection between lack of sympathy and self-centred preoccupation with private concerns.

In pre-blitz London, while death still seems unreal to the firemen, personal advancement is a stronger motivation than solidarity. Those auxiliaries who can afford it compete to buy the Regulars beer in the hope that it may win them special advantages. 'Those Auxiliaries so inclined, who could not afford to buy the Regulars beer, sought favour in doing more work than the rest' (pp.48–9). Piper, the oldest member of the squad, considered a trouble-maker with a glib tongue, seeks personal advancement by offering to redecorate District Officer Trant's house, for whom he serves as an informer on his colleagues in the fire station. Despite his similarity to his egocentric mates, Piper is never admitted as an individual worth respect. For one thing, he cannot afford to bribe the Regulars by buying them beer.

Human beings who share the predicament of being human in a fragmentary world, suffer from a self-absorbed separation from and a lack of identification with fellow individuals. Highly aware of this, Green is anxious to evoke the reader's tolerance for pushers such as Piper by providing glimpses from their private worlds. He focuses on this old soldier, hungry, tramping home to his spartan two-roomed flat only to be thrown out on the street again by Mrs Piper, who, 'bitter by nature', refuses to give him supper. Dismayed, but with no anger, Piper must find supper elsewhere. By means of a montage arrangement of visual details, Green asserts the emotive image of Piper as a solitary figure, cared for by no one, and for whom Green therefore tries to awaken the reader's sympathy.

> Outside, street lighting, shop displays, electric signs made Piper's heavens dull pink, the houses brown, only their upper floors and gables were shrouded in that half dark which is night over a town in times of peace.
>
> As he went under a street lamp with its yellow pride of light there stood a guardsman, by the coffee stall painted the same colour as his scarlet coat. Many smells were about Piper at this cross roads, from the fishmonger's, closed now, but with a stack of boxes piled outside drenched in kipper, from the local each time someone came in or out of the swing doors fanned a sickly waft outside, from the fish and chip round a corner that, when frying, as now, spread high over this street, and, last of all, boiling water in the urns extruded steam on to the laden air, creating a comfort in which these various smells were marshalled, and so damped down that they could not be lifted on the warmth a little way toward the high, chill, faint stars.   (p.53)

Colour, light and darkness in this passage are used by Green not primarily for their descriptive value, but mainly as a means of conveying a mood and of generating an emotional response in the reader. Many Expressionist artists have based their art on the assumption that particular colours effect certain sensations on the spectator or reader, and Green seems to seek this kind of perceptual result. However, attempts to schematize his use of colour in *Caught* in accordance with such affective principles do not disclose the full meaning of his narrative. There may be passages in the novel where a particular colour is so intimately connected with definable content that it seems to take on a definite meaning. As in previously examined passages from other novels, however, individual colours in *Caught*, if they are abstracted from their particular context, do not have independent symbolic meanings. The sun is consistently seen as a vitalizing symbol, but this does not attach a specific meaning to the colour yellow.

For Green, the symbolic implications of certain colours do not act as the sole constituent of meaning, but as components which, only in a wider context, combine to manifest Green's true intent. Their meaning, as Stokes argues, 'may be compared to a vague resonance, an undertone which gives the description a note of mysterious depth, but defies definition'.[4] In accordance with this idea, sensations and associations produced by specific colours serve to enrich a certain created atmosphere and to magnify the affective impact of a passage. Thus, a conflict of scales determines the basic tone of Green's passage. The image of the coffee stall surrounded by a cone of lamp light against a dark and 'dull' background produces a sense of enclosure, of confinement, enhanced by the 'laden air' of steam, which is 'damped down' under the 'high, chill, faint stars'. In this 'sickly' 'warmth' Piper seeks a little consolation in a cold world, but it is a comfort inadequate to his need. Green's broadening of the perspective increases the magnitude of the scene, placing Piper in a position of cosmic loneliness by the contrast with the void around the 'high, chill, faint stars'; to Green a position capable of inspiring empathy.

In this context, it is difficult to identify a specific independent 'meaning' in the occurrence of the 'yellow pride of light' and the scarlet coffee stall and coat. In a general sense, red is a highly dramatic colour, sometimes alarming colour, often used by Green in connection with war and sex, but it may also be used more generally to amplify any experience of strong affective quality. It is this latter function that red serves in the above passage.

The tone of the scene emerges from a series of montage conflicts which together produce a precise meaning. Green's description of how Piper enters the yellow light from a street lamp and then confronts a scarlet coffee stall and a man dressed in a scarlet coat is intended to express disparity and conflict because, in visual terms, scarlet collides with yellow, creating an uncomfortable tension through the harsh contrast. Furthermore, shop displays and electric signs and lights create a 'dull pink' which merges with brown houses and a 'shroud' of half-dark surrounding the upper floors and gables, producing a saturated atmosphere of oppressiveness, which then, in a conflict of masses, contrasts with the bright 'yellow pride' of the street lamp and with the scarlet. A strong sense of discord ensues.

Green's technique is essentially representative of montage as defined by Eisenstein. Eisenstein does believe that certain colours elicit specific sensations in a spectator, but that actual meaning is determined by 'those *arbitrary* relationships within a system of images dictated by the particular work of art'. In other words, combinations of colours and images will achieve greater expressiveness and specificity than individual colours presented independently. In accordance with this idea, Eisenstein suggests, for example, that 'many characteristics we ascribe to the colour yellow derive from its immediate neighbour in the spectrum – green'. Furthermore, Eisenstein cites an artist named Allen who describes a certain painting, an example of montage of colours that correlates with the way in which Green has arranged individual colours and combinations of colours in the preceding scene. Eisenstein suggests how a 'terrifying' image is created when the '"fateful" tone' of a combination of dark and dull colours of which yellow is the central one is accentuated through collision with intense red:

the colours are all dark and dull, lighted only in the centre. This centre is a combination of dirty green and yellow grey, mixed with faded brown; the rest is almost black. . . .

This yellow scale, melting into dirty greens and a faded brown, is emphasized by contrast with the lower portion of the canvas:

. . . only below some reddish tones can be seen; muffled and overlaid upon each other, but, more or less aided by thickness and their comparatively great colour intensity, they create a clearly expressed contrast to the rest of the painting.[5]

In order to emphasize the issue of cosmic loneliness, Green switches the focus from Piper on to another lonely figure seeking consolation. 'Standing up against the counter, and she was so frail in dark clothes she seemed part of the shadow, he saw Mary Howells, the old friend, a char' (p.53). Green's portrayal of Mary Howells's plight emphasizes, through montage, another aspect of life that calls for sympathy and understanding. Throughout *Caught*, this strong concern is opposed by human relations based on superficial, romantic self-gratification. The widow, Mrs Howells, has managed to get a job with the fire service, thanks to Piper. She enjoys work in the kitchen, is in fact content with her modest lot in life, were it not for her daughter, Brid, who causes her constant worries. Brid, unhappily married, with a baby she barely knows how to take care of, turns up at her mother's one morning, mentally overwrought, having left her husband. Mary Howells, gravely concerned, sets off to Doncaster to speak some sense to Brid's husband. But, as she tells Arthur Piper after her return,

'Sometimes I feel me head goin' round and round. For she can't go h'out to work, not in the state she's in. The expense. An' I've got to see about 'er allotment, or whatever they call it in the army these days. She can't do nothin' for 'erself. Some mornin's I'm afraid to leave 'er with the baby. If it wasn't for the neighbours I wouldn't, honest.'

She came to a stop.

'So there you are then', Piper said gloomy.

At that instant, in great haste, on leave, and for only the second time, Richard tumbled into bed with Hilly. The relief he experienced when their bodies met was like the crack, on a snow silent day, of a branch that breaks to fall under a weight of snow, as his hands went like two owls in daylight over the hills, moors, and wooded valleys, over the fat white winter of her body.

'But I told 'im, Arthur, you should've been there to 'ear. I said to 'im, I says', she went on, imagining every word, 'You're no good to no-one, and I got a daughter, I 'ave, 'oo you took, an' when you'd used what you wanted you sent 'er back, I

says, more shame to yer, call yerself a man, I said, 'E went
white, Arthur, even if 'e didn't say nothink. But I wouldn't
spare 'im. Yus, I said, yus, you 'as your pleasure of a gel, and
then what, I says, why, you want another dish.'

(pp.116–17)

The conflict of planes produced by the insertion of Richard's
and Hilly's love-making, makes this scene basically ironic. It is
important to note that the pleasure Richard, subjectively, finds
in the episode does not determine the tone of the scene. This
passage is a valuable example of the way in which tone is
produced by montage, not on the basis of an independent scene
within the montage trope, even if this scene in itself may have
positive or negative value to the character or characters involved.
Through immediate juxtaposition, Mary Howells's concern and
care for Brid and her criticism of sexual self-gratification maintain
direct reference to the scene between Richard and Hilly. Richard,
it will appear, is at this stage emotionally insulated from his
fellow beings. Later, one finds that 'secretly, and he had not
even put it to himself, he was irritated, mainly because she had
gone to bed with him. He found it made her of no account'
(p.130).

The argument that the tone of the preceding passage is
determined by the montage context is supported by other scenes
involving Richard and Hilly as well as by Green's return to
the first 'love' scene. In the glimpse Green provides of them
immediately preceding this 'love' scene, they are presented
together in a night club. The quality of shallowness and deceit
in their relationship is accentuated through conflicts of masses.
Richard can only commit himself half-heartedly to Hilly, for he
is also interested in having an affair with Prudence, who, Hilly
tells him, has started seeing Pye.

So Pye saw her every night. He felt excited and jealous.
At this moment all the lights went out. A blue lime was
turned on, sizzling, on to the small stage.   (p.111)

The conflict of masses between the audience and the coloured
singer bathed in 'intense blue light' is intended to deepen the
sense of disparity between Richard and Hilly in the dark and
what is spotlighted on the stage: the lady's song which awakens

dreams of love and beauty in the audience that Richard 'could see only as the less dark below her and whose clouded heads, each one, drew nearer to a companion's in this forced communion, this hyacinthine, grape dark fellowship of longing'. The lady becomes a symbol of truth: 'The music floated her, the beat was even more of all she had to say, the colour became a part, *alive* and *deep*, making what they told each other, with her but in silence, simply repeatedly plain, the truth, over and over again' (p.112, emphasis added). Ironically, the two 'lovers' in the dark cannot surrender to the music. To Hilly, 'the stage grew impossibly brilliant. She shut her eyes and settled down, not, as she told herself, for long, to love Dickie' (ibid.). In fact, the whole performance is just play-acting with no sincerity. Thus, when the conflict of masses has ceased, the lack of truth is revealed:

> When she had done, and the lights went up, the singer stood revealed *as what she was not*, a negress with too wide a smile. The same with Hilly. As he looked at her he thought it wild that the touch of the unseen inside of her arm should have been so, and *saw her not as she was*.
>
> (Ibid. emphasis added)

Several scenes involving Hilly and Richard stress the disparity between the reality of their lives and basic emotional needs, unfulfilled as a result of their disengagement.

> They lay now on a sofa, naked, a pleasant brutal picture by the light of his coal fire from which rose petals showered on them as the flames played, deepening the flush spread over contented bodies. She wiggled over on top, held his dark face and drank it with her eyes. She had never been to Venice. She murmured to herself, 'This man's my gondola.'
> Brid at that instant was crying. She missed her Ted, so feckless in everything except when he loved her ... he was everything to her who had had to come back she wouldn't know why exactly, something to do with mum, and of course there was baby.   (p.120)

The picture of the miserable Brid yearning for the lover on whom she depends, is contrasted through a conflict of planes with a deceptively romanticized picture of the two love-makers, a 'pleasant' but 'brutal picture'. Richard's and Hilly's lack of love is suggested and intensified by this stark contrast. Besides, a conflict of masses is created as the romantic flush of light from the coal fire, showering on their bodies like rose petals, contrasts with Richard's 'dark face'. The montage conflict deepens an underlying thematic conflict. Ironically, when Hilly drinks his dark face with her eyes, she finds not love, but escape. She is transported to Venice; he is her vehicle, her 'gondola'.

Green has again provided an elucidating example of the way in which tone is created by montage and not by single images or symbols. Roses often have connotations of love, but, depending on the particular context, this colour or image may be used ironically by Green. This is clearly demonstrated in another example. When Brid, dejected, enters her mother's kitchen after running away from her husband, Mrs Howells, bewildered, astonished,

> with shaking fingers, put down the china teapot covered with pink roses her sister, Aggie, had given as a wedding present; which had reflected Brid's conception by that liquid rose flower light of a dying coal fire twenty-one years back; which now witnessed Brid's return, deflowered, but married, and with the fruit, a child.
> 'If I didn't nearly drop the pot. Oh me girl. . . .'   (p.78)

The change of focus from the wretched Brid, who has indifferently put her baby down and stands with her suitcase, 'holding it with both hands in front of her knees', to the teapot covered with pink roses, nearly dropped by Mrs Howells, deepens thematic conflicts through association montage. Despite Green's sympathy for Brid, the sense of disparity inherent in the juxtaposition of pink roses and Brid's present position serves as an ironic comment on the fragility of romantic dreams. The parallel between this scene and the one involving Hilly and Richard is clear. 'Brid's conception by that liquid rose flower light of a dying coal fire', symbolized by the rose-covered teapot, relates to the rose-showered picture of Hilly and Richard 'by the light of his coal fire', a beautiful image which only enhances, by contrast with her thoughts of Richard as a means for escape, the hollowness of their liaison.

On the basis of the preceding montage conflicts, it may be argued that Green by no means shows a casual attitude towards sex and romance. Throughout his fiction, sexual impulses are seen as natural and vital, because they are the very source of a creative and viable response to life. For Green as for Lawrence sensual and spiritual fulfilment implies a self-expanding communion with the natural flow of 'living'. In his portrayals of the relationship between man and woman, Green repeatedly draws attention to deeper, underlying needs. These may find fulfilment through sex, but, just as often, sex only magnifies the lack of contact which may exist between human beings as well as the lack of an affirmative response to 'living' in general. It is lack of emotional fulfilment and of mutual understanding due to the characters' egocentric detachment that is ironically focused in *Caught*. With his acute awareness of the tragic aspect of life, Green's concerns involve the need for full commitment to vital human feelings in a world threatened by disorder and estrangement.

As in *Back*, the cause of human isolation (that is, to the extent that the individual is responsible for his own isolation and is not primarily a victim of a reality which cannot be amended) lies in man's inability to recognize a palpable reality outside his own private sphere. Richard's lack of warmth is largely the result of 'his ever present loss', his preoccupation with an idealized dead wife, with whose inaccurate memory the living cannot compete. In a conflict of planes, Green stresses the irony of Richard's position as he rejects reality in favour of the romanticized memory of his wife's first visit to his parents' country place.

The roses, when they came to the rose garden, were full out, climbing along brick walls, some, overpowered by their heavy flowers, in obeisance before brick paths, petals loose here and there on the earth but, on each bush and tree of roses, rose after rose after rose of every shade stared like oxen, and came forward to meet them with a sweet, heavy, luxuriant breath.

Sitting as he was on the back step of a heavy unit pump, with a mangy kitten swiping at flies attracted by a cod's head in the gutter at his feet, the nine years that had passed, the position he was now in, all this lifted him as though in a balloon made lighter than air by the scent of roses.

(*Caught*, p.64)

Again, images of roses are used to enhance the romanticized beauty of Richard's fantasy, its unreal, dreamlike nature expressed by the surreal quality of the entire scene. The brutally realistic glimpse of a cod's head in the gutter, surrounded by flies, surpasses mere objective description. The coarseness of reality is aggravated as a result of Richard's biased outlook. It collides with his dreamworld to produce a grim tone of escapism.

Richard's inability to commit himself to the immediate reality centred around human beings is more specifically exemplified in the following conflict of planes. Still imagining himself to be with his wife in the garden of his past, he sees that

> Roses had come above her bare knees under the fluted skirt she wore, and the swallows flying so low made her, in his recollection, *much taller than she had ever been.*
>
> Back in his present, he heard a tap of high heels. Looking up, he saw Prudence, dressed in green as of dark olives like to the colour of that cod's head. She smiled, but did not stop. Still under the influence of his memories, he thought how sharp she appeared against the black wall with AMBULANCE painted in grey letters three foot high.
>
> (pp.64–5, emphasis added)

Richard's image of Prudence, when compared with the saturated luxuriance of his wife, becomes too unbearably dull and crude, and he lapses back into his dreamworld. In yet another montage conflict, in which the concrete image of Prudence interrupts Richard's absorption in his past, Green incorporates values and ironies that elucidate the central themes of the novel.

> Here, as Prudence drifted quickly off, infinitely young, so much the opposite of his heavy serge in the lightness of her dress that he broke violently out swearing, here, where he had seen Prudence lit up from under her frock by a blaze of the midday sun directed through her window, and he broke out sweating, he poured with sweat, here again he thought he broke the spell of what had been and, accepting his new life for the first time, he momentarily determined to join in the delights he imagined men and girls were sharing out to each other in the desperation of the times.   (p.65)

In order to make sense of the various qualities of tone inherent in this last scene, it is necessary to bear in mind that montage juxtaposes incongruous aspects of life, thereby testing the validity of contradictory attitudes, but only with reference to the concrete situation presented. Tone basically is a function of the 'camera' angle and is defined by the special sequence of interacting aspects of life that are presented in the specific context. This principle enables Green to give different impressions of the same character depending on the 'camera' angle, context, and the particular values he wants emphasized. Thus, in the preceding passage, Prudence, whose attitude to life is repeatedly seen as shallow, appears as an image of vitality. That scene, however, does not incorporate any evaluation of her attitude to life. Prudence appears as a symbol of vitality primarily from the point of view of Richard's life-excluding self-absorption in the memory of his wife. Prudence suddenly penetrates Richard's abstract fantasy world with her youth and freshness, necessitating his commitment to all that can be derived from the palpable present moment. It is in this manner Green stresses the values which represent the truly vital constituents of human existence.

To Richard, Prudence, then, becomes a symbol of vitality, challenging his benumbing submergence in the past. The sight of her in the street immediately evokes another image in Richard's mind: his first meeting with Prudence, 'lit up from under her frock by a blaze of the midday sun directed through her window'. The scene from Richard's first meeting with Prudence is worth citing for the light it sheds on Green's montage technique, and also for the way in which it provides insight into the relation between technique and vision. Richard is accompanied by Ilse, whom he has just met in the street:

> She went inside a *white* room. An acetylene lamp triangle of sunlight cut into the floor. At the apex stood another girl, *dark*. This light, reflected up the bell of her skirt, made her translucent to the waist. She said, 'Oh a fireman.' He turned his eyes away, burned. He chanced on a rectangular table set back against the wall. It had a *black* glass top on which, in a scarlet bowl, was a cactus, painted *white*.
>
> At once he noted that he had passed a glass tank in the lobby, filled with cut daffodils. This made him uneasy.
>
> (p.50, emphasis added)

A sterile and lifeless atmosphere is created in the room by the starkly contrasting pattern of white and black. Sunlight, used throughout Green's fiction as a life-giving symbol, lights up Prudence's skirt with a vitality Richard finds hard to confront. He turns away, and escapes to a table by the wall. Significantly, Richard's withdrawal from the sun, and from Prudence, assumes an ironic tone expressed in visual conflicts of colours and forms. The table to which he turns has a 'black glass top', and, on it, a 'cactus, painted white'; the 'scarlet bowl' not only enhances the stark, sterile contrast between those two colours but collides with them by its alarming intensity. Furthermore, turning away from the 'triangle of sunlight', directly associated with the 'bell' of her skirt, he retreats to a 'rectangular' table, the asymmetry of the two forms accentuating the conflict of values caused by his reaction.[6] Richard's uneasiness in the moment of withdrawal at the thought of the daffodils he has just passed in the lobby further suggests the irony of his attitude. The connection between his withdrawal from the sun and his discomfort, for the same reason, at the thought of the daffodils forms a dissonant link with the impression of nurturing life surrounding Mrs Eames's act of placing her flowers so that they turn their faces to the sun (*Living*, p.232).

Back in his present, filled with his vivid associations of Prudence, Richard decides 'again' to emerge from the influence of his past and accept his present life. Green, however, informs the reader of the delusion of Richard's determination by noting that it is not the first time he makes this decision. Furthermore, Richard's orientation towards new values, Green suggests, implies no real recovery from his self-centredness. Green points out that Richard now wants to take part in the joys he 'imagines' men and women are desperately 'sharing out to each other'. In the harsh reality Green creates, there is no 'sharing'. Richard's misguided efforts to commit himself to 'his new life' are exposed in a couple of montage conflicts following his new decision. The first indication of the shallowness of the life-style to which he now consciously aspires occurs at the party for firemen and girls. Prudence is cheerfully flirting with the firemen. 'Pye was laughing gargantually into her face. His sly pig's eyes assessed his chances' (*Caught*, p.71). In this callous atmosphere, Richard, talking to Hilly, thinks to himself that he has discovered her as a human being:

He felt he regarded her now as a real person, not just the girl
for a drink when the evening's training was done. By this time
both of them had had a few drinks. Then another crash of
laughter dragged his eyes away.

> Prudence was being a success. She liked firemen.... She felt
> firemen must be very brave, but particularly the professionals,
> which was where Pye had the advantage. They had those
> funny hats.　(p.73)

Green stresses his great concern with the need for love and
understanding between people by repeatedly devoting scenes
towards the elaboration of this theme. Richard's misconception
that he now recognizes Hilly as a real human being, 'not just
the girl for a drink', is immediately undercut by Green's comment
that they by this time 'had had a few drinks'. The audio-visual
counterpoint produced by a crash of laughter from Prudence
and a group of firemen interrupts Richard's thoughts, thereby
heightening the irony of his position. By focusing on Prudence,
whose admiration for professional firemen revolves around their
'funny hats', Green highlights her ridiculous superficiality and,
furthermore, suggests a lack of sincerity common to them all.

Man's essential isolation is the central issue Green tries to
explore in *Caught*. To highlight individuals' separation from each
other and to reveal their deeper, unrealized needs is the main
function of this party. Just prior to its commencement, 'Richard
stood *lonely* by the door to bring both girls in when they arrived,
they were so very late, under the high brilliant stars, he wondered
if they would ever come' (pp.67–8, emphasis added). The conflict
of scales accentuates Richard's isolation and his need for contact.
Adopting the point of view of the detached observer, Green
includes all the 'party goers' in an atmosphere of isolation. As
in a modern play, he confines a group of people in one room for
close scrutiny in order to disclose the truth about them. His
picture is oppressive. The room in which they are gathered,
overheated and completely without ventilation, has its windows

> coated with black paint.... The room was painted yellow
> orange. The floor was done out with flags of artificial stone
> which, whatever the scrubbing, gave off a thick grey dust. All,
> as they sat in this bare room, had purple shadows hacked out

beneath their eyebrows, chins and noses by the naked, hot spotlights in the orange ceiling. (p.69)

Rigid, unyielding colours combine with the 'naked, hot spotlights' and stuffy air to create an atmosphere of conflict and of menacing barrenness and separateness. It is a scene where self-seeking individuals do not seem to comprehend the extent of their own isolation and are therefore precluded from extending fellow feeling to one another. Only active participation in the inhumanity of the war will alleviate this condition, and the confrontation with war becomes the significant turning-point in *Caught*.

Only in retrospect, when the threat has passed and Richard, with his sister-in-law, is walking peacefully in his parents' garden, far away from London, does he try to convey the profound significance of his experience in the night raids. In response to Dy's queries about Hilly, Richard, with a shrug, minimizes the significance of their relationship. ' "Hilly? She's about still. Yes", he went on rather fast, "the great idea is to be on your own" ' (p.176). It is his profound recognition of human community that Richard now feels has made him a new person. He explains to Dy: 'In some fantastic way I'm sure you only get in war, we were suddenly alone and forced to rely on one another entirely. And that after twelve months' bickering. Each crew was thrown upon itself, on its own resources. The only thing to do was to keep together' (pp.182–3). To Richard, the experience of the blitz becomes 'almost like an explanation of the whole of our life in the war, waiting in the sub-station for just this. I do so want you to get the whole thing' (p.180). Richard attempts to recount, but the vividness of it all fails to be transmitted. Significantly, his compelling experience of the dynamic beauty that life contains has been as important as the discovery of his own isolation and his new sense of the value of solidarity. Green, as author, tries to communicate the emotive quality of Richard's experience through visualization. Richard begins:

'The first night', he said, 'we were ordered to the docks. As we came over Westminster Bridge it was fantastic, the whole of the left side of London seemed to be alight'.
(It had not been like that at all. As they went, not hurrying, but steadily towards the river, the sky in that quarter, which happened to be the east, beginning at the bottom of the streets

until it spread over the nearest houses, was flooded in a second sunset, orange and rose, turning the pavement pink. Civilians hastened by twos or threes, hushed below the stupendous pall of defeat until, in the business quarter, the streets were deserted.)

(These firemen at last drove out on to the bridge. Here two men and a girl, like grey cartridge paper under this light which stretched with the spread of a fan up the vertical sky, were creeping off, drunkenly, defiantly singing.)   (p.176)

Green intrudes to animate Richard's visual impressions, which have already been readjusted in his mind and become memory, into an inaccurate account of his real experience. This intrusion serves not as an explanation of Richard's ordeal, but as a dramatization of his true experience. The meaning Green wishes to communicate is deepened by the conflict of perspectives. It is a meaning that cannot be defined, because it deviates from an authentic transcription of actuality. The significance of the author's depiction is contained in its striking vividness, in contrast to Richard's more one-dimensional recollections. Dy, like Green, is aware that Richard's memory has altered reality into something abstract: 'there was nothing in what he had spoken to catch her imagination'. It is eventually a metaphor that does catch Dy's attention: Richard describes their taxi as 'a pink beetle drawing a pepper corn', a picture to which Dy responds 'because she thought it vivid'. She wonders, 'the real thing ... the real thing is the picture you carry in your eye afterwards, surely? It can't be what you can't remember, can it' (p.179). The image of the beetle is important in that it surpasses a conventional, 'prosaic' apprehension of reality. Similarly, Green's re-creation of the scene Richard describes as 'fantastic' attains a poetic vividness and intensity that exceeds the function of prose. Green seeks to give this world of disintegration a fabulous, poetic quality rather than describe or explain that reality. The composition of vivid colours, 'a second sunset', attains a poetic dynamism of its own, a projection of an artistic sensibility that perceives Life despite a pall of destruction. This reading is elucidated by Green's statement in *Pack my Bag*, 'there must be a threat to one's skin to wake what is left of things remembered into things to die with'; vivid images we should 'take with us like a bar of gold'.[7] Green's striking re-creation of Richard's

actual perceptions is motivated by his conviction of the necessity
of constant commitment to the poetic visual moment. As Green
says in *Pack my Bag*, 'the crime is to forget'. Vividness belonging
to the past cannot effect vital experience.

On a prosaic level, Green's visualization of the war scene
creates difficulties in interpretation. The scene cannot be
explained in terms of colours and their possible symbolic meanings. There seems to be no justification for classifying pink, for
example, as primarily used for creating a threatening atmosphere
of war. Although pink transforms London during the bombard-
ment, it is not an invariably negative colour. Nor can the scene
be explained by strictly defining rose and pink as the colours of
love (which they sometimes are). Yet this latter interpretation
comes closer to the intent behind Green's utilization of these
colours. Pink, rose and orange, in this context, are vigorous,
sparkling colours as opposed to grey or black. From this point
of view, the blitz scene may be approached to advantage in terms
of montage, notably as a conflict of masses. An examination of
several related scenes will support such an approach.

In the scene depicting Richard's first night as a fireman, the
vibrant orange, rose and pink as from a 'second sunset' contrast
with three lonely drunken figures, grey like 'cartridge paper
under this light' surrounded by 'deserted' streets. In purely
visual terms, it is a stark contrast between vivacity and 'death'.
Significantly, it is the sudden recognition of this close competition
between 'living' and death that brings about Richard's change
of heart, and which shapes the thematic structure of *Caught*.

A previously presented scene (the only eye-witnessed war
scene included before Richard's retrospection) provides insight
into the real significance of Green's use of colour. The montage
structure is employed again as a means towards achieving the
same goal, but through a different process. What is important
to Green is the optimal evocation of the parallel existence of life
and death, each achieving the greatest impact when portrayed
side by side so that the antithesis is emphasized through the
contrast. In the previous scene, the contrast between the colours
has the same effect as a different kind of montage, the conflict
of masses apparent in the following passage.

He found the driver had brought them to a statue, which
still *looked blindly on*, in the centre of a London square. . . . Two

thirty-foot high sprays or fans of flame lit the face of ornate hotel buildings, or what may have been the east and west sides of a vast block of flats ... and illuminated them so well that, at the distance, he was able to pick out details of brickwork and stone facings more easily, and in colours more natural, than would have been possible on a *spring morning, in early sunlight*.

Against this livid incandescence stood the *old* war horse, *pitch black*, his bronze rider up, *pitch black*, both, as always, facing south.   (p.95, emphasis added)

The play of flames, illuminating buildings as if 'on a spring morning, in early sunlight' (a regenerative image), opposes the 'pitch black' war horse, 'old' and 'blind'. Green seems intensely alert to the poetic quality of this antithesis, to the image of Life despite death. In terms of montage, the bright light accentuates the blackness of the horse, its 'blind' age, its isolation where it is situated 'as always, facing south', setting the mood of static loneliness and death, and furthermore, establishing a close thematic link with the central theme of the immediately succeeding scenes, reflecting Richard's own isolation.

Lighting his torch, Richard at once hears 'a cry that was *lost*, "Put it out, put that light out"' (p.96, emphasis added). Richard is left in dark isolation by 'the bronze horse, black on one flank, rose coloured on the other towards the now spreading fire'. Again, as the vivid rose colour collides with the pitch black, thereby increasing its intensity, it heightens the sense of Richard's loneliness. The profound experience of his own isolation, the appalling magnitude of meaninglessness and human distress about him, his thoughts then of Pye who has taken cover 'willy nilly, in his coffin, eaten by worms six foot underground', provoke Richard's regeneration.

Confronting the ultimate existential void, there is only one solution for Richard: participation in Life. In the same way that Green has used light and vivid colours in montage conflicts as contrasts in order to heighten a sense of human isolation, and of death, he also juxtaposes these darker aspects of reality with the most vivid play of colours to intensify the vital essence of life. Green re-creates Richard's experience that first night:

(The firemen saw each other's faces. They saw the water

below a dirty yellow towards the fire; the wharves on that far side low and black, those on the bank they were leaving a *pretty rose*. They saw the whole fury of that conflagration in which they had to play a part. They sat very still, beneath the immensity. For, against it, warehouses, small towers, puny steeples *seemed alive* with sparks from the mile high pandemonium of flame reflected in the quaking sky. This fan, a roaring red gold, pulsed rose at the outside edge, the perimeter round which the heavens, set with stars before fading into utter blackness, were for a space a trembling green.)

(pp.176–7, emphasis added)

Richard can only recollect the immensity of the flames' destructive power, 'like a huge wood fire on a flat hearth, only a thousand times bigger' (p.180). Green's correction heightens the poetic quality of the scene; the roaring fire is transformed in Green's imagination into 'red gold', a correlative of his vital image, in *Pack my Bag*, of 'a bar of gold'. The reality he presents is filled with vividly interacting details of visual beauty. He creates a vibrant moment of vivacity counterpointing the darker aspects of death. A 'pretty rose' together with 'a roaring gold' and a 'trembling green' over towers and steeples that 'seemed alive with sparks' under a 'quaking sky' 'set with stars', play against the 'low and black' wharves before 'fading into utter blackness'. No colour symbolism can explain the meaning of this scene; it is not a representation of actuality, but an impassioned artistic vision. The vivid mosaic of colours evokes life in all its immediacy as a counterpoint to the dark undertones of physical as well as spiritual death. Green can imagine joy in the destructive fires: blazing flames and a glow of 'rose' that 'toyed joyfully' with 'black stacks' of timber in the 'pink of that night' (*Caught*, p.180). It is the commitment to life, in all its perceivable immediacy, that he finally offers to the reader, before it 'fades' into 'utter blackness'.

Green's vision of life in *Caught* may be further illuminated by the close similarity of the preceding scene with one from Joseph Conrad's *Youth*. The young Marlow and the crew on board the barque *Judea* are fighting desperately to keep the doomed ship afloat. Marlow reports,

It was our fate to pump in that ship, to pump out of her, to pump into her; and after keeping water out of her to save ourselves from being drowned, we frantically poured water into her to save ourselves from being burnt.

And she crawled on, do or die, in the serene weather. The sky was a miracle of purity, a miracle of azure. The sea was polished, was blue, was pellucid, was sparkling like a precious stone, extending on all sides, all round to the horizon – as if the whole terrestrial globe had been one jewel, one colossal sapphire, a single gem fashioned into a planet. And on the lustre of the great calm waters the Judea glided imperceptibly, enveloped in languid and unclean vapours, in a lazy cloud that drifted to leeward, light and slow; a pestiferous cloud defiling the splendour of sea and sky.[8]

Like Richard Roe in his moment of revelation, Marlow's exhilaration at the beauty and vitality of sea and sky makes him insusceptible to the destructive force of the fire. By their contrast rather, the 'pestiferous cloud' enhances the splendour of the 'terrestrial jewel'. Richard embraces life when confronted with undeniable destructiveness and loneliness; Marlow rejoices in the vitality of youth, acutely aware of the surrounding dark forces and that life can only continue as long as man continually re-creates for himself the living present moment.

Oh, the glamour of youth! Oh, the fire of it, more dazzling than the flames of the burning ship, throwing a magic light on the wide earth, leaping audaciously to the sky, presently to be quenched by time, more cruel, more pitiless, more bitter than the sea – and like the flames of the burning ship surrounded by an impenetrable night.[9]

As for Richard, Marlow's active participation in the fire-fighting becomes 'the endeavour, the test, the trial of life' on a voyage towards self-discovery. Significantly, in recounting the ordeals of their protagonists, both Conrad and Green are trying to isolate the essence of this vital response to the test of life. Marlow wonders at the crew's courage after the explosion. They 'had in them the right stuff', given to them, he thinks, by the vastness of the sea, 'the loneliness surrounding their dark stolid souls'.[10] Green's critical scrutiny of the group 'caught' by the war ends with a sign of faith in the human potential. The

firemen, faced with destruction, experience the value of co-
operation. The bravest of them is Shiner Wright. Richard
remembers him attacking the fire, 'right up in it, mouth wide
open, snarling, drooling at the flames'. '(He had said, "Hi, cock.
Boy, am I enjoying this")' (*Caught*, p.185). Richard also looks
strengthened. Dy 'decided his face was thinner, while his neck
had thickened. His shoulders were broader' (p.179).

Tantamount to the men's positive assertiveness when threatened by the war's destruction, is Green's underlying awareness
of his characters' capacity for sympathy and understanding.
Pye reveals his benevolent tendencies on several occasions.
Superintendent Dodge, Green's chief personification of
officialdom, shows unexpected tolerance when Mary Howells,
threatened with dismissal for having run away from work,
appeals to him as a human being. At one point, Richard
seems close to breaking through his self-constructed emotional
barricades to a more fulfilling assertiveness. There is 'beginning
warmth', perhaps potential love:

> As with the return of summer, a beginning warmth ran in
> their limbs where they lay together, on leave, in naked bed.
> Richard fetched a great sigh. What he had now, and had only
> held before when drunk, was so much to his contentment that
> he wanted nothing more.   (p.118)

In the final analysis, Green does not condemn his characters
for lacking the actual potential to demonstrate benignity. Their
problem is that they are 'caught' in some way, their vital feelings
restrained by outer and inner circumstances. Accordingly, Green
never presents his characters as completely cynical and
superficial, but always probes, often ironically, their deeper,
unfulfilled needs and longings. These yearnings ultimately reflect
what is human in man, which can only be released by confrontation with a palpable reality.

Most of the characters in *Caught* act with misdirected responses
to their natural instincts. 'It was danger Prudence sought in this
lull of living, before the enemy went into Norway', Green remarks
(p.122). Prudence haphazardly seeks the same kind of 'joy' that
Richard eventually discovers during the blitz. Hilly is convinced
that 'this war's been a tremendous release for most', but Green
discloses how his characters, in reality, become more 'caught' in

their desperate efforts to really live (p.99). What finally binds all the characters together is Green's conviction that humans share a common fund of basic needs and longings, a common potential. The central themes of *Caught* (i.e. Green's insistence on the value of 'living' and his underlying faith in the potential for vitality of his characters) converge in the affinity of perception revealed by Richard and his son, Christopher. The nature of Richard's revitalization clearly corresponds with Christopher's liveliness demonstrated at the beginning of the novel, a parallel which strongly suggests common, healthy instincts. Christopher's natural sprightliness, unthwarted by the forces of socialization or by the stasis caused by too much introspection, reflects Richard's younger self. 'Christopher was like any other child of his age, not very interested or interesting, strident with health. He enjoyed teasing and was careful no-one should know what he felt' (p.5). Christopher's youthfulness springs from the same fervent need for 'living' that is his father's underlying inducement for joining the Auxiliary Fire Service. Significantly, it is Christopher's perceptual sensitivity Richard regains in the fire scenes. It becomes a vital stimulus in the development of Richard's more reflective consciousness. Passing by the shop where his son had been abducted, Richard is struck by the toy display which had so mesmerized Christopher:

> Fire engines attracted the father, but deer, then sailboats, had bewitched the son. For both it was the deep colour spilled over these objects that, by evoking memories they would not name, and which they could not place, held them, and then led both to a loch-deep unconsciousness of all else.

The joyful play of colours in the shop window as well as in the fire scenes reflects Christopher's and Richard's acute artistic sensibilities. It does not contain an objective symbolic meaning. Rather, it represents a reality created by the subjective consciousnesses of the spectators. The toy display functions as a piece of art. Green accounts for this artistic process thus:

> The function ... of a good painting or piece of sculpture is to appeal by or through the eye to the memory of things seen. This does not mean to say that the appeal is by any means to the ideal, but the result is probably to carry the viewer's ability

to see, which is after all appreciation, to a new reality beyond his experience, thereby creating something which, however abstract, has a life of its own.[11]

So with the present scene:

> The body of the shop was inundated with colour, brimming, and this colour, as the sea was a predominant part of each window, was a permanence of sapphire in shopping hours. Pink neon lights and the high ceiling wore down this blue to some extent, made customers' faces less aggressively steeped in the body of the store, but *enhanced, or deepened* that fire brigade scarlet to carmine, and, in so doing, drugged Richard's consciousness.   (pp.12–13, emphasis added)

Though Christopher is kidnapped by Pye's sister inside this shop, the scene does not simply express a mood of foreboding, in which pink and red combine with other sinister hues to create a corresponding atmosphere. Considering the emphasis Green places on the play of colours in the shop window as well as in the thematically related fire scenes, it is clear that these passages have a more profound significance than what merely derives from their atmosphere. Rather, their dramatic intensity is a mystical projection of the spectator's 'loch-deep' subconsciousness. As Green says, the appeal of art is not principally to the 'ideal', but to man's natural need for sensuous exploration, 'which is after all appreciation'. In fact, to view Pye's sister as a major threat to Christopher bears no meaningful relation to Green's central thematic concerns in *Caught*. She is primarily an unhappy victim of circumstances beyond her control and so does not really influence the novel's tones.

The dynamism of colours reflects Richard's and Christopher's innermost needs and their spontaneous enjoyment of the toys' vividness. The tone of the scene does not derive from the colours' 'meanings', but from their purely visual qualities: 'pink neon lights' impinge on the sapphire blue only to 'enhance' and 'deepen' the effect of that 'fire brigade scarlet' to which Richard is most attracted. The intensification of a scene's visual impact due to the juxtaposition of two or more colours, or of different intensities of light, represents precisely the central principle of montage. Green, in the preceding scene, employs montage in order to heighten the evocative kinesis that penetrates Richard's senses. The effect of this technique highlights Green's central concern with the need for full 'living'. Richard, inspired by his vision, empathizes with his son's needs, no different from his own: ' "I want, I want". He said to himself, it is not for us to measure the dark cupidity, the need.' Prosaic explanations cannot account for 'the spell which held his [Christopher's] eyes. Words were no means of communication now' (p.14). Just as Richard, after the fire raids, fails in his attempts to convey the vividness of his revelation, so here can Christopher's exhilaration only be transmitted through the natural vigour of prismatic colours. From this point of view, the use of pink or of red, in this context (acknowledging that the same colours do not have a defined meaning and that they may serve different functions in other contexts), reflects their natural 'cupidity'. The following scene stresses not only Christopher's longings, but also those of Pye's frustrated sister, thus suggesting the common source of their personalities:

> He [Christopher] became dazzled by the pink neon lights beyond her features. Caught in another patch of colour, some of her chin was pillar-box red, also a part of the silver fox she wore ... when, to make him do as she wanted, she caught full at him with her eyes that, by the ocean in which they were steeped, were so much *a part of the world his need had made*, and so much more a part of it by being *alive*, then he felt anything must be natural.   (Ibid., emphasis added)

Green's characteristic focusing on the nature of his characters' needs prevents Christopher's and Richard's respective perceptions of the toy display and of the colourful fire scenes from producing a mere aesthetic effect. Green, unlike Joyce, does not seek an abstract aesthetic pattern which, says Stephen Dedalus, 'awakens, or ought to awaken, or induces, or ought to induce, an aesthetic stasis, an ideal pity or an ideal terror, a stasis called forth, prolonged, and at last dissolved by what I call the rhythm of beauty'.[12] To Green, beauty does not lie in an abstract, patterned harmony inducing stasis, but in a natural, living dynamism which counteracts pattern. Dedalus argues that 'Beauty expressed by the artist cannot awaken in us an emotion which is kinetic or a sensation which is purely physical.' However, it is precisely such a response to beauty Green seeks, for Green designates beauty not as an object for aesthetic contemplation, but as a kinetic projection of vigorous, human needs. In this way, his evocation of beauty and vitality does not abstract itself from the plane of human suffering and imperfection. With the aid of montage, Green integrates these aspects of life into a vision based on sympathetic communion with things 'living'.

Richard's revelation of the firefighting scenes, as 'almost like an explanation of the whole of our life in the war', has certain affinities with Lily Briscoe's epiphanic vision in *To the Lighthouse*, but differs in its essential dynamically inspired quality. Lily Briscoe's completion of her painting is prompted by a sudden compassion for mankind, based on her intuitive recognition of man's loneliness, 'the truth about things'. Lily shares old Mr Carmichael's thoughts: 'He stood there spreading his hands over all the weakness and suffering of mankind; she thought he was surveying, tolerantly, compassionately, their final destiny.' Filled with renewed inspiration, she turns to her canvas: 'There it was – her picture. Yes, with all its green and blues, its lines running up and across'.[13] Like Lily's, Green's artistic vision arises from his intuitive, sympathetic appraisal of life and humanity. Lily's canvas of variegated colours and crossing lines reflects the amorphous nature of life. When she adds the final stroke, however, a line in the centre which unites the elements, she reveals her underlying allegiance to a static, contemplated order. Virginia Woolf's vision is essentially tragic, an artistic ordering of her characters' subjective realities for the purpose of counteracting flux; an artistic order based on compassion and understanding for individuals because they share the same tragic destiny. Green's vision, however, surpasses tragedy and evolves into a comic affirmation of reality by advocating community with the essence of 'living'. Commitment to living brings hope of reintegration through human sympathies.

Green's appeal for humanism extends to criticism of certain attitudes conditioned by an institutionalized society. In a dream, Pye sees himself going to visit his sister in hospital. He is refused the opportunity to speak to her in private by 'dry, striped men' inside a hall of bars.

Then, from above, he heard her cry low, 'Bert'. Looking up, he could see Amy on the third floor of the cage, hanging to

bars like they do in pictures, dressed all in yellow.... 'Amy',
he called, 'but we can't speak like this.' 'Excuse me', he said
to the one expressionless man who now remained, 'we can't
speak like this, in public, shouting top and bottom to each
other. This lady's my sister.' 'Them's the regulations, Mr
Pye.' 'But man, it's not human.' 'Sorry, there it is.' 'But, by
God, this ain't right.' 'You know what they are, you're in a
service, Mr Pye, an' they won't have it.'   (p.85)

No doubt the impersonal treatment Pye receives from officials
is one of the factors that contribute to his victimization. Pye is
convinced that 'any system that can send an unfortunate woman
into what is jail really, is vile, a filthy system'. As he tells
Richard, 'they told me I must sign her away like a bit of furniture
or they would prosecute' (p.38). In light of Green's great concern
with the nature of his characters' private needs and yearnings,
Pye's discontent signals criticisms shared by the author. Yet
there is no consistent examination or criticism of social or
political institutions in *Caught*. What criticism exists applies
primarily to the attitudes of individuals in relation to other
individuals 'caught' within a 'system'. In accordance with
the central themes of *Caught*, individual responsibilities and
sympathies should not suffer in deference to conformity to
regulations. As Richard realizes when surrounded by the inhumanity of the war, 'you have to disobey if you're any good'
(p.182). Green's stress is not on social or political principles; he
is concerned with human relationships in terms of the individual's
confirmation of his own humanism.

Accordingly, *Caught* ends as it began, with scenes from
Richard's private garden. Richard's estranged relationship with
his son shows signs of improvement. Still overwhelmed by his
war experiences, Richard dismisses Christopher, but only until
after tea. The garden of his past, which has separated him from
reality, has lost its firm hold on him. He is even ready to begin
forgetting the war raids. Soon, 'it had come to seem out of date'
(p.178).

Richard, at the novel's end, is but beginning to emerge from
his own preoccupations towards the recognition of a 'living'
reality. 'He warmed to her [Dy] for a moment, then turned back
to himself again' (p.189). Inconclusive, the implications of
Richard's revelation only intimated, *Caught* compels the reader

to derive his own meaning, his own judgement. A specified, resolved conclusion would conflict with Green's primary objective, that of making fiction an effective medium for communication between the 'life' of the whole novel and the reader. In order to understand the ending, the reader must view it as a consequence of the novel's total 'life'. Richard's war experience is the climax of the novel, offering 'an explanation of the whole of our life in the war'. Significantly, that life is the life most vividly portrayed in *Caught* through a network of juxtaposed scenes. It cannot be fully explained by the intrusions of an author or by Richard's subjective recordings; it must speak for itself. On the level of realistic representation, the reticulation of scenes (see Griffith's film device) creates atmosphere and exposes different aspects of reality in the London of 1940. However, objectivity of presentation is counterpointed by the author's subjective sensibilities. Montage arrangements in *Caught* accentuate Green's central concerns, provoking the reader's affective response to vital themes. Accordingly, the 'meaning' of Richard's moral and emotional development echoes the tone created in different contexts throughout the novel. It is essentially montage that elucidates the full significance and implications of Richard's revelation about life.

BACK (1946)

Thematically, *Back* possesses close affinities with *Caught*. It will therefore be examined, rather briefly, in connection with the other. As in *Caught*, the central character of *Back* is haunted by a dead woman. Charley Summers only recovers from this debilitating state of mind when he rejects the idealized memory of his late mistress, Rose, and accepts a 'living' reality. A repatriated prisoner just back from the war, he is initially unable to distinguish the real from the unreal. When he meets Rose's half-sister, Nancy Whitmore, Charley is convinced that she is, in fact, Rose and that the story of her death has been fabricated. However, aided by Nancy's patient understanding, Charley becomes increasingly aware that Nancy is not Rose. He gradually becomes conscious of his own needs and, finally denying his dead mistress, realizes that he loves Nancy.

As in *Caught*, the protagonist can only be reintegrated with

life through confrontation with death, from which he has tried
to insulate himself in a fantasy world. Cultivation of life despite
the immanent proximity of pain and death, Green suggests, is
possible through mobilization of sound natural instinct, as
represented by the Grants' cat. Charley is visiting old Mr Grant,
Rose's and Nancy's father, when Grant dies of a stroke in the
middle of the night. Charley, who is about to despair, discovers
the cat, which, like most animals in Green's novels, is unperturbed
by disintegrating forces. 'It didn't even raise its ears.' Charley
finds it incredible 'that this animal could ignore crude animal
cries above, which he had shut out with his wet palms' (*Back*,
p.186). The image of the cat's instinctual self-sufficiency precipi-
tates Charley's final recognition of his own natural needs. A sign
of this is that, moments after Grant's death, 'instinct' makes him
switch off the light while waiting for his woman to come to his
bed. The cat, with its careful pregnancy and motherhood, seems
to reflect Nancy's and Charley's need to fulfil their natures.
Nancy will marry a man only on the condition that he accept
the cat and her kittens with her (p.206). By means of his montage
technique, Green stresses his belief in the 'comic' possibility for
human fulfilment despite an underlying tragic vision.

The close interaction between Green's vision and technique
is apparent in the following scenes. Charley and Nancy face a
physical wasteland:

> Autumn was the season, most roses were dead. Petals that
> had dropped some months back and rotted, traces of a summer
> now gone, were covered by the brown leaves which even in
> this still air rocked down to lie deep on the ground as they
> walked, so that their feet rustled. Where a flying bomb had
> dropped recently, the drift of leaves was still green underfoot,
> the trees bare as deep winter. Then, just as they were passing
> this spot, the syrens set up a broken wailing.
> 'Come on', he said, turning off the road into the garden of
> a house in ruins.   (p.176)

The audio-visual counterpoint at once signals the irreconcilability
between the withered wasteland and the garden, and is a warning
to the two lovers to escape the former and to seek the growth of
the latter. It is significant that both of the gardens in *Back* and
in *Caught* are places to which are attached the treasured memories

of a bygone past. However, those 'briars that had borne gay rose, after rose, after wild rose' are now dead, 'brown' and 'leafless'. There is new life: 'as they turned again to themselves in the garden, the briars wreathed from one *black* cypress to another were aflame, as *alive* as live filaments in an electric *light* bulb, against the *night*'s quick agony of the *sun*' (p.177, emphasis added). In visual terms, the juxtaposition of light and dark generates a sense of polarity within a spatial framework. A perceptual synthesis is produced whereby the darker aspects, through contrast, intensify the import of Charley's and Nancy's present commitment. It creates the sense of a life-giving instant separated from the diurnal processes.

> The *night*, on its way fast, was *chill*, and now he had again that undreamed of sharp warmth moving and living on his own, her breath an attar of roses on his deep *sun-red* cheek, her hair an animal over his eyes and *alive*, for he could see each rose *glowing* separate strand, then her *dark body* thrusting heavy at him, and her *blood dark* eel fingers that fumbled at his neck.
> She cruelly spoiled it. She took her sweet lips off his.
>
> (Ibid., emphasis added)

Green's evocation of this vibrant moment causes the lovers to merge into a sensuous and spiritual unity. The image of Nancy's 'blood dark eel fingers' is not insidious but a metaphorical expression which, together with the darker aspects of the external world, enhances the mystic sensuality of their embrace. It is significant that the tone of the passage does not derive from a referential meaning belonging to individual images within the montage structure. It springs from the scene's total sensory impact. Like the Grants' cat in the moment of death, Charley at this instant has a strong, 'warm' sense of instinctually 'moving and living on his own'; Nancy is associated with an 'animal', 'alive'.

Differences between the first and last scene of the novel reveal the inconsistency of colour symbolism; the meaning of colours is largely determined by context. The initial picture – a road which is 'asphalted blue' and a church of 'blood coloured brick' – enhances a dominant atmosphere of emotional conflict. In the final love scene, these colours form a much happier scheme of contrasts. Now the darkness outside is a 'marvellous deep blue'. Roses do not 'stare', they 'spill a light ... over her [Nancy] in all their summer colours, her hands that lay along her legs were red, her stomach gold, her breasts the colour of cream roses, and her neck white roses for the bride'. Red and blue here are not sinister colours; they intensify the vivid beauty of the moment.

The contradictory aspect of life and death in *Back* envelops various characters in some unreal region between these two poles. One may argue that what makes life in *Back* unreal is Green's characters' inability to respond creatively to life's contradictory quality, the possibility for life despite the immanent presence of death. There are distinct differences between the perceptual immediacy produced by Green's montage technique in the preceding scenes and the dreamlike, surreal atmosphere surrounding Charley's regressive search for his dear Rose. As he enters the cemetery where Rose is buried, Charley

> had his cheek brushed by a rose, and began awkwardly to search for Rose, through roses, in what seemed to him should be the sunniest places on a fine day, the warmest when the sun came out at twelve o'clock for she had been so warm, and amongst the newer memorials in local stone because she had died in time of war, when, or so he imagined, James could never have found marble for her, of whom, at no time before this moment, had he ever thought as cold beneath a slab, food for worms, her great red hair, still growing, a sort of moist bower for worms.   (pp.7–8)

The juxtaposition of sunlight and fragrant roses with cold gravestones and other images of death might have evoked sensory polarity. Green's style, however, creates no perceptual immediacy which may make the reader's impressions visually 'real'. Instead, the objects of contemplation recede into intangibility. The juxtaposed images do not collide in a montage manner, but intertwine grotesquely in some unreal region between life and death. Green's use of one long run-on sentence without natural pauses creates a stream-of-consciousness effect, as in a Joyce novel. The style becomes a mimetic projection of Charley's fumbling attempt to separate between dream and reality.

Two interesting aspects of Green's technique have been examined in the previous discussion. Montage is used in order to produce a sense of sensuous or affective immediacy between scene and reader. For the completely opposite effect, juxtaposed images suggesting either 'reality' or hallucination are inextricably entangled in an uneasy borderland between life and death. This close connection between technique and content explains why Green makes use of montage, in *Back*, almost exclusively in the introduction and conclusion. The function of the introduction is to set the tone of the rest of the novel through the construction of an atmosphere and to present the reader with the central themes. The ending, as has been demonstrated, conveys the central character's reintegration with reality and his revitalized interrelationship with Life. Throughout the bulk of the novel, the reader sees the world of *Back* as warped by Charley's hallucinatory vision. Stokes says that

> Green's method fully creates Charley – inarticulate, bemused, unable to feel anything except as it is distorted by his self-pitying obsession. *Back*, in fact, is the nearest that Green has ever come to a novel in which the viewpoint is that of a single character, of, to use James's term, 'the fool'. It is perhaps the most remarkable of Green's many *tours de force*, because although so much of the novel consists of scene, the reader sees always through the eyes of Charley, and ... the reader's 'vision is distorted by Charley's faulty spectacles'.[14]

Compared with *Caught*, with its multiple points of view and intricate flashback technique, *Back* is far more conventionally constructed along a chronological narrative line. Since the author, for the most part, tends to keep close to the protagonist's consciousness, there is insufficient objective detachment for the central ironies (because the novel is basically ironic) to spring from occasional montage effects. The irony is implied in the overall structural duplicity of the novel. 'One common device of this sort', states M. H. Abrams of a feature which applies to *Back*,

> is the invention of a naive hero, or else a naive narrator or spokesman, whose invincible simplicity leads him to persist in putting an interpretation on affairs which the knowing reader – who penetrates to, and shares, the implicit point of view of

the authorial presence behind the naive *persona* – just as persistently is able to alter and correct.[15]

Irony as a quality arising from the compositional structure of a concrete context occurs mainly in the novel's introduction. By means of a few montage arrangements, Green sets the tone which conditions the interpretation of the ensuing narrative. Charley is introduced on the opening page as a young man who lost his leg in the war 'for not noticing the gun beneath a rose'. This image has a broader symbolic meaning than its literal signification. In terms of the novel's central theme, the rose refers to Charley's dead girlfriend, Rose, who, in Charley's mind, is idealized and associated with fragrant roses. The gun suggests the destructive quality of Charley's obsession with the past. His search for Rose is a lethal trap. This meaning is first clarified in a montage conflict involving audio-visual counterpoint. Making his way through the cemetery, Charley is surrounded by 'trees of mourning', and by 'rose after rose after rose' (p.5). The atmosphere reinforces the unreality of his dream. Its abstraction finds expression in Gertrude Stein's famous poem, 'A rose is a rose is a rose is a rose.'[16] Reality, however, intrudes to rouse Charley. His progress is interrupted by

a sudden upthrusting cackle of geese in panic, the sound of which brought home to him a stack of faggots he had seen blown high by a grenade.... So, while the geese quietened, he felt what he had seen until the silence which followed, when he at once forgot.
But there was left him an idea that he had been warned. (p.6)

Two incongruous pictures collide in a montage fashion generating a third image, a new concept. The incident is a warning to Charley not to pursue his quest. This passage is an interesting one since the author himself explains the effect intended by the audio-visual counterpoint. He thereby reveals the ideas underlying his scenic technique which apply to the basic principles of montage, a factor which encourages a montage approach to his fiction. Furthermore, the preceding passage parallels similar scenes in *Loving* and *Concluding*. Peacocks' shrieks warn the lovers, Edith and Raunce, against lurking dangers; the cries

of Rock's goose during his nocturnal walk through the woods
are directed against his life-denying irreconcilability. These
parallels indicate that montage offers a valid interpretation of
central themes in these novels.

Charley's disregarding of the first warning necessitates a
reminder, which increases the irony of his pursuit. When again
he heads for the graves, he is disturbed by a 'bicycle bell, ringing
closer and closer by the church, clustering spray upon spray of
sound which wreathed the air much as those roses grew around
the headstones, whence, so he felt, they narrowly regarded him'
(Back, p.6). Charley's feeling of being 'narrowly regarded'
corresponds with the sense of warning given by the bicycle bell.
It 'caused him to stop dead'.

A new montage conflict immediately draws attention to other
aspects of Charley's delusions involving Rose. A boy of about
six comes on a tricycle past the porch then, 'as the machine got
up speed, he stood to one side, in spite of the gate still closed
between the two of them'. The conflict of planes emphasizes the
separation between Charley and the boy, who turns out to be
Rose's son, whom Charley later mistakes to be his own. Rose
and her son belong to a world from which Charley is excluded.
The conflict is heightened through a combined conflict of graphic
direction and audio-visual counterpoint. When Charley enters
this secluded world through the gate, the boy comes in the
opposite direction: he 'shrilly rang the bell as he dashed past'.
Charley is 'irritated' by the noise, which, like the cackle of geese,
serves as a warning, a signal intended to awaken him and make
him face reality. Ironically, he disregards this sign as he did the
warning given by the geese: 'he forgot the boy who was gone,
who spelled nothing to him'.

Green's characterization of the geese in the introductory
chapter as warning messengers illuminates the meaning of the
following incidence. It starts raining, and Charley seeks shelter.

> Misery kept his mind blank until he turned the porch. Then
> he had a bad shock when he found who was sheltering before
> him. For of all people, of all imaginable men, and fat as those
> geese, was James. They stared at each other.   (pp.9–10)

The suddenness of the two men's confrontation renders the
impact of a conflict of graphic direction. Unwittingly, Charley

is confronting the boy's *real* father. The irony of Charley's position is heightened when he associates James with the geese without recognizing that their underlying function is to awaken him to reality.

Having acquainted the reader with the dominant tone and central themes of *Back*, Green seems to turn his interest more towards an involved recounting of Charley's slow, incredulous progress towards an acceptance of reality than towards evoking Charley's ironic position before the reader by dynamic visualiz- ation. The lack of dramatic intent (and hence the lack of tone derived from the compositional structure) is also evident in the various characters' verbal interactions. Stokes observes that 'a great deal of the novel (more than of any preceding novel except *Loving*) consists of scene' – and he goes on to mention a network of characters involved in dialogue – 'But all of these conversations Green keeps firmly on the prosaic level.'[17] One might argue that, since reality in the middle part of the novel is largely modified by Charley's subjective vision, the lack of dynamic counterpoint mirrors Charley's abstraction and lack of vigour. Green manifests a close connection between form and content in *Back*. From this point of view, the novel's overall structure, consisting of a prosaic narrative section introduced by objectified compositional ironies and succeeded by a dynamic reintegration of life's contradictory impulses, fulfils its most important function.

4   *Loving* (1945)

Compared to the previously examined novels, *Loving* is more consistently committed to Green's theory on 'non-representational' art. Stokes observes in a statistical survey of Green's various techniques that in *Loving, Nothing* and *Doting* there is no 'formal character exposition' nor 'informal character revelation'. This means that Green does not interpret or record his characters' thoughts and impressions. In his other novels, by contrast, this method accounts for between 15 and 21 per cent of the text.[1] In *Loving*, then, Green has largely abandoned the 'inner' view and presents his characters through the disengagement of a mere observer. A greater degree of objectivity is sought through the de-emphasizing of description in favour of dialogue. Non-representational dialogue implies, to Green, a kind of communication which provides the oblique and elusive quality he experiences in real life. Rosamond Lehmann captures the essential nature of the dialogue in *Loving*; there is

> on the Servants' Hall's side the class language of circumlocution, ambiguity, rhetorical flourish, of devious sly approach to the end in view; all the verbal taboos and traditional tags and saws; on the drawing-room side the habit of incoherence, tentativeness, over-emphasis, the obsessive modish portmanteau words. Rarely do any of them speak out with certainty and clarity, even to their own.[2]

Characteristic speech patterns intimate the nature of various characters' temperaments, feelings, thoughts and social interaction. The suggestive power of *Loving* also encompasses the more abstract, intangible dimensions of human existence. Imagery and symbolism serve as objectification of the characters' inner worlds.

Green's imagery and symbolism have central thematic significance. Different aspects of reality are consciously arranged according to the subjective evaluations of the author. The reticulation of metaphors is employed to enrich the expressiveness and suggestiveness of the different facets of life. Since Green writes 'from his innermost beliefs', symbolism and imagery will also reflect the author's private visions, needs and longings. In the final analysis, his use of metaphors will indirectly relate to his attitudes towards characters and events within his work. To a greater extent than his other works, *Loving* is a symbolic novel. However, since Green endows his motifs with various shades of meaning, tone may be traced mainly in the structural interaction of metaphors and contexts. This analytical approach is necessitated by previous critics' inability to detect a consistent moral consciousness in *Loving*. A major objective in the analysis of this novel is the attempt to distinguish the meanings of the various elements, to examine their function in relation to one another, and to the novel as a whole. This method is based on the view that, despite the divergent levels of reality contained in *Loving* (objective, subjective, metaphorical, etc.), it is possible to discern an underlying compositional pattern that produces a statement about experience as well as a dominant tone.

The assumption that Green injects an overall moral tone into the composition of *Loving* is strengthened in light of the novel's fully intentioned fairy-tale structure. It begins with, 'Once upon a day an old butler called Eldon lay dying in his room', and ends with the two lovers, Raunce and Edith, having left the old Irish castle, the setting of the novel's plot: 'Over in England they were married and lived happily ever after.' If *Loving* is modelled on the established fairy-tale tradition, its content construes an artistic pattern which suggests Green's interest in moral or ethical edification.

The central plot of *Loving* concerns the love relationship of Charley Raunce and Edith, both servants at Kinalty Castle. This English-staffed castle, situated in neutral Ireland, is unaffected by the war which ravages England. It seems to have some obscure symbolic implication, pervaded, as it is, with a sense of unreality and functionless remoteness. An archaic remnant of the past, the castle is a monument of conformity to customs and fashions that merely mimic natural vitality. It is a museum of false pretensions which, in its attempt to preserve a dead past, has become an empty shell of artful decoration. Its form pretends to be genuine Gothic, but is really composed of several faked details – a façade with a pseudo-Greek temple and a deliberately ruined wall to give the appearance of authenticity. Several rooms are unused, covered with dust and cobweb.

Constant references to this background of obsolete, functionless splendour are obviously of great importance in the total effect of the book. This fact requires an account of the specific ways in which the castle, as a compositional motif, interacts structurally with other motifs, with the novel's network of symbolism, and so with its plot. In terms of plot, *Loving* begins with the death of Eldon, the old, dishonest but reliable butler, and Charley Raunce's succession to his post. The continuance of the old hierarchy and its effete traditions seems to have been secured. However, Raunce and Edith, after falling in love, unexpectedly escape the old order and finally return to England. Despite the novel's sense of resolution, the ending has confused many critics. Immediately prior to Raunce's and Edith's depar- ture, there is a poetic scene in which Edith is feeding the peacocks and the doves. Raunce calls her name, using 'exactly that tone Mr Eldon had employed at the last when calling his Ellen. "Edie", he moaned' (p.204). It may seem that the novel ends where it began, that Raunce throughout the novel has merely completed a circle and has finally been equated, by Green, with the dying, old butler. The implication of such an interpretation would be that Raunce is not escaping to a better life in England, but is instead going to an early death as a result of deteriorating health (his dyspepsia is gradually getting worse) and the possibly insidious effects of 'loving'. The further implication might be that there is a cold, deliberate irony in Green's fairy-tale ending, that Edith, with whom the peacocks and the doves are in complicity, has perhaps ensnared Raunce by a senseless, animal eroticism. The interpretation sketched here is based on the possible existence of a complex and coherent negative symbolism: recurrent images and elements – everything enveloped in the decayed atmosphere of the castle – are aspects of a degenerating force which entangles Raunce's and Edith's integrities.

It is questionable that this structure is indeed a function of Green's actual method and intent. The analysis is interesting, however, for it reveals crucial weaknesses that suggest the relevance and necessity of a montage approach. To ascribe to the different elements of *Loving* an invariable symbolism and to determine meaning on the basis of their recurrence is too

categorical. Such a method fails to account for the visual
dynamism and poetic vividness pervading many of the settings.
Verification of the various elements' different effects can only be
satisfactorily approximated if symbols and images are examined
in relation to their contexts (for example, in terms of montage)
and not as vehicles with predefined meanings that cannot be
altered or modified according to their structural function.

In the vivid montage that terminates the novel, Green includes
the major characters and images.

> She [Edith] began to feed the peacocks. They came forward
> until they had her surrounded. Then a company of doves flew
> down on the seat to be fed. They settled all over her. And
> their fluttering disturbed Raunce who reopened his eyes. What
> he saw then he watched so that it could be guessed that he
> was in pain with his great delight. For what with the peacocks
> bowing at her purple skirts, the white doves nodding on her
> shoulders round her brilliant cheeks and her great eyes that
> blinked tears of happiness, it made a picture.
>
> 'Edie', he appealed soft, probably not daring to move or
> speak too sharp for fear he might disturb it all. Yet he used
> exactly that tone Mr Eldon had employed at the last when
> calling his Ellen. 'Edie', he moaned.   (pp.203–4)

There is no sign that Raunce's moaning is a symbolic symptom
of any malignant affair with Edith. Neither the separate images
nor their coalescence seem to carry any clear message so as to
provide a premonition of the hero's fate. Green indicates that
Raunce's fits of dyspepsia after falling in love with Edith, have
no sinister thematic implications: 'In this particular case, not
unusually, the husband had been made ill – his stomach had
been upset – by being in love.' In fact, Green himself was
unaware of any deliberately ironic ending at the time he wrote
Loving. 'I have often been asked how soon after they got to
England the husband died . . . my answer invariably is "Whenever
you think", although when writing the book I had no idea but
that they were to have anything but a long and happy life
thereafter.'[3] The possibility of a 'happy ending' is strengthened
in view of *Loving*'s design. The beginning, 'Once upon a day',
repeated in Nanny Swift's symbolic story of life in the dovecote –
'Once upon a time' – suggests a parallel with Elizabethan

comedy as well as the fairy-tale tradition. This structural cliché envelops the story in an unreal atmosphere of timeless present which makes past and future irrelevant. Northrop Frye says of *Cymbeline* that 'the only phrase that will date such a play is "once upon a time"'. Comedy is also suggested by Edith's anticipation of *Loving*'s optimistic concluding statement: 'all's well that ends well' (p.187) (this prediction is repeatedly stressed in *Concluding*). Frye claims that ' "all's well that ends well" is a statement about the structure of comedy, and is not intended to apply to actual life'.[4] In the same manner, the structure of *Concluding* does not represent life after the book.

One may argue that, since Green stresses the equivocal nature of his characters' destiny, an attempt to determine a logical outcome is not essential to the comprehension of the novel's central issue. Ambiguity and uncertainty are inherent in various scenes and images. When viewed in juxtaposition with contrary elements, these images contribute to making a statement about present experience. They cannot *symbolize* events or the outcome of events.

The difficulty involved in seeking logical explanations of Green's poetic scenes stems from the fact that they are not primarily intended to function as symbolic mirrors of reality. Images which may, separately, contain certain general symbolic meanings, produce a unity whose visual totality determines the functions of its parts. In a world of disintegration and uncertainty, Green seeks to evoke life rather than describe it. Meaning is a quality which resides not within the linguistic medium itself, but in a region beyond, where language is conceived anew in the poetry of vision. Beauty achieves its impact by the power of words to produce contrary images that converge in a different dimension. The poetry of vision does not explain reality but is embodied with a life of its own. It eludes the systems of cognition, destroys the classification of conventional language, and reassembles the pieces into a dynamic whole.

Still, the final scene depicting Edith with the doves and the peacocks is imbued with important thematic implications. It portrays Raunce, whose mind has formerly been imprisoned by the conventions and systems laid down by the old traditions of the castle, now able to perceive the radiant beauty of the moment. There is good reason to believe that his experience in this scene coincides with a greater sensibility, effected by his love for Edith.

The revitalization of Raunce's mind refers back to his statement
in the middle of the novel: 'Just lately I been wonderin' if my
life weren't just starting' (p.104). Raunce's utterance concerns
his feelings about life; it does not stress the question of a
prolonged life as a crucial factor in *Loving*. Green, in reference
to *Loving*, supports this view:

> It may be that the reader, in a hangover from Elizabethan
> days, expects all his heroes to be killed, but it certainly is
> extremely difficult to leave in his imagination a life continuing
> beyond the book, and the future of novels must surely be to
> leave characters alive enough to go on living the life they have
> led in the book; failing which you cannot have a book which
> has a life of its own. It follows, therefore, that catharsis, the
> purging through pity, sudden death and the rest, is not a
> theme with much future.[5]

Green's themes are committed to the Life of the present moment.
If viewed on this poetic level, his final association of Raunce and
Eldon does not symbolize identical fates; it links their ultimate
humanness. Raunce's soft moaning expresses his love, for which
also Eldon is yearning when moaning Ellen's name on his
deathbed.

A fundamental objective of montage, as defined by Eisenstein,
is 'emotional dynamization' or 'emotional intensification'. The
montage conflict produced by the shift of focus in the last scene
heightens in various ways the intense beauty surrounding Edith.
It is intensified by the audio-visual counterpoint deriving from
Raunce's soft appeal, 'Edie'. Moreover, whatever sombre associations Raunce's position may awaken do not affect the essential
reverential tone of the passage. Rather, one's suspicions about
Raunce's health and the uncertainty as to their future enhance
the preciousness of the present moment. What Green actually
presents is a blissful moment in which various elements mingle
into a beautiful harmony. Green's technique springs from his
realization about life which can best be explained in terms of
Dorothy Van Ghent's characterization of Sterne's vision in
Tristram Shandy:

> It is because of Sterne's acute awareness of time passage and
> of the conundrums of the time sense, that he is also so acutely

aware of the concrete moment; or, conversely, we could say that it is because of his awareness of the preciousness of the concrete moment, that he is so acutely aware of time, which destroys the moment.[6]

Loving is not a tragic novel in which man's incorrigible sensual nature represents a serious threat to his own existence. Nor is it altogether comic, although this impression seems to be the main reason for many critics' puzzlement over Green's work. There is much humour in Loving, but not of the comic-strip type. Green's use of humour places reality within an artistic structure where man's instinctual nature as well as the darker, threatening, imperfect aspects of life appear in a redeeming light. Green is a realistic writer who recognizes the imperfection of both life and man. Life is contradictory, and so is man; the good is interspersed with the bad. Green deals with both the comic and the tragic sides of reality. At times he is critical of characters and events, sometimes accepting, or he may portray them with a combination of humour and cutting irony. His mixture of criticism and approval, grimness and comedy, prose and poetry, shapes the contradictory appearance of Loving. By means of a montage approach, however, these divergent aspects can be weighed in central contexts, and consistent theme and tone deduced. Whichever technique Green chooses, each seems to be utilized in defiance of forces which restrain the development of human qualities and retard an affirmative participation in the living present.

In connection with Green's creation of humour, a comparison of Sterne's and Green's ideas is useful in its elucidation of Green's central themes. Both authors use similar means to undermine life-restraining preoccupations by the invocation of humorous montage. A valuable clue in the understanding of the thematic concerns of the two writers is provided by Coleridge's discussion of 'one humorific point common to all that can be called humorous', a common point he believes to reside in

a certain reference to the general and the universal, by which the finite great is brought into identity with the little, or the little with the finite great, so as to make both nothing in comparison with the infinite. The little is made great, and the great little in order to destroy both; because all is equal in contrast with the infinite.   (p.94)

As Dorothy Van Ghent says with reference to Coleridge's definition, 'our understanding of the "seriousness" of Sterne's humour can prepare us for a larger understanding of those authors nearer our time, who are concerned seriously with the problems of our time, but who are sensitive also to the sources of laughter'. *Tristram Shandy*, like *Loving*, ridicules man's preoccupation with abstract ideas that preclude his participation in the immediate present. Phutatorius, in the course of making a pompous speech, for example, is disconcerted by the presence of a hot chestnut in his breeches. Van Ghent states that 'What we shall look for here is the equating of "great" and trivial, which resonates in humour because of the strange balance contrived between these incommensurables.' Sterne's idea of humour is to let the trivial and whimsical puncture pathos and so ask 'finite judgment to suspend its intoxicated action for a moment in a healthy smile at its own potency for exaggeration, hysteria and error'.[7]

The following passage from *Loving* demonstrates how Green, in a similar manner, greets regression and life-negating, exaggerated scepticism with a 'healthy smile'. It is a passage crucial to the understanding of his vision. The dovecote, where the scene is enacted, represents an encapsulation of the entire novel. Just as Green has framed his story about life in *Loving* within the structure of the fairy tale, so Nanny Swift begins hers about life in the dovecote with 'Once upon a time'. The dovecote is the arena of play, courtship, struggle and murder.

Despite this violence, the structural parallel between the two 'fairy tales' does not necessarily reflect the author's preoccupation with the destructive implications of the characters' inclinations and involvements. Again, one must distinguish between the reality which Green objectively describes and the reality he creates. It is from the latter that the tone of the passage derives. In fact, the way in which Miss Swift's innocent, moralistic story is repeatedly interrupted, through cross-montage, by unexpected, bizarre events, heightens the humour of the entire passage.

'Once upon a time there were six little doves lived in a nest', she began. . . . Miss Evelyn and Miss Moira each put a

finger to their mouths as they went on bowing to each other. . . .
Miss Swift continued;

'Because they were so poor and hungry and cold in their
thin feathers out there in the rain.' She opened her eyes.
'Children', she said, 'stop those silly tricks' and the girls
obeyed. 'But the sun came out to warm them', she intoned.

'Jesus', Albert muttered, 'look at that.' . . . Now that the
birds had settled again they seemed to have taken up their
affairs at the point where they had been interrupted. So that
all these balconies were crowded with doves and a heavy
murmur of cooing throbbed the air though at one spot there
seemed to be trouble.

'You're very, very wicked boy', said Evelyn to Albert looking
where she thought he looked. What she saw was one dove
driving another along a ledge backwards. Each time it reached
the end the driven one took flight and fluttered then settled
back on that same ledge once more only to be driven back the
other way to clatter into air again. This was being repeated
tirelessly when from another balcony something fell.

'That's ripe that is', Albert said.

'I didn't see', Evelyn cried. 'I didn't really. What came
about?'

'And then there was a time', the nanny said from behind
closed eyes and the wall of deafness, 'oh my dears your old
nanny hardly knows how to tell you but the naughty unloyal
dove I told of.'

'It was a baby one', Albert said.

'A baby dove. Oh do let me see'. . . .

'It was a baby one', Albert said, 'and nude. That big bastard
pushed it.'

'The big what?' Evelyn asked. 'Oh but I mean oughtn't we
to rescue the poor?'

. . . a rustle made them turn about on either side of Miss
Swift who sat facing that dovecote shuteyed and deaf. They
saw Kate and Edith in long purple uniforms bow swaying
towards them in soft sunlight through the white budding
branches, fingers over lips. Even little Albert copied the gesture
back this time. All five began soundlessly giggling in the face
of beauty.

'Did you see Mr Raunce?' Kate asked at last.

''E went that way'. . . .

'And then they were in great peril every mortal one', Miss Swift continued.   (pp.58–9)

What constitutes the 'finite great' is the solemnity with which Miss Swift narrates her story in face of matters concerning life and death, before doves 'quarrelling, murdering and making love again'. Miss Swift's confusion at the many interruptions caused by the fascinated cries of the children while she is sitting 'shuteyed and deaf' constitutes that part of the equation which is termed the 'finite little' (the diction also heightens the humour: when one of the doves pushes a baby dove, a 'nude' one, Albert calls the aggressor a 'bastard', which surprises Miss Evelyn, because she has never heard that word; ''e fell down right on 'is nut', Albert exclaims).

'And now where was I?'
'You were at that bit where the kind old father says he can marry her 'cause he's getting too old to know better.'
'Well now that's right', Miss Swift began once more.... Then one more small mass fell without a thud, pink.
'There y'are', said Albert.
'Where? I didn't see. Oh I've missed again', Evelyn said. 'Did you?' to Moira.
'You're none of you listening you naughty children', the nanny said. 'Here's poor nanny wasting her breath and you don't pay attention.'   (p.59)

Since the dovecote must be seen as the major 'symbol' in *Loving*, the structural irony of the preceding scene has thematic implications important to the interpretation of the entire novel. Raunce's and Edith's intrusion gives the nanny's moralistic story a precise reference; for, as soon as Raunce's whereabouts are mentioned, Miss Swift concludes that the white doves were 'in great peril every mortal one'. The symbolic connection between the doves of Miss Swift's fairy story and the characters is also suggested by the equal number of doves ('six little doves') and characters. That is, Raunce is the sixth 'dove', a connection which is intimated through direct association: 'All five began soundlessly giggling in the face of beauty. "Did you see Mr Raunce?"'
Significantly, the humour and compositional irony marking

the actual events in the dovecote suggest that the perils are exaggerated. Whatever grimness is inherent in the image of fighting doves is alleviated by other images reverently celebrating the instinctual responses of both birds and humans. Ironically, Miss Swift's tale is abstracted and oversimplified; like its narrator, it is 'shuteyed and deaf' to the very essence of reality. The girls are not as innocent as the Nanny's 'white' doves, and the world not as bad as she seems to believe. The essence of life cannot be perceived by a closed, concept-ridden mind. It can only be intuited in a childlike, natural response to 'living', as demonstrated by Moira and Evelyn, who, copying the doves bowing beak to beak, nod deeply to one another past Miss Swift. Watching Edith and Kate, who, imitating the doves' dance, 'bow swaying towards them in soft sunlight through the white budding branches, fingers over lips . . . all five began soundlessly giggling in the face of beauty'. The final image of doves and peacocks bowing and nodding around Edith confirms Green's reverence for natural beauty.

Reality, if approached with an affirmative, childlike curiosity, is not as frightening and bizarre as it may appear if interpreted through a conceptual bias. Green emphasizes this comic conflict between healthy sensuality and Nanny Swift's stagnancy in his portrayal of Edith's and Kate's rapturous enjoyment of the doves' 'kissing'. Edith and Kate warn Miss Evelyn not to pay attention to the doves,

> 'Because they're very rum them birds', Kate said also *whispering*. . . .
> 'Sssh', said Edith watching *rapt*. . . .
> 'And then there came a time when this wicked tempting bird came to her father to ask her hand', Miss Swift said, passing a *dry* tongue over *dry* lips, *shuteyed*. . . .
> 'Oh what are they doing then?' Miss Moira cried.
> 'They're kissing love', Kate answered *low*.
> '*Hush* dear', said Edith.   (pp.59–60, emphasis added)

The humour, as well as the irony, is accentuated by the fact that the doves are just as rapturously enjoying their game which they have been 'tirelessly' pursuing. In fact, when the doves are suddenly disturbed by the children, they flee, 'apart', 'filling the air with sighing' (p.60). As in Sterne's *Tristram Shandy*, Green's healthy attitude towards the bizarre in *Loving* must be taken as 'one term of a structural irony, and a provision for keeping the sentimental and the emotional and the pathetic in the same human world with the obscene and the trivial and the absurd'.[8]

From an ideological point of view, then, the centrality of the dovecote scene suggests Green's world as a 'human' world in which the vital aspect of natural human impulses is recognized. Destructive effects of free, instinctual response are certainly also implied, but, again, montage alters tone by emotionally emphasizing specific aspects. Thus, the sensual vitality and fulfilment contained in the dovecote scene are enhanced despite contradictory forces. It is important to note that, in this scene, the humour produced by the incongruity of Nanny's moralistic fairy story and the children's excitement at the doves' behaviour does not really result from Green's juxtaposition of the real against the unreal. That is, Nanny Swift's innocent story is not meant to accentuate, through a sense of disparity, the horror of the real world, portrayed with grotesque realism. The most important effect of Green's ironic montage of the 'finite great' and the 'finite little' is that the humorous incongruity transforms 'grotesque realism' into a positive statement about a world which is essentially comic as long as what is 'living' is approached through a healthy, instinctual perceptiveness.

One crucial theme in Green's work is his desire to encourage man's full response to vital human needs and impulses. Failure to perceive or respect the nature of man's essential humanness induces the complex combinations of farce and grim irony. Humour may draw attention to the joyful or merely amusing aspects of life. At other times, Green utilizes humour for the purpose of ridiculing unresponsiveness to human values. In the latter cases, Sterne's practice of equating the 'finite great' and the 'finite little' in order to produce a tone of merry absurdity is not as easily applicable. Green's merging of humour and tragic irony in the following scene may appear paradoxical. A closer examination, however, reveals that both tonal qualities serve the articulation of an overriding theme.

Once upon a day an old butler called Eldon lay dying in his room attended by the head housemaid, Miss Agatha Burch. From time to time the other servants separately or in chorus gave expression to proper sentiments and then went on with what they had been doing.

One name he uttered over and over, 'Ellen.'

The pointed windows of Mr Eldon's room were naked glass with no blinds or curtains. . . .

Came a man's laugh. Miss Burch jerked, then the voice broke out again. Charley Raunce, head footman, was talking outside to Bert his yellow pantry boy. . . .

'. . . on with what I was on with', he spoke, 'you should clean your teeth before ever you have anything to do with a woman. That's a matter of personal hygiene. Because I take an interest in you for which you should be thankful. I'm sayin' you want to take it easy my lad, or you'll be the *death* of yourself.'

The lad looked sick. (p.18, emphasis added)

The 'finite little' is represented by Raunce's obsession with the necessity of cleaning one's teeth before having anything to do with a woman, and his ridiculously inappropriate assertion that, if Bert does not observe this elementary rule, he may prepare his own death. Raunce's advice is decidedly funny, and the humour clearly an echo of Green's attempt to create ambiguity, since occurring in such a grave context. Nevertheless, Raunce's trivial concerns do not relieve or ridicule the solemnity or 'pathos' of death. Eldon's demise cannot be labelled under the denominations of the 'sentimental and the emotional and the pathetic', which lose their seriousness by being matched 'in the same human world with the obscene and the trivial and the absurd'. The tragic image of Eldon, utterly lonely and dying, is emphasized by Green's attention to the 'pointed windows' of 'naked glass with no blinds or curtains'. Hence, Green's image of Eldon connotes not the 'finite great', but the 'infinite', in relation to which Raunce's idea of what is vitally important becomes 'nothing'; because, says Coleridge, 'all is equal in contrast with the infinite'. Because of Green's acute awareness of the close competition between life and death, Coleridge's idea concerning the interrelation of the 'finite great', the 'finite little' and the infinite provides a useful frame of reference for determining whether Green stresses the comic aspects of a concret context (that is, whether he accentuates the positive qualities of life) or whether he asserts the dominance of tragic irony. These differences are subtly pronounced in the dovecote scene and in the impressions from Eldon's sick-room.

In the latter scene, then, Green focuses the routine indifference towards the dying displayed by Raunce and the other servants. Raunce rides his 'hobby-horse', his obsession with dental hygiene, which he has magnified to become a matter indeed more considerable than life or death. Such 'hobby-horses' may provide temporary escape from pain and death, but no viable solution when they lead to withdrawal from sympathetic involvements. True enough, Green wants his characters to oppose detrimental preoccupation with loss and sorrow, but those people leading the most meaningful lives are generally those who are acutely aware of the surrounding forces of darkness and who, with that knowledge, therefore consciously commit themselves to a life of love and growth. Green's best example is probably Mr and Mrs Eames in *Living*. The major point to make is that Green is not predominantly concerned with mere survival, with a regressive protection from death, but with 'living' and fulfilment.

In conclusion, one may argue that only such hobby-horses as can be transcribed 'loving' or 'living' are acclaimed by Green. Raunce's hobby-horse, to climb in the hierarchy of the castle, is associated with stasis and death. It is typical that the servants are more interested in getting on with their routine chores than giving expression to 'proper sentiments' with concern to the dying Eldon. Raunce's and most of the servants' hobby-horses serve the prolonging of an outmoded, artificial order which, a hobby-horse in itself, restricts the free expansion of vital human sympathies. The fact that Raunce finally abandons his hobby-horse, therefore, supports the assumption that his love for Edith has stimulated a greater human sensitivity. Correspondingly, the epiphanic last scene incorporates sentiments that, in their affirmation of life at that moment, would embrace Eldon as a fellow human being. In fact, Green does stress the importance of human sympathy as a central theme in *Loving*'s plot. Miss Burch touches the truth subtly implied by Green: 'Mr Eldon he died of a broken heart Miss Swift. There was a lot he told nobody' (p.112). Green has Miss Swift predict that the characters may sooner or later disclaim routines and traditions and perhaps follow their private intuitions:

there's big changes under way. I shouldn't wonder if things

were never the same say what you will. But don't mistake me.
I wouldn't put myself above a doctor. Though we can all bear
witness about Mr Eldon how that poor man lay calling on a
name and Doctor Connolly no more than paid him a call
every so often, when we all know what we had under our very
eyes with him growing weaker each day that passed, I don't
say but someone might have taken matters into their own
hands.   (p.113)

The 'big changes' predicted by Miss Swift – which she, in reality,
fears – are, in accordance with Green's values, changes for the
better. What she fears most is vigorous human instincts which,
because natural, counteract the false security of artificially
imposed patterns. It is to the pattern of ancient traditions that
Raunce has become heir. He has remained indoors for so many
years that he nearly faints when persuaded to go for a walk so
as to breathe some fresh air. Like a spectre, his appearance
merges with the decayed atmosphere of the old castle. In the
post of butler, Raunce embodies the stagnant effeteness of the
castle which restrains new life. One day he is seen to move
through 'sombre' doors in the 'white-wrapped dimness' of unused
'dust-sheeted rooms'. 'High windows muted by white blinds'
witness relics of past life 'sheeted in white and to which he had
never raised the cloths'. Raunce is part of this ghostly, 'shadowless
castle of treasures', shrouded in lifeless white. He dips his fingers
into a bowl and then sniffs at 'the dry bones of roses', an act,
Green points out, which Raunce has made a ritual. A loud sound
disturbs this context of deathlike silence. 'The music came louder
and louder as he progressed until at the white and gold ballroom
doors it fairly thundered.' Raunce poses himself defiantly 'against
the thrust of music'. Inside the room, he sees Edith and Kate

wheeling wheeling in each other's arms heedless at the far end
where they had drawn up one of the white blinds. Above from
a rather low ceiling five great chandeliers swept one after the
other almost to the waxed parquet floor reflecting in their
hundred thousand drops the single sparkle of distant day,
again and again red velvet panelled walls, and two girls,
minute in purple, dancing multiplied to eternity in these
trembling pears of glass.   (pp.64–5)

The gyrating spell is abruptly terminated. Raunce switches off

the music, making the needle grate. Edith sighs, 'It's over now.'
Like the actions of doves in the dovecote scene at being disturbed,
the two girls disappointedly disengage. Green introduces the
audio-visual counterpoint in order to produce a sense of collision
between the dead silence of the old castle and the thunderous
music. As in *Concluding*, in which the significance of the dancing-
scenes is far more elaborated, Green employs audio-visual
counterpoint to intensify the dancing girls' animation. The
trembling music and the centrifugal dynamism of the dancing
echo a 'hundred thousand drops' of sparkling daylight to create
an instant impression of 'eternity', a momentary bliss which
surmounts time and decay, and shatters the stagnant tranquillity
of history.

This and similar passages in *Loving* are dreamlike scenes that
suffuse symbols and action in a complex, involved manner, a
curious commingling of fantasy and realism, resulting from a
Modernist interweaving of an inner world and the everyday
factual world. Its function is not a mere presentation of disparate
facets of experience in an abstract artistic form, a mental or
artistic process by which bits of reality are reordered into a new
combination which becomes the sum of its parts, resembling the
qualities Coleridge attributes to 'Fancy'. The qualities of the
dancing-scene resemble qualities which Coleridge attributes to
'Imagination'. Both Green and Coleridge display a strong urge
to capture the instant luminosity of love and beauty. The
dancing-scene represents an attempt to create a poetic moment
of Truth. Essentially romantic, it 'struggles to idealize and to
unify. It is essentially *vital*, even as all objects (*as* objects) are
essentially fixed and dead.' The animation of all the antique
treasures in the whirling dancing-scene is intensified by its
juxtaposition with the lifeless, dust-sheeted silence through which
Raunce has just passed. These two incongruent worlds collide
in a montage fashion to produce poetry of 'a higher order'.
Coleridge's idea of the 'Imagination' possesses precisely this
'synthetic' power which is revealed 'in the balance or reconciliation of opposite or discordant qualities'. In this manner, Green's
Modernist projection of a fantasy world into the everyday world
not only objectifies mental pictures produced in a symbol-making
mind. Death collides spatially with life to create a transcendent
unity, a synthesis which is glimpsed as the momentary experience
of 'eternity'.[9]

Similar scenes in *Loving* support the view that Green's unreal
or fantastic images do not only form integral parts of an abstract
whole. Rather, the tension produced by the mingling of real and
unreal may create the kind of dynamic unity which Coleridge
would label 'vital'. One day Edith, Albert and the children enter
the castle's sham Greek temple, into 'another darker daylight,
into a vast hall lit by rain and dark skylights and which was
filled with marble bronze and plaster statuary in rows'. In this
strange, time-worn sepulchre, past life has petrified. As they play
blind man's buff, they are surrounded by 'witnesses in bronze in
marble and plaster' which echo their excited shrieks 'from stone
cold bosoms to damp streaming marble bellies, to and from huge
oyster niches in the walls in which boys fought giant boas or
idled with a flute, and which volleyed under green skylights
empty in the ceiling' (pp.107–11). This imagery, together with
Green's choice of words for sounds, Davidson suggests, is 'that
of war and of love repelled'. Albert seeks Edith, but 'for answer
he had a *storm* of giggles ... which went *ricochetting* ... and *volleyed*
... he could hear *feet slither* ... they *shrieked* ... in a *tumult* of
these words'.[10] The imagery and sounds may suggest parallels
between the lives and experiences of the youngsters playing blind
man's buff and those mimed by the ancient statues – some
fighting, one indulging in beautiful music, or others 'kneeling
with heads and arms raised to heaven', or worshipping the 'half-
dressed lady that held a wreath at the end of her two long arms'.
The statues display the multiplicity of life, of man's conflicts,
longings and struggles. There is a parallel between the lives of
the youngsters and the former lives depicted in the ancient
statues, but also between the participants in the blind man's
buff and the doves' mating and fighting. This game of blind
man's buff is a love game. Edith has brought, as the most
conspicuous symbol, her red I-love-you scarf which is used for
blindfolding. Bert is the rejected beseecher whose courtship is
countered by Edith's complete indifference, and the tumult of
their contest is echoed in Green's use of war imagery. However,
as particularly revealed by the parallel with the doves' quarrelling
and love-making, conflicts are an integral part of life, and do
not prevent the participants from deriving a rapturous moment
from their game. This is the reason for the primarily humorous
portrayal of the dovecote scene. Magical moments may be
captured among the turbulence of life; their intensity is in fact

enhanced by life's contradictory impulses. It is precisely this aspect that links Green's technique with Coleridge's idea of a 'vital', 'synthetic' combination of life's discordant qualities. From this point of view, Green's images are not just integral, symbolic components enriching the expressiveness and suggestiveness of the passage. The statues, as inhabitants of the castle, represent past life now dead and cold as stone. The transfixed mimic real life. In contrast, Edith 'was brilliant, she glowed as she rang her curls like bells without a note'. And, when Albert kisses Miss Moira, 'Her child's skin was electric hot under a film of water.' This mausoleum reverberates with new life at the excited shrieks of the children, and as they urge Albert to kiss Edith, 'Kiss her then ... kiss her.' He does, for a second, 'and in spite of being so short more brilliant more soft and warm perhaps than his thousand dreams'. Although darkness is surrounding them – 'it had become almost too dark to see his face' – Albert, in a conflict of masses, 'seemed absolutely dazzled' in a state of supreme bliss. The sense of a 'vital', unifying liveliness is strengthened, through an audio-visual counterpoint, by the interruption of a discordant rusty hinge; then 'Raunce entered upon a scene which this noise and perhaps also his presence had instantly turned to more stone.' Edith is left 'blind as any statue', before Raunce walks back 'into grey dust-sheeted twilight'.

Green's reason for depicting Raunce as a stone-cold intruder into the vividness of the game is immediately intimated by a conflict of planes. 'Back in his room Raunce unlocked the drawer in which he kept the red and black notebooks. He verified that they were there' (p.111). These books, in which Eldon used to keep meticulous account of debits and credits in the household, promise the perpetuation of the old order. As if in reaction to the 'frivolity' of the playing youngsters, Raunce wants to reassure himself that he is still in possession of the books upon which the security of his future relies. The value conflicts implied here are more conspicuously enacted in Dickens's *Hard Times*. The natural spontaneity and fulfilment of the circus people clash with Bounderby's calculating, materialistic ambition, and the lack of a vital imagination demonstrated by the square-minded Gradgrind, whose utilitarian abode is appropriately named Stone Lodge. Raunce's utilitarian bent, augmented by the butler's role as custodian of the old order, is revealed when he refuses to join in the blind man's buff on the grounds that 'I chucked this blind man's buff before I'd lived as many years as my lad here. In my time if we had nothing better to do than lark about on a half day we got on with our work' (*Loving*, p.110). Raunce discloses the same utilitarian attitude in the previously discussed dancing-scene, when opposing the girls' rapturous enjoyment for fear they may damage the old treasures that are not to be used.

'They'll break it', he said aloud as though in explanation, presumably referring to the gramophone which was one of the first luxury clockwork models. 'And in a war', he added as he turned back to these portals, 'it would still fetch good money', talking to himself against the thrust of music.   (p.65)

The following intricate combination of various images illuminates more specifically the nature of the conflicts which initially segregate Raunce from Green's main values. Eldon's fastidiously kept notebooks, ordered into two categories with starkly contrasting colours, seem to express the same life-restricting qualities as the rigorous black and white squares of the carpet across which Raunce walks on his way to steal Eldon's notebooks, the same exact black and white pattern of Miss Edge's tiled floor in *Concluding*, of the black and white farm where Miss Baker was brought up, and even Edge's regimentation of flowers into categories of red and white. Otherwise, flowers are invariably associated with growth and fruition in Green's fiction. Still on his way to Eldon's sick-room, Raunce stops abruptly. 'In one of the malachite vases, filled with daffodils, which stood on tall pedestals of gold naked male children without wings, he had seen a withered trumpet. He cut off the head with a pair of nail clippers' (*Loving*, p.23). As indicated by the context, Raunce's beheading of this single flower symbolizes his denial of the withering Eldon. Birds, in Green's fiction, also suggest freedom and vivacity. The lack of understanding for such qualities by the proprietors of the castle is indicated by the fact that the children's wings are broken.

In his role as butler, Raunce's violation of values of growth is suggested by the way in which 'he punted the daffodil ahead like a rugger ball.... He was kicking this flower into his pantry not more than thirty inches at a time when Miss Burch with no warning opened and came out of Mr Eldon's death chamber. She was snuffling. He picked it up off the floor quick' (pp.23–

4). The conflict of graphic directions between Raunce and Miss
Burch, who is trying to attend to Eldon's needs, defines one
aspect of Raunce's estrangement from vital values: his lack of
sympathy. His cynicism is evident when he asks, 'When's the
interment?' and in the next moment wonders what time is dinner.
By a significant symbolic gesture, he dumps the daffodil in a
bucket, then sneaks into Eldon's sick-room to annex those red
and black notebooks, with his face averted from the mass of
daffodils beside Eldon's bed.

Another central symbolic scene requires explication in order
to elucidate Raunce's function in the dynamic world of *Loving*.
One day Edith and Kate muster enough courage to enter Paddy
O'Conor's lamp room.

> It was a place from which light was almost excluded now by
> cobwebs across its two windows and into which, with the door
> ajar, the shafted sun lay in a lengthened arch of blazing
> sovereigns. Over a corn bin on which he had packed last
> autumn's ferns lay Paddy snoring between these windows, a
> web strung from one lock of hair back onto the sill above and,
> which rose and fell as he breathed. Caught in the reflection of
> spring sunlight this cobweb looked to be made of gold as did
> those others which by working long minutes spiders had drawn
> from spar to spar of the fern bedding on which his head rested.
> It might have been almost that O'Conor's dreams were held
> by hairs of gold binding his head beneath a vaulted roof on
> which the floor of cobbles reflected an old king's molten
> treasure from the bog. . . .
> Now, through a veil of light . . . Edith could dimly see,
> not hear, a number of peacocks driven into view by some
> disturbance on their side and hardly to be recognized in this
> sovereign light. For their eyes had changed to rubies, their
> plumage to orange as they bowed and scraped at each other
> against the equal danger.　(pp.56–7)

For all the old dust, cobwebs, withered ferns, antique treasures,
and the prostrate Paddy beneath a vaulted roof, the total visual
impact of the scene is not of stasis. True, the peacocks are
imprisoned by Paddy in this 'dusty case', where they 'sheltered
in winter, nested in spring, and where they died of natural causes
at the end'. Their uneventful lives seem to mirror the routine

existences of the castle's inhabitants. However, in the immediate
present moment evoked by Green, these dust-covered, 'heavy
days' form the visual background from which the birds emerge,
in a conflict of masses, with blazing ruby eyes and orange
plumage. 'Now'! Green emphasizes, they catch the reflected
'sovereign' light. Similarly, the image of Paddy snoring, like an
old Irish king, on 'last autumn's ferns' in the dim dark, shrouded
by cobwebs, creates the inertia of a dead past. But Green points
out how 'O'Conor's life was opened, as Kate let the sun in and
Edith bent to look'. Before the girls enter Paddy's room, they
are depicted in 'the great shaft of golden sun which lighted these
girls through parted cloud'. The blazing shaft of sun affirms the
girls' natural, vigorous sensuality. 'You aim to make him a
bishop?', Kate says to Edith, 'Well if I 'ad my way I'd strip
those rags off to give that pelt of his a good rub over.' 'Don't
talk so. You couldn't.' Then they burst into excited giggles. The
half-dark room is filled with a revitalizing 'spring sunlight' from
the 'shafted sun', which 'lay in a lengthened arch of blazing
sovereigns', and by 'movement in the sunset of that sidewall
which reflected glare from the floor in its glass'.
    Suddenly the peacocks, again,

> were gone with a beat of wings and in their room stood Charley
> Raunce, the skin of his pale face altered by refraction to red
> morocco leather.
>   The girls stood transfixed as if by arrows between the
> Irishman dead motionless asleep and the other intent and
> quiet behind a division. Then dropping everything they turned,
> they also fled.   (pp.55–7)

The meaning of Raunce's intrusion is ambiguous. Again, Green
juxtaposes dynamic and static qualities by the contrast between
Paddy's lethargic figure and Raunce's intent appearance. Like
the peacocks' ruby eyes, Raunce's always gaunt face has now
taken on a luminous 'red morocco leather' glow from the
refraction of the blazing sunlight. Green's combination of discordant qualities, of masses and of stasis and dynamism, synthesizes
the whole into a 'vital', poetic unity in the sense defined by
Coleridge. Raunce's intent appearance may suggest the intrusion
of his silent, repressed sexuality upon the enthralled girls, or his
repressed need to participate in the displayed beauty. His

entrance adds dramatic intensity to the magic scene, but there
are also strong intimations that Raunce interrupts with the kind
of purposefulness that makes him insensitive to the moment of joy
and beauty, and which thereby dissipates it. This interpretation is
potentially accurate, because, with his heightened sensibility at
the novel's end, he watches Edith among the bowing peacocks,
'not daring to move or speak too sharp for fear he might disturb
it all'.

What the scene in Paddy's lamp room really emphasizes is
the values of an instinctual, intuitive responsiveness to the
dynamic quality of life. Other scenes, similar in their composition,
reveal how Green repeatedly juxtaposes masses as well as
vividness and stasis, not to accentuate disparity between decep-
tive dream and reality, but to give 'verisimilitude' to a poetic,
synthetic moment. Raunce and Edith, now in love, have found
their way to the seat by the dovecote where Edith 'that first
afternoon of spring' had watched 'the birds love-making'. The
doves are now playing high in the air in 'declining light',
'wheeling' like the ecstatic girls in the dancing-scene.

> Edith laid her lovely head on Raunce's nearest shoulder
> and above them, above the *great shadows* laid by trees those
> *white* birds *wheeled* in a sky of *eggshell blue and pink* with a remote
> sound of *applause* as, circling, they clapped their stretched,
> starched wings in flight.
>   That side of Edith's face open to the reflection of the sky
> was a *deep red*.
>   'She passed my books all right this mornin'', he murmured.
>   'What books?' she asked low and sleepy.
>   'Me monthly accounts', he replied.
>   'Did she?' Edith sighed content. They fell silent. At some
> distance peacocks called to one another, shriek upon far
> shriek.   (p.170, emphasis added)

Edith's resting figure is animated by her 'deep red' face, which,
like the peacocks' ruby eyes and Raunce's 'red morocco leather'
face, reflects the poetic dynamism of the context. The meaning
of the peacocks' shrieks is not precise. On one level, their calls
to one another may be interpreted as an analogue of Edith's and
Raunce's unspoken communication, accentuating the poetic and
the erotic in the scene. Thus, the intrusion of the distant shrieks

into the idyll heightens the fragile preciousness of the moment, which is 'applauded' by the wheeling doves. However, the shrill shrieks may also seem to carry a note of warning, suggesting the presence of a world not quite as poetic. They occur just as Raunce mentions his red and black notebooks, his accounts and monthly savings, on which depend his plans of buying the old butler's house within the grounds of the castle. It is possible that the peacocks are warning against repressive forces which for so long have conditioned Raunce's life. At the end of the book, after the lovers' decision to escape the castle, both peacocks and doves 'applaud' the poetic moment.

The peacocks have a central although obscure symbolic function in the structure of *Loving*. Although their symbolism evades precise definition, the examination of their possible meanings as facets of concrete montage contexts is worthwhile. Determination of the peacocks' general symbolic functions is particularly important in order to refute suspicions that their constant intrusions into the novel's poetic scenes may emphasize Edith's and Raunce's eroticism as an insidious mechanism. Their natural impulses are healthy. In an interview with Alan Ross, Green is asked: 'Could you define the compulsion behind your writing?' His reply is, 'Sex.' Green remarks that

> I got the idea for *Loving* from a man I served with in the Fire Service during the war. He'd been a man-servant and he told me he'd once asked the elderly butler who ruled below stairs what he liked most in the world. The reply was: 'Lying in bed with a woman on a summer morning, with the window open, eating buttered toast'.[11]

In light of Green's statements, the peacocks may in fact be seen to urge a deeper commitment to 'loving' and, therefore, escape from the stagnant castle. It is necessary to examine the peacocks' function in relation to different levels of meaning.

The cries of the peacocks seem to reverberate the erotic in the book, and peacocks and doves surround Edith in some arcane, poetic pact with nature. In various contexts, however, the birds accentuate a more complex meaning, as in the scene in which Kate and Edith tease one another about what they would do if they found Raunce or 'Raunce's Albert' in their room, and the peacocks outside begin to parade.

Though they could not see them the peacocks below were beginning to parade.

'And if it had've been Charley Edie?'

Edie gave a screech then slapped a hand over her mouth. A peacock screamed beneath *but they were so used to this they paid no notice.*   (pp.45–6, emphasis added)

Like the cackling geese in *Caught* and *Concluding*, the peacocks seem to serve as warning heralds. Their shrieks seek to draw the girls' attention to some ambiguous threat which they, at this stage, disregard. Green may juxtapose images and scenes, not necessarily to pass ironic comment or value judgement on the attitudes or activities of the characters involved, but more as a catalytic device for warning them, or the reader, of the actual precariousness of reality. In other words, it is a warning to Edith and Kate that they should mobilize their resources to challenge a more threatening reality than their own little bedroom world. Mrs Tennant and Mrs Jack are addressed by the peacocks in the same manner. This time, however, the montage carries a strongly ironic note.

'Why, listen to those birds', Kate said.

Edith looked out. A great distance beneath she saw Mrs Tennant and her daughter-in-law starting for a walk. The dogs raced about on the terrace yapping which made the six peacocks present scream. The two women set off *negligent* and well dressed behind their bounding pets to get an appetite for tea.   (*Loving*, p.34, emphasis added)

Since the peacocks' warning signals are being ignored, they are insistently repeated. Green even stresses the peacock motif in a grotesque, violent manner. Mrs Welch's grandson, Albert, an invader from the outside world, arrives and before long strangles a peacock. Yet Green's characters attempt to ignore the symbolic significance of the incident. 'Mrs Welch buried it away where none should see' (p.105). The greyhound, Badger, retrieves it and presents to Edith and Raunce 'a plucked carcass that stank'. Edith orders Badger away. 'On which the dog deposited this carcass at Raunce's feet.' Raunce hangs it in Mrs Welch's larder – Miss Burch tells Miss Swift – 'swarming with maggots' and 'infecting all our food'. Again the carcass disappears; Raunce's Albert reports that it has been incinerated by Mrs Welch in the boiler. The peacocks' message and the nature of their complicity with Edith may be deduced in terms of the traditional concepts of conflicts and dénouement. At the story's end, as peacocks and doves cluster around Edith in a moment of perfect bliss, there is no longer any opposition between values embodied by the peacocks and Edith's position. The resolution of conflict is obviously related to Edith's and Raunce's decision to leave the castle and to face the threat of war in England. Despite the insecurity of Edith's and Raunce's position, the novel ends on a happy note. In the interview with Alan Ross, Green answers a central question: 'Yet, all your books have, I think, happy endings. Would you agree that this is in essence because they are love stories, inspired by the belief that love is the most absorbing human experience of all, and therefore the most hopeful?' Green: 'Yes, indeed yes.'[12] Edith's and Raunce's escape implies freedom to meet a 'living' reality, freedom to confront the challenge of death, but also of 'loving'. In this outcome, the peacocks not only show their complicity with Edith; they function as a symbolic counterpart. Edith's and Raunce's release coincides with the peacocks', to some degree, new-won freedom: ' "Come on out and feed the peacockth", she [Edith] proposed, for Paddy had at last consented to free these birds again' (p.192). The peacocks, now free, rally to partake in Raunce's celebration to Edith's fecund beauty.

> 'Why', he said, 'I love you more than I thought I was capable. I'm surprised at myself, honest I am. If my old mother could see her Charley now she'd never recognize 'im, he murmured. . . . He leant forward, gazed awkward into her face. 'I never seen anything like your eyes they're so 'uge not in all my experience', he announced soft. 'Yet for eighteen months I didn't so much as notice them. Can you explain that?' Then, perhaps to distract her attention, he invited her to witness what he saw, the peacocks that had been attracted. (p.198)

The peacocks' imprisonment by Paddy in his room ('As though stuffed in a dusty case they showed themselves from time to time as one after another across the heavy days they came up to look

at him') mirrors all the characters' captivity in the castle. What
is more, there are suggestions that Paddy's motives for restricting
the peacocks' freedom may correspond to Mrs Tennant's reasons
for maintaining the stagnant, superficial order. Mrs Tennant
would rather the peacocks be let out of their cages – not for their
own sake, but because 'They're a part of the decoration of the
place.' Paddy is reluctant, for, as Raunce suggests, 'O'Conor
was afraid of something or other' that is never explained (p.185).
In the passage describing Paddy asleep in his room, he is depicted
as a decayed, ancient Irish king shrouded in cobwebs. His
attachment to the peacocks is motivated by his fear of such forces
as may disturb the stasis effected by legend's rituals. 'It's priest-
ridden love', Charley concludes before his escape (p.202). It is
fear of human forces which may cause turmoil of the kind into
which the castle is thrown at the loss of the ring, another key
motif in *Loving*. The artificiality of life in the castle is suggested
by the way in which the peacocks are reduced, in Mrs Tennant's
mind, to mere museum pieces. 'Having established there was no
dust she rearranged the peacocks' feathers that for years had
stood in a famille rose vase' (p.30). The peacocks' feathers are
carefully *arranged*, surrounded by various animals that have been
turned into what they are not. Mrs Tennant possesses an
'imitation pint measure also in gilded wood and in which
peacocks' feathers were arranged. She lifted this off the white
marble mantelpiece that was a triumph of sculptured reliefs
depicting on small plaques various unlikely animals' (p.184).
Mrs Tennant's formalism suggests her estrangement from natural
human impulses, and also a lack of interest in human beings.
'My dear what do we know about the servants', she sighs, 'it's
quite bad enough having them die on one' (p.36). The traditions
on which the castle depends represent something inhuman and
cold, like the marble statues. In Mrs Tennant's eyes 'there was
something hard and glittering beyond the stone of age' (p.184).

If the peacocks' shrieks are viewed as warnings against forces
that threaten natural, instinctual 'living', they constitute a
clarifying leitmotiv. The nature of the contexts in which the
peacocks are heard strengthens the possibility of such a meaning.
The montage conflicts deepen the incompatibility between 'loving' and the life-style of the aristocracy in Ireland. In addition
to the examples previously discussed, there is one scene in which
Edith and Kate are lying on their bed in their room. The girls

giggle about men. Edith is lying almost naked while Kate is stroking her till she begins to drowse. Suddenly there is a 'real outcry' from the peacocks, and in the drive below they discover Mrs Jack and Captain Davenport, with whom Mrs Tennant's daughter-in-law is having an adulterous affair. 'I do wish I could get you out of my system', she is heard to say (pp.47–8). The audio-visual counterpoint fashioned by the peacocks' 'real outcry' is decidedly a warning against some threat which is not immediately defined. Mrs Jack, however, is not in a state of 'loving', which, to Green, implies an affirmative communion with 'living', and with what is alive. Her fears and guilt are overpowering. When Mrs Tennant recounts to her daughter-in-law Raunce's suspicion that O'Conor has locked up the peacocks because he is afraid of something, Mrs Jack's face 'appeared stiff with apprehension' (p.185). Her feelings are not warm, but impersonal passion – she wishes she could get the Captain out of her 'system'. Her preoccupations also cause her to neglect her children. Edith's first reaction at seeing the adulterous couple outside her window is: 'But won't the children be disappointed. I know they was counting on their mother taking them out the little loves' (p.47). Mrs Jack's attempts to conceal her illicit desires behind a façade of decorum bring her no peace of mind. She is 'caught' in the 'system'. Her unfulfilled needs, her guilt-ridden conscience and her compulsive defensiveness make her a victim of the castle's regressive atmosphere which the peacocks warn Edith and Kate to escape.

In a similar way, the peacock motif may also be read, in the following passage, as a warning against dehumanizing conditions. Raunce and Edith are talking about marriage.

'I mean after we're married', she whispered, her voice gone husky.... 'I'll make everything you want of me now so much more than you ever dreamed that you'll be quit imaginin' for the rest of your life.'

'Oh honey', he said in a sort of cry and kissed her passionately. But a rustling noise interrupted them.

'What's that?' he asked violent.

'Hush dear', she said, 'it'th only the peacockth'.

And indeed a line of these birds one after the other and hardly visible in this dusk was making tracks back to the stables. (p.173)

Again, the meaning of the peacocks' interruption is ambiguous. The glimpse of peacocks returning, in rigid formation, to their 'dusty case' suggests the peacocks' captivity in a 'system'. Their condition represents a counterpoint to fulfilment and 'loving'. This does not mean that the peacocks' interruption carries negative symbolic implications concerning Edith's and Raunce's marriage. Green's intent is obviously different, considering his suggesting that his themes are committed to the life within the novel; scenes do not symbolize the characters' destinies after the book. There is no evidence that the author attempts to discourage Edith's and Raunce's union. Edith is not a naïve and innocent victim of Raunce's advances; she knows well how to attract him. Raunce does not seem to remain an aggressive character. Confused by Edith's beauty and confidence after his intrusion into the dancing scene and the blind man's buff, he apologizes and retreats, complaining about his neck to attract sympathy, and sighing because he misses Edith's company (p.110). Edith, by her maternal, feminine vitality, is able to soften and conquer him, to make him 'sick' with love. Hence, the peacocks' interruption may simply be read as a warning to Edith and Raunce to beware of repressive, dehumanizing forces that may condition their relationship. The peacocks are in 'conspiracy' with Edith; they accentuate the erotic in the novel; but they also bring notion of life's fragility.

The various incidents with the weathervane unify all the motifs and layers of conflict in the novel. One day, Raunce is standing in front of a map of Ireland which has a pointer connected to a weathervane. He notices that the device is stuck in one position, 'with the arrow tip exactly on Clancarty, Clancarty which was indicated by two nude figures male and female recumbent in gold crowns. For the artist had been told the place was a home of the old kings' (p.49). Mrs Jack, walking in and noticing how the arrow is indicating the scene of her adulterous affair, breaks the pointer in her agitated attempt to move it away from those 'disgusting people'. Clancarty, a monument over ancient kings, is a metaphor for the decadence of its inheritors who cultivate a dead past. At Clancarty, Captain Davenport 'digs after the old kings in his bog' (p.39). In some obscure way, Paddy is also involved with the ancient history of the place. Paddy 'knows Clancarty', Kate points out (p.40).[13] The connection between the episode with the weathervane and the shrieks of the peacocks is focused as Edith and Kate accompany Raunce to examine the works of the weathervane. Caught in the gear wheels, 'held by the leg was a live mouse'. Edith lets out a shriek, like those peacocks, and faints; the mouse responds in a 'paper-thin scream' (p.52).

The mouse does not echo Raunce's desperate predicament at being caught in any insidious mechanism of loving. In fact, this incident takes place before Raunce has fallen in love with Edith. It signifies the 'living', the human, entrapped by the cold machinery of artificiality, condemned by conformity to a petrified order which lovers must escape. Its symbolism is pertinent to all the inhabitants of the castle. As suggested by the map's two nude figures recumbent in gold crowns, Mrs Jack and the Captain's carnal affair implies a regressive search for old kings' treasures in Davenport's bog. 'Do they dig for it ... or pry long sticks into the ground or what?', Raunce muses, which makes Edith blush with embarrassment (p.40). She may be associating Raunce's remark with her unfortunate intrusion on the two nude figures in Mrs Jack's gold-boat bed. The gold theme, Davidson points out, is used to 'suggest falseness or deception by covering or mimicking the real thing, carnality, by its association, and an entrapment, a transfixed helplesssness that is quite Midas-like'. Thus, Mrs Jack and the Captain's relationship 'seems as cold, joyless and perilous as Mrs Tennant's precious world, wherein at the end she sits entrapped in a hammock of gold wire netting, forlorn, plumb in the centre of the dairy room'.[14] The image of the ensnared mouse obliquely alludes to the threat poised against Edith and Kate. Mrs Welch refers to them as a 'pair of two-legged mice' and Kate is worried there may be a mouse in Paddy's room (p.55). Raunce, before his falling in love with Edith, is not only a captive of the old machinery; he is the one trusted to operate it. When Edith goes to show him where to find the mechanism holding the mouse, he 'came smoothly out, automatic'. When Raunce hears the gramophone in the previously discussed dancing-scene, his real worry is that the girls may break the machine. Emotionally repressed, he follows the music 'like the most silent cat after two white mice' (p.65). At the beginning of the book, when Raunce, insensitive to Eldon's feelings, slinks into his sick-room to steal his whisky, Albert 'looked to listen as for a shriek' (p.18).

The shrieks of the peacocks, as well as other shrieks associated with the peacocks, form a meaningful pattern of warnings against dehumanizing forces. In addition, it is important to examine the peacock motifs with regard to their function in each particular context. They also recur outside montage arrangements as apt devices for enriching the suggestiveness of the narrative, and to create the desired degree of ambiguity. When Edith first appears in the novel, she is wearing 'a peacock's feather above her lovely head, in her dark-folded hair' (p.19). She is carrying a gauntlet glove full of unbroken peacock's eggs which she is going to smear on her skin as a love charm. Rapturous shrieks from playing children or from Edith's and Kate's delighted giggling about men pervade the book. In such contexts, the peacock motif may seem to express the peacocks' 'complicity' with natural vitality.

Images and motifs associated with peacocks are employed for their connotative, metaphorical potentials, to enrich the symbolic suggestiveness of the narrative. On a different level of meaning, they serve as structural elements. One may argue that the equivocal effect of Green's use of the peacocks stems mainly from their different functions in relation to different contexts. If this aspect of Green's technique is closely examined, one finds that the peacock motif does not exist in symbolic randomness, but accentuates the novel's structure and its value statement about experience.

Another key motif in *Loving* is Mrs Tennant's ring, a valuable antique. Raunce provides an important clue to the real significance of the ring when, in response to Edith's question as to whether they are going to leave the castle, he replies, 'No ... we're not. Not so long as we can find that ring.... And keep the house from bein' burned down over our heads. Or Mrs Jack from running off with the Captain so Mrs Tennant goes over for good to England' (p.149). Raunce and the other servants associate the ring with the preservation of the status quo. Loss of the precious ring may entail losing their jobs, and, in a symbolic sense, the breakdown of the old order. The ring belongs to the 'shadowless castle of treasures' which, Green points out, 'had yet to be burned down' (p.65). Earle Labor notes how the circuit of disappearance made by the ring 'is remarkably similar to the rounds made by the tainted carcass of the dead peacock', which is first buried by Mrs Welch, then found by the dog Badger, returned to Mrs Welch by Raunce, who hangs it in her larder, and finally obliterated by Mrs Welch, who throws the carcass in the boiler.[15] The constant reappearance of the dead peacock and the continual disappearance of the ring increase the feeling of insecurity among the castle's inhabitants. In the tumult that ensues, Mrs Welch anxiously removes all signs of disturbing forces, while the servants, either out of a dislike for change, or from a sense of duty, search for the lost ring which may restore stability to the household.

The trial of having to cope with threats of disintegration, both from the inside and outside world, accompanying Mrs Tennant's long absence abroad and the loss of the ring, changes Raunce's plans for the future. The sense of continuance provided by the castle proves an illusion. Raunce tells Edith that 'it wouldn't come as a surprise if places such as this weren't doomed to a natural death so to say' (p.195). Raunce's and Edith's escape, despite the final return of the ring, is motivated by this recognition.

It is the repeated loss of the ring, then, not its retrieval, that is important in an existentialist sense. Having been the petty-minded butler in the castle, content to preserve the *status quo*, Raunce gradually recognizes the immanent precariousness of existence. His love for Edith is strengthened by a new awareness of the preciousness of life, which is slowly being destroyed by the passage of time. 'I didn't realize I could love anyone the way I love you. I thought I'd lived too long.... Why I'm altogether changed ... but the years fly fast.... To think of Albert old enough to enlist' (p.149). Significantly, it is Albert's dangerous decision to join the air force as a tail gunner that finally prompts Raunce's revaluation of his position. Edith wonders why he has now changed his mind to leave the castle. '"It's Albert", he explained. "My Albert to want to do a thing like that. Why it's almost as if 'e was me own son"' (p.151). Raunce's great concern for the boy arises partly from the stirrings of his awakened humanness. 'He began to clear away the dinner things for his lad Albert. He surprised himself doing it' (p.150). (In keeping with the strong humorous element in the novel, Raunce's affection for his lad characteristically suffers whenever he thinks of him as a rival lover.)

An important thematic point is missed, however, if Raunce's inchoate need to participate in life is not recognized at the same time. His adolescent anxiety has been evident in his regressive attachment to his mother, to whom he has conscientiously been

writing letters imploring her to come and stay with him in
Ireland. His worries concerning the recovery of the lost ring
have been aggravated by other fears. 'An' you went on that
they'd clap you in the Army soon as ever you stepped off the
boat over in Britain', Edith challenges him (p.151). What worries
him now, on the other hand, is the feeling that his mother
'reckons we're 'iding ourselves away in this neutral country'.
' "It's that bit about being afraid that gets me", he muttered'
(p.197). Raunce's return to England despite the war may be
partly the result of an awakened sense of duty to his country, as
several critics have suggested. His growth, however, is more
satisfactorily explained in terms of the existentialist theme that
pervades all of Green's novels. Having experienced that security
is actually an illusion and that dependence on the *status quo* is
just an abstract bulwark inevitably undermined by the non-
coherence of reality, Raunce senses the need to confront insta-
bility. The certainty of his material and social position is
sacrificed for more fulfilling objectives – ' "it's no manner of use
hanging on in a place where you're not valued", he said' (p.195).
Whether Raunce will eventually join the army over in England
is uncertain, like everything else concerning their future. Green's
major issue is Raunce's incipient willingness to accept uncertainty. Dependence upon precedent, precisely the idea against
which Raunce is reacting, is lastly propounded by Edith, who
nourishes second thoughts about leaving. ' "Stay in what you
know, that's what I always maintain", Edith announced although
she had never before expressed an opinion one way or the other'
(p.196). The symptoms of Edith's conformity, however, are easily
overrun by more attractive incitements. She is delighted once
Raunce suggests that they elope together, which is far more
romantically exciting than just leaving. ' "Oh I can love you for
this", she murmured' (p.200). Their determination to escape
suggests hope for the future. Raunce's activated mental state,
'loving', provides hope that he will be able to participate in a
more 'living' reality.

Although Raunce shows signs of personal growth, it is Edith
who represents the crucial values in *Loving*. Green's poetic
characterization of her 'glowing', 'brilliant', 'sparkling' beauty
reflects her inner qualities. She adores Mrs Jack's children, who,
in return, love Edith above anyone else. She handles Mrs Jack's
garments with a delicacy and devotion radiating from her

vigorous femininity. Edith's extraordinary capacity for joy derives from her devotion to life in a broad sense. She proceeds from girlish giggles with Kate to a womanly maturity that encompasses her whole being. She rejects Albert's regressive calf love: 'A child like that? He wants his old mother, that's his trouble. But live an' let live is what I always say' (p.130). On another occasion she tells Raunce, 'I like a man that's a man and not a lad' (p.149). For Raunce, she wants to be both mother and mistress, bringing him comfort and joy. Whether the nervous, dyspeptic Raunce, on his part, can quite live up to Edith's idea of a man, is left uncertain. At the end, he still seems concerned with his duty towards his mother. However, Raunce's possible inadequacy does not alter the principal value statement of the novel, centring round Edith's maternal sensuality.

Besides creating a radiant moment of fecund beauty, the final scene clarifies the organizing principle of *Loving*. It brings Edith into the dovecote in both a literal and a symbolic sense. Just as Lily, at the end of *Living*, is identified with the one pigeon which courageously responds to its instincts, so Edith is alternately associated with both peacocks and doves. Raunce may also attain certain characteristics of these birds. In Edith's darkened room, the two lovers embrace and become doves:

> Their two bodies flowed into one as he put his arms about her. The shape they made was crowned with his head, on top of a white sharp curved neck, dominating and cruel over the blur that was her mass of hair through which her lips sucked at him warm and heady.   (*Loving*, p.180)

Green's linking of the doves with Edith's and Raunce's sensual world of loving confirms the symbolic centrality of the previously examined dovecote scene. Raunce's fervour, 'dominating and cruel', like that of the doves, reveals man's animal nature. As in the doves' rapturous 'kissing', however, Green perceives the vital aspect of natural impulses; animal instinct is an integral part of human love. Green's equation of Edith (and Raunce) with the doves suggests that the entire plot of the novel is modelled on the fairy-tale structure in order to crystallize basic truths in symbolic form. All events correlate (however indirectly) with values associated with the two key symbols in the novel, the dovecote (including the functions of the peacocks) and the ring, the former connoting vitality and instinctual 'living', and the latter, automatic, life-excluding conformity.[16] Meaning is produced by the juxtapositions or intrusions of elements pertaining to these two incongruous poles of values in relation to particular contexts.

Hall suggests that 'Most of the characters in *Loving* are more easily worried by symbols than by events – they have established methods for dealing with events.'[17] Hall's perceptive observation aids the delineation of central themes in the novel, and the detection of an underlying montage structure. Most of the confusions and anxieties in *Loving* come because of someone's preoccupation with events, objects or duties that are related to the two main symbols. It is the constant juxtapositions of the characters' symbolically related preoccupations and a contrary reality that produce both the humorous and the grim statements of the book. The servants most resistant to change – Raunce, Miss Burch, Miss Swift, Mrs Welch – are repeatedly puzzled by absurd situations which deviate from their narrow conceptions about life, demanding readjustment. Green may caricature these characters so that their blindness and, to them, irrational events lose their underlying seriousness and become hilarious. As Coleridge says, 'all is equal in contrast with the infinite'. The relevance of these words indicates that *Loving*, with all its humour, is an existentialist novel, and therefore basically serious. A scene like the one in which Raunce declares his 'big' love for Edith, whereupon the dog comes and deposits the stinking carcass of a plucked peacock at his feet, is decidedly comical. However, the humour only alleviates the sense of warning given by the dead peacock. All events in *Loving* are enacted against the imminent threat of death, either physical or spiritual. At the end, the dead peacock is symbolically resurrected in the hopeful image of live ones being fed by Edith. Structurally and thematically, the connection of the dead peacock and the ring centres on the question of life and death. The glimpse of the ring hidden under half an eggshell suggests lurking danger (p.135). In some symbolic way, the rotten, stinking peacock, buried by Mrs Welch, connects with the meaning of the ring, the important difference being that, whereas Mrs Welch wants to bury the peacock, she needs to disinter the ring. She is intent on opening the drains in which she thinks the ring is stuck, for, almost as if it came from the rotting peacock, she notices 'a terrible stench of drains' (p.161). Symbolically related to the theme of decay, Bassoff notes 'in connection with the *underground* that "Captain Davenport seeks after treasure in a bog"' (emphasis added).[18]

In this secluded world of decay, Green does not overlook some characters' great capacity for spontaneous merriment. Burdened by sinister premonitions, the servants may all surrender to joyous giggling when imitating the IRA man's lisp – because in such a grave context, his 'th's really are funny. At the table, as the servants are discussing Edith's sensational discovery of Captain Davenport trying to hide under the silk sheets in Mrs Jack's bed, uneasiness and confusion yield to laughter. Even Paddy emerges from his usual lethargy:

a great braying laugh started out of the lampman. It swelled. It filled the room. Raunce said, 'Look what you've done', and in his turn began to laugh. Kate joined in. So at last did Edith. These two girls did not giggle this time, they both deeply laughed. (p.81)

Green's description of the contagious laughter, the way in which it swells, fills the entire room, is remarkably similar to his technique for evoking the storming intensity of wheeling, dancing girls both in *Loving* and *Concluding*, or, for example, the expanding swarm of starlings filling the air in a musical crescendo in *Concluding*'s oft-referred-to sunset scene. The servants' joy relieves the gravity of daily anxieties and disagreements, presenting Mrs Jack's amorous misadventure with the redeeming touch of ludicrousness that it merits. It is characteristic that the servants do have a 'human' dimension to their personalities, in addition to the more mechanical square-mindedness conditioned by their positions. They do not copy the petrified decadence of Mrs Tennant. Everybody nourishes strong affections for someone. Eldon loves Ellen. Miss Burch, the spinsterish housekeeper, loves Eldon. Edith and Kate relax from their routine chores by indulging in intimate, feminine communion. Mrs Welch runs her domain, the kitchen, as an authoritarian guard of order and morality. Frivolity somehow taints the food. When reprimanding her obnoxious grandson, however, 'her voice was thick with love' (p.54). And Miss Burch adores Edith: 'I love that girl of mine Edith, I love that child Miss Swift' (p.116). Even Raunce's

Albert loves, in his adolescent way – he accepts the blame for
the theft of the ring, which he has never seen, in order to shield
Edith. In fact, the impersonal forces which they serve are
countered by liberating human impulses. As Raunce remarks,
'"Miss Swift is a difficult woman whilst she's up in her nursery.
But she can be nice as you please outside." "That's right", Miss
Burch said, "and as I've often found, take someone out of their
position in life and you find a different person altogether, yes"'
(p.42). The girls' giggling suggests that Miss Burch's remark is
aimed at Raunce, another indication that he ought to escape his
position as butler of the castle. When they all gather around
their table, they seem human beings who agree, disagree, laugh
and love. Their humanness, in all its intrigue, displays traits
reminiscent of the book's central symbolism, life in the dovecote;
it is not a static conformity that is presented, but more like a
living reality.

From a structural point of view, *Loving* is a novel in which
healthy human impulses are in competition with a life-restraining
dependence on *status quo*, either externally or personally imposed.
The servants' capacity for joy is a sign of their humanity, but
may at times be submerged in a mindless indifference towards
vital human concerns, owing to their preoccupation with triviality
and superficiality. Only a montage approach can indicate the
tone intended in the interaction between certain attitudes and
different contexts. The servants' contribution to the maintenance
of the castle is, symbolically, a manifestation of their regressive
folly. It is ultimately a metaphor for their private fears concerning
'living'. Despite their inherent capacity for loving, most of the
characters suffer as a consequence of unfulfilled needs. And it is
the fulfilment of vital human needs in an existentialist context
that is Green's preoccupation. It is the effect of the loving on
Edith and Raunce that resolves the novel. Since, on a metaphorical level, the curious tension between realism and fantasy stems
from Green's and his characters' projections of longings and
fears (represented by symbols and images) into the everyday
life, Edith's and Raunce's escape is not exclusively a physical
escape from one place to another. It implies their symbolic
rejection of a static order (associated with the ring) and Green's
celebration of 'living' (his symbolic identification of Edith with
the birds in the final scene). Similarly, in the intersection between
symbolism and narrative structure in *Loving*, montage reveals

disparities and contradictions that produce both the comic and the tragic statements of the novel.

Only a montage approach can fully illuminate Green's artistic order. Contradictory images act against one another to crystallize the importance of humanly sustaining values. The reader's perception of values is reinforced by the sense of life's uncertainty and fragility. In this manner, Green's montage method heightens the comic tone of the novel despite his recognition of tragedy and conflict. Moments of poetic significance reflect the author's creative commitment to his world. Accordingly, his utilization of montage stimulates the reader's affirmative participation in a living present, a present with a 'life of its own'.

5   *Concluding* (1948)

Concluding is probably the most unresolved of Green's novels. It stresses the complexity of contradictory human impulses and conflicts. Edward Stokes finds that 'in *Concluding* . . . Green has developed even further the poetic methods which enable him to present, at the same time, several different aspects or levels of reality – the contemporary and the timeless, the specific and the universal'.[1] The incorporation of many aspects of reality in the record of a day in the life of old Mr Rock reflects Green's recognition of man's entrapment in a fragmentary universe. The world of *Concluding* is one in which no fundamental questions are answered. We do not know whether Rock will lose his cottage; his fears of becoming homeless will continue. The disappearance of the two schoolgirls Mary and Merode remains a mystery; Merode is found in the forest, but explains nothing; Mary never reappears. Nor do we know who haunts the woods in the middle of the night, yelling Mary's name and playing tricks on both the Principals and on Rock. As Rock concludes at the end of the novel, 'We shall never know the truth' (p.253).

Green does not resolve the major conflicts in *Concluding*, or answer its central questions, because this is not his chief concern. On the contrary, the world he creates here is intentionally ambiguous. The possibility of a clarified meaning which binds together the different aspects of a single day is ultimately obscured in the darkness of intangibility. In this world, therefore, it is more important to assess the structural functions of the elements as artistic expressions than attempt to explain the inherent meaning of elusive fragments. *Concluding* abounds in visual expressions such as colour, light, darkness, circles, spirals, sea and water imagery. Within these groups of images there are subdivisions: images of light, for example, consist of sunlight, moonlight, torchlight, reflected light in rich prism colours – each with some individual but never fully revealed meaning. The technique is used to transmit emotional experience, which, according to Green, may only be expressed through visual imagery and poetic metaphor. This imagery is important as it expresses the more pervasive contradiction which formulates life itself.

A close examination of Green's sea and water images reveals that they have by no means a clear, consistent denotative meaning, nor do they necessarily refer to a realistic, empirical representation. Very often, sea images are used to evoke the sensuous complexity of a subjective experience which is too rich to be expressed in clear descriptive statements. Thus the girls Mr Rock meets at breakfast invade his senses with sensual, 'flowing' vitality:

> the sleep from which they had just come a rosy moss upon the lips, the *heavy tide* of dreams on each in a *flow* of her eighteen summers, and which would *ebb* now only with their first cup they were fetching, as his tea made his old blood run again, in this morning's second miracle for Mr Rock.
> (p.22, emphasis added)

At other times, water imagery serves as a connective tissue by which Green expresses a sense of unification. An illustrative example is provided in the scene in which Rock, courageously challenging the dark to mount the steps of the Institute, unites three 'alien, glistening, frozen-eyed, alone' people into 'one hydra-headed body' (pp.189–90). Green may employ water imagery to connote drowning, but the imagery is not a direct, objective representation of actuality:

> 'I haven't been quite well, I had a breakdown at work', Elizabeth told Miss Winstanley, as they set out along a great hill of rhododendron twelve foot high with flowers the colour of blood, and the colour of the flesh of *bathers* in open air in sunless country. Winstanley, as she bent her head to listen, took her companion's hand in hers as a sort of tribute to this woman's being *drenched* with love.   (p.98, emphasis added)

The two italicized words in this passage serve indefinable functions. The surreal quality of the scene suggests that it is principally a metaphorical projection of Liz's subjective feelings. Her reminiscence of her nervous breakdown, from which she has more or less recovered, evokes the picture of 'bathers ... in sunless country'. However, Liz's 'being drenched with love' is no symbolic testimony of the lethal quality of her relationship with Sebastian. Green does not reveal the cause of her nervous breakdown. Moreover, there also are passages in the book which stress the beauty of the lovers' relationship. If the flowers in the previous scene are recognized as being different colours, it is possible that the red rhododendrons – 'the colour of blood' – express the intensity of Liz's love, and contradict the bloodless, colourless ones. The fact that Winstanley 'let go of that hot hand' supports this interpretation. Liz's 'hot' blood corresponds to the blood-red flowers. It is possible that the scene reflects her subjective immersion in love rather than an objective representation of drowning. This possibility is strengthened by Miss Winstanley's question, 'Would you like my mirror?'

If Green's images were only seen as integral elements in the novel's ordained cyclic movement from morning till night, the dominant tone of *Concluding* would indeed be that of a tragic vision. The preceding examples indicate, however, that his images do not simply infiltrate the different levels of reality in the novel so as to give it a coherent pattern of general disintegration and dark, sinister mysticism. They do not primarily reflect a verifiable ulterior reality. Instead, they are technical devices which enrich the novel's style. In order to provide a precise meaning, they will consequently have to be examined as part of a larger context. This approach is validated by Green's previously cited statement that 'it is the context in which they [words] lie that alone gives them life. They should be used as painters use colour, to give tone.'[2]

Visual imagery is rarely divorced from some determining context so as to attain complete autonomy of texture. Metaphorical texture provides the flavour of the narrative, whereas montage highlights the significance of context in which sentence rhythm, juxtaposition of images and filmic devices play an essential part. When two scenes or images collide in the generative way characteristic of montage, they create an intensified perceptual awareness of and a deepened sense of disparity between those aspects of the narrative that are emphasized, thereby modifying the meaning of the surrounding context. Despite Green's recognition of tragedy, montage works as a counteracting, reintegrating force. Montage strives to crystallize meaning and significance. The montage effect in *Concluding* deepens the disparity between fragments in order to bring vital human values into relief. In this manner, Green strengthens the didactic aspect of the novel at the expense of purely realistic presentation.

Meaning as a function of montage is best approached by an examination of the imagery of darkness and light. Darkness and light are contradictory aspects of reality and are bound up with *Concluding*'s cyclic movement. The thematic importance of these images in specific contexts may be discovered through a montage approach. A sense of heavy weariness, enhanced by a misty semi-darkness before sunrise, sets the mood at the opening of *Concluding*. Rock 'groaned a third time. – Early morning comes hard on a man my age, he told himself for comfort, comes hard. – How hard? Oh, heavy' (p.5). Rock's mood is in consonance with the silent treetops surrounded by mist,

> beneath which loomed colourlessly one mass of flowering rhododendron after another and then the azaleas, which, without scent, pale in the fresh of early morning, had not yet begun, as they would later, to sway their sweetness forwards, back, in silent church bells to the morning.   (p.6)

The two old men, Rock and Adams, are concerned with complaining and worrying about old age and the passage of time. 'Why I lost her [his wife], sir, the winter just gone', Adams says. 'I'm getting an old dodderer', Rock complains. '"You're a ripe age now", George Adams agreed.' 'It's my legs', Rock goes on. '"Nothing anyone can do for the bends", Adams said at last, out of an empty head.' A conflict of masses, created by a dazzling sunlight, suddenly interrupts the old men's conversation:

> At this instant, like a woman letting down her mass of hair from a white towel in which she had bound it, the sun came through for a moment, and lit the azaleas on either side before fog, redescending, blanketted these off again; as it might be white curtains, drawn by someone out of sight, over a palace bedroom window, to shut behind them a blonde princess undressing.
> 'It's not fair on one to grow old', Mr Rock said.   (pp.6–7)

These scenes from the opening pages of *Concluding* present a crucial problem for consideration: to what extent does the two characters' position reflect a tragic preoccupation on the part of the author, and to what extent is Green's arrangement of details intended to emphasize human values?

It is important to note that Green's attention in the opening pages of *Concluding* does not dwell solely on life's oppressive cyclic movement towards eternal darkness. On the contrary, he strikes an optimistic note by affirming that the bleak morning will later be chased by sun, birds and flowers. In fact, this conviction is shared by Rock when getting out of bed that morning: 'It will be a fine day, a fine day in the end, he decided' (p.5). The truth of these optimistic statements is finally reassuringly confirmed at the end of the novel. Rock, although surrounded by darkness, can then conclude that he is 'well satisfied with his day' (p.254). Liz has just echoed Rock's previous assertion that 'All's well that ends well' (p.252). Most significantly, this statement signals *Concluding*'s similarity to the genre of Shakespearean comedy. Northrop Frye suggests that 'the "all's well that ends well" formula is deeply involved with a structure in which redemption from death, or even revival from death, is a central element'.[3] Green seems to suggest that there is hope as long as one concentrates on the positive aspects contained in one single day at a time, without looking too far beyond into mute darkness.

Green's anticipation of a 'happy ending' deepens the incongruity between the positive aspects of life and Rock's and Adams's negativism and fears about life here and now. Montage emphasizes precisely this meaning, for, when the sun suddenly breaks through the mist, Green makes sure that it does not go on shining. For only a moment it transforms the world around Rock before he goes on grumbling about the injustice of growing old. Thus the main function of this conflict of masses is suddenly to interrupt the flow of complaints by a glimpse of beauty. The resultant incongruity produces a sense of irony which marks Rock's outlook.

Various similar devices are used by Green to draw the reader's attention to the tone of the novel. Rock's and Adams's attentions shift to Liz, Rock's granddaughter, with whom Rock lives alone in a small cottage. Liz has just recovered from a nervous breakdown, and Rock blames it all on Sebastian, Liz's lover, of whom Rock is irreconcilably jealous; 'she would never get well while she could meet that man, he knew' (p.7). When Adams questions if Rock does not find his granddaughter a blessing to have with him, Rock grunts to himself, 'a blessing and a curse ... then repented this last so violently that he could not be sure he had not spoken out loud'. This 'loud' rush of feeling that seizes Rock is intensified by a call heard by Adams. Its function is that of an audio-visual counterpoint (although one does not actually hear the call). As in the previous montage trope, this counterpoint is obviously intended to arrest and bring Rock's negating attitude into relief. Again, however, he fails to be profoundly affected. He does not hear the call; he does not comprehend its personal relevance: 'The sage looked blank at his companion. But it was too dark with sudden mist to read the expression on his face.... "I'm a mite deaf", Mr Rock answered.'

The call probably comes from someone searching in the woods for the lost Mary, the young woman who has disappeared without a trace from her boarding school. Some indication of its symbolic meaning is given by the great importance Rock attaches to whether there is an echo or not. He tells Adams that 'if you ... call away from the place down this ride behind, you won't get a whisper in return' (p.8). The lack of reply seems to reflect man's entrapment in flux and uncertainty. The predicament of human existence accounts for the underlying tragic vision of *Concluding*. In this void, man can either commit himself to growth and beauty, or surrender to the dark forces which will transport him through the solitary journey from the semi-darkness of morning to the long sleep of dark night. Green's montage technique accents the precariousness of existence and the need to comprehend life through love.

Green emphasizes the significance of the calls for the lost girl by making them an integral part of *Concluding*'s structure. During Rock's and Adams's morning conversation, the call is repeated thrice. Significantly, Rock groans, not once, but thrice. Similarly, Rock has three animals which, at the end of the novel, each lets out a squeal to assert some obscure message. The recurrence of the number three, and the fact that the name shouted is Mary, indicate some biblical allusion. Simon Peter denies Christ thrice; Peter's name means 'Rock'; at the end of the novel, after Rock's vehement denial of the girls and Edge, he exclaims the word 'Petra' (p.245). The possibility that some events relate to basic Christian values or to man's (notably Rock's) denial of them is stressed in *Pack my Bag*. Green's citation of a sermon remembered from childhood reveals his concern with this theme.

> Brethren you know the time Jesus told Peter that he would deny him thrice and then the cock would crow and I expect you remember how Peter did deny that he had been with Jesus and how after three times denying of having been with Jesus the cock crew and how he went out and wept.

Green offers Christ's love as a contrast to Peter's denial, 'his wonderful love for Peter not only for Peter but for the whole world'.[4] *Concluding*'s biblical images or allusions do not possess a consistent, self-sufficient symbolic meaning. Whether they emphasize basic values or characters' affirmation or denial of these can only be determined in relation to each concrete context. It may be significant that, after Rock has failed to respond to the appeal of the first call, Green describes Rock and Adams as moving like 'suiciding moles in the half light' (p.8).

The values to which Green points are specifically implied in connection with the following montage conflict. Adams hints at how hard Rock works carrying buckets full of swill. 'I do this for Elizabeth, Mr Rock told himself.' At that instant there is a conflict of masses: 'His glasses were misted, fog still hung about, but the sun coming through once more, made it for a second so that he might have been inside a pearl strung next the skin of his beloved ... – Elizabeth, Eliza, Liz, Mr Rock thought.' The conflict of masses counterpoints values linked with the sun and the sense of confinement associated with mist. This conflict is further accentuated by the fact that Rock pronounces Liz's name three times, an act which intimates the religious significance of love. That there is a vital necessity for love in the midst of unfathomable darkness is again stressed after the second call, when Rock learns from Adams that there is no echo, just a void. Realizing this, he 'let his love for Elizabeth, and fear that he might lose the cottage, sap what ability was left him' (pp.8–9).

Rational obsession with empirical reality, with disorder and flux, is life-denying. Consequently, Green stresses the need to comprehend life through love. This dichotomy provides a basic clue to the understanding of *Concluding*. Ways in which values of love apply to the relationship between the individual and nature are expanded upon in connection with a new series of audio-visual counterpoints involving the attitudes of Miss Edge and Miss Baker, the spinsterish headmistresses of the Institute that trains girls to become state servants. Human nature, to Miss Edge, represents a disintegrating force and must therefore be brought under the control of the state. For this reason, she fears individuals who will not bend to the interests of institutional life. She distrusts Rock's strong individualism, and wants him evicted from his state-owned cottage, which is situated in the grounds of the Institute. Around her mansion (the throne of regimentation), Edge has arranged a well kept, symmetrical garden, a shield against the mystic forest beyond and, symbolically, against her repressed natural needs. The calls in the woods signal the disturbing presence of a reality which her uniform order is intended to exclude. Standing by the window in her house, she looks out on her big lawns,

> which, in the dew, over long grass, all down the *three* descending Terraces, had strings of brilliants garlanded now between the blades and which flashed prism colours at her from the sun, against a background of mist. 'I love it', she repeated.... She was about to move away, out of danger, when she was halted. 'There', she exclaimed. 'Did you not hear this time?'
>
> (p.16, emphasis added)

An essential function of the call is obviously to 'halt' Edge's withdrawal from the 'danger' she perceives. Green uses various devices to heighten the dynamism of this passage. Effects similar to a conflict of graphic directions are produced as the *three* regularly arranged 'Terraces' (the fact that 'Terraces' is capitalized emphasizes and increases its visual impression) are counteracted by dazzling prism colours from the sun, which also create a conflict of masses against a background of mist. Enhanced by a rhythm which Eisenstein and Vendryes would term 'emotional speech', these conflicts accentuate a tone of disparity between natural vividness and formal order. Edge's attempted withdrawal from this vivid display of natural splendour is abruptly arrested by the call for Mary. The call functions as an audio-visual counterpoint, a warning that Edge's self-restraint is life-denying.

Viewed against the number of examples given so far, there is clearly a recurrent pattern of montage conflicts in *Concluding*. There can be no doubt that the use of montage accentuates the

novel's tone. Green entreats an affirmative response to reality,
implying the values of love, care and tolerance. On the other
hand, he makes no clear distinction between these values and
sexuality. Sexuality is not isolated as a force that immerses the
self into the disintegrating rhythms of flux. Rather, Green
emphasizes its vital potentiality. Affirmation of human nature
counteracts the dark, disintegrating forces that threaten to
quench 'living'. Denial of sexual impulses is ironically dramatized
through montage in the following scene. Green's technique in
the first part bears much resemblance to what Eisenstein would
call a conflict of event and its duration. The deliberate slow
motion of Green's description only increases the underlying
conflicts in the passage. It reveals Edge's fear of life; it increases
the reader's expectation that something will suddenly break up
the slow progress; and it makes the collision of incongruous
images all the more powerful when that does happen. Slowly,
Edge

> moved across to draw one pair of curtains, merely to look at
> the weather, or to lower a window perhaps, she did not know,
> but the room influenced her to act on graceful impulse. She
> took hold on velvet, which had red lilies over a deeper red,
> and paused, as she gently parted the twin halves, to admire
> her hands' whiteness against the heavy pile. Delicately, then,
> she proceeded to reveal window panes ... to disclose glass
> frosted to flat arches by condensation, so that the Sanctum
> was reflected all dark sapphire blue from electric light at her
> back because it was not yet morning. She could even see,
> round her head's inky shade, no other than a swarm of
> aquamarines, which, pictured on the dark sapphire panes,
> were each drop of the chandelier that she had lit with the
> lamps switched on in entering.   (p.12)

The restraint of Edge's movements is dynamized by sexual
undertones. This technique highlights the headmistress's
repressed sexual proclivities. Very delicately, she 'took hold on
velvet' and 'gently parted the twin halves'. In doing this, Green
makes her pause while he pictures the whiteness of her hands
against deep red velvet, a contrast intended to heighten the
underlying sexual tension of the description, not only because of
the contrast in colours, but also because deep red is a dramatic

colour evoking associations of blood, and because velvet has a delicate quality that appeals to the tactile senses. This depiction of latent energy is counteracted by the image of 'glass frosted to flat arches'. Moreover, Green creates tension and suspense due to the incongruity produced by highly dynamic, vivacious images – such as 'dark sapphire blue' reflections and a 'swarm of aquamarines' – and Edge's slow disaffectedness which is enhanced by negative expressions: Edge sees *'no other* than a swarm of aquamarines' (emphasis added).

It is at this very instant that Green's style suddenly changes into a highly energetic vehicle for conveying dramatic action. 'Excited emotional speech', as Eisenstein would term it, provides the sensory impact of a sudden filmic close-up which accentuates conflict between Edge's attitude and vital values.

> She also caught a glimpse of matter whisk across behind, then dart back to hide. She turned. Held her breath, or she might have screamed. And it was, as she had feared, a horrid bat.
> She made one dive for the wicker basket and put that on her. (Ibid.)

The image of the bat serves, on one level, a similar function to the repeated calls for the disappeared Mary. It clashes with attitudes in the preceding context – here with Edge's distrustful cautiousness. After the incident, her still strong desire to open the curtains wrestles with her fear that she may see more bats, that they might even 'flicker up her skirts', so she merely 'peeped at the day as if by stealth' (pp.12, 15). Her reaction to the bat reflects not only her sexual repressions, but also (since the bat appears in the context of brilliant, light-reflected aquamarines) her more general denial of natural dynamism. Facing this scene, Edge dives for a wicker basket and puts her head into it, thereby creating a conflict of scales. (Similarly, Gates, in *Living*, puts his head into the basin.) The wicker basket has the same functional meaning as the pot, the sink and the basin, all extensively discussed in the analysis of *Living*. The conflict of scales produces a sense of confinement, of repression, and of alienation from the sun. This tone is immediately strengthened by a new conflict of scales and masses between the wicker basket and the outside world. Baker opens the window. 'A light came through, so grey it was doomed, together with a wisp of mist. The bat flew outside at once' (p.13).

By concentrating on new visual details, Green reinforces the connection of Edge's misanthropy, her denial of natural vividness, and her sexual repressions. Edge, removing the basket from her head, cynically remarks, 'If we could as easily rid ourselves of Rock.' She is referring to her symbolic equation of Rock and the bat. Immediately, Baker notices a piece of paper which has been in the basket on Edge's head. It reads, 'FURNICATES'. The piece of paper on her head (with the word misspelt) makes Edge look ridiculous. It ironically points to her repressed sexuality, perhaps even to a repressed attraction for Rock. When she drops the 'word' and lets it 'spiral to destruction', she implicitly defies Rock, the bat, the forest, and all nature.

In order to find a measure of stationary security in the midst of nature and flux, Edge mistakenly chooses to view life as a static, repetitive pattern which brings hope in terms of calculated intervals. After dropping the piece of paper to rotate to the ground, she remarks to Baker, 'Each Wednesday that you and I go up to Town . . . the weather we have here, Baker, is exquisite, truly exquisite. There may be black fog outside, just now, this minute, but we shall be cheated, dear. The sun will shine' (ibid.). The sun will certainly shine some time during the day; this is what both Rock and Adams also tell themselves for comfort. However, renewal of human life is not the inevitable result of the diurnal pattern. *Concluding* exposes life's habitual yielding to the tragic flux of formless, cyclic propensity, which can only be challenged through participation in the living present.

> Day was committed to night; the sequence here is light then darkness, and what had been begun in this community under the glare of morning, is yet to be concealed in a sharp fresh of moonlight, a statuary of day after sunset, to be *lost*, *at last*, when the usual cloud drifts over the full moon.
>
> (p.109, emphasis added)

Green emphatically equates artificially imposed patterns and the cyclic pattern in the following scene. Edge is facing a new day:

> sun up, a lovely day had opened and, as she watched, a cloud of starlings rose from the nearest of her Woods, they ascended

in a spiral up into blue sky; a thousand dots revolving on a wave, the shape of a vast black seashell pointed to the morning; and she was about to exclaim in delight when, throughout the dormitories upstairs, with a sound of bees in this distant Sanctum, buzzers called her girls to rise so that two hundred and eighty nine turned over to that sound, stretched and yawned, opened blue eyes on their white sheets to this new day which would stretch on, clinging to its light, until at length, when night should fall at last, would be time for the violins and the dance.   (p.19)

As in the sunset scene watched by Rock and Liz (quoted in the Introduction), the spiralling fluctuation of a swarm of starlings fills up the entire scene, uniting sea and sky, conquering and transcending time. This instant revelation of life, which reflects Green's sensuous commitment to the present moment, is shattered by buzzers from the Sanctum. They produce an audio-visual counterpoint which abruptly reasserts chronological time and signals a conflict of scales between freedom outside and institutional order within the school. 'Two hundred and eighty nine' girls wake up to the commencement of a day filled with domestic chores and institutional schedule. Resembling flowers, they open 'blue eyes on their white sheets' only to enter into the preordained direction of a day which, in desperation, will 'cling' to its light until it is doomed by night. Due to the way in which the audio-visual counterpoint signals a collision of timeless present with the temporal, Green's equation of repetitive institutional patterns and a tragic cyclic pattern is emphasized by their contextual closeness to one another. The organizing of the dance referred to represents the culmination of Edge's attempts to fit human impulses into a controlled pattern.

The suggestion that *Concluding* affirms the value of natural human impulses, which significantly are linked to sexuality, may be countered by sceptical critics finding irrational inclinations in the characters. There are hints that Adams is lurking in the deep woods and may be exploiting the girls sexually. However, there is never any evidence that he really does. Similarly, it is rumoured in the novel that Sebastian meets the girls in the dark woods at night. But as Edge admits, despite her fears about Sebastian, 'There's never come even a hint of trouble, the five years he's been here, between him and one of our girls' (p.18).

Adams himself suspects Rock of having done away with Mary;
Rock suspects Adams. Green never gives any sign that might
confirm the actual presence of active perverse forces in the woods,
or in Adams and Rock. Mary's disappearance, the calls in the
woods, and the deep, muddy lake certainly have ominous
undertones, but the fears they evoke are primarily caused by the
characters' sense of insecurity in face of the inexplicable darkness.
Nor can the girls' sexual impulses be called corrupted or
destructive because they find mystic outlets; their natural needs
have become all the stronger due to excessive control of the
human spirit. On the whole, the fears are reduced to the level
of evil forces subjectively imposed. Despite multiple intrigues in
the world of *Concluding*, linked with characteristic human motives
of egotism and jealousy, these aspects do not shift the impartiality
of the narrative tone.

The previous montage approach has revealed the vital distinction Green makes between objective reality and subjective
attitudes. He does not dwell on a tragic objective reality of
which major motifs are symbolic, integral components. He creates
a reality of contradictory facets. Different contexts emphasize
different aspects of life in relation to the author's or characters'
subjective evaluations. Comic and tragic images coexist; it is the
subjective conception of their interaction that determines their
tone.

This approach is based on the view that Green's world is not
simply cyclic, but also dialectical. Northrop Frye's analysis of the
counterpoint of comic and tragic phenomena in Shakespearean
comedy (*Concluding*'s affinity with Shakespearean comedy has
already been indicated) elucidates Green's vision. Frye suggests
that the first half of the cycle of nature, 'the movement from
birth to death, spring to winter, dawn to dark, is the basis of the
great alliance of nature and reason, the sense of nature as a
rational order in which all movement is toward the increasingly
predictable'. Against the tragic direction of the objective world
is set the comic power of the subjective imagination:

> We can see that death is the inevitable result of birth, but new
> life is not the inevitable result of death. It is hoped for, even
> expected, but at its core is something unpredictable and
> mysterious, something that belongs to the imaginative equiva-
> lents of faith, hope, and love, not to the rational virtues.[5]

In *Concluding*, these mystical, even magic values, are associated with the forest, whereas the contrary image of the State Institute is confined in a rational, unimaginative order. Significantly, the sense of the forest is modified by being a metaphorical reflection of various characters' subjective imaginations, their dreams and fears. *Concluding*'s most poetic scenes in the forest capture a world of instant eternity. The green world is also represented by the Eameses' 'garden of Eden' in *Living*, Green's most conspicuous metaphor for man's spiritual aspiration. Growth and fertility contrast with the black factory town beyond. When Mrs Eames reproaches her husband for listening to Bentley's complaints in the garden, Mr Eames replies that 'if Eve hadn't've started off clacking the serpent wouldn't 'ave caught 'er in his trap'. Mr Eames's question, 'What's Adam and Eve got to do with Bentley?', suggests the biblical implications of their values (*Living*, p.248).

The comic vision, according to Frye in 'The Archetypes of Literature', generally centres around a 'garden, grove or park', or the forest in Shakespeare's comedies. In the tragic vision, the vegetable world is a 'sinister forest'.[6] The forest in *Concluding*, inhabited by Rock, has qualities of fertility and magic that pertain to the comic vision. Its sinister mysticism, however, reflects Green's awareness of contradictory forces. Consequently, Green employs montage to emphasize the value of comic, subjective perception and imagination, against a background of conflict. Frye says that 'it is the separation between redemption and destruction which constitutes the dialectic of romantic comedy'. Despite the difference in structure between Shakespeare's and Green's work, their visions are similar. The dialectic in Shakespeare's comedies works along a traditional narrative line: beginning, middle section of complication, and dénouement. According to Frye, 'the renewing power of the final action lifts us into a higher world, and separates that world from the world of the comic action itself'.[7] In contrast, most of Green's novels lack a conventional plot; the 'renewing power' is evoked through dialectical montage – in the image of contradiction, in the sensuous commitment to the present moment.

The main symbolic conflict in *Concluding* is between the forest and the house. The garden of the Institute does not correlate with the archetypal comic garden image. Here even flowers are confined into categories, of white and red. In contrast, the forest

contains qualities of free, instinctual nature. The significance of
life in the forest is enhanced through biblical allusions. Green
repeatedly refers to Rock as the 'sage', and Adams's name is
biblical. Adams is a forester; Rock has withdrawn from the
'civilized' world where he was once a famous scientist, refuses
to open mail, and has now retreated to 'nature'. He lives a life
of simple pleasures, a shepherd tending to his three animals – a
pig, a goose and a cat. Viewed from the Institute, everything
beyond the third terrace of the garden is concealed in mysticism
and mist. As Mrs Blain, the cook, remarks to Rock, 'you're one
who's never in the light, is he girls?' (p.26).

Different attitudes to Rock's animals provide an important
clue to the nature of conflict between the forest and the Institute.
In the animal world within the comic vision, Frye says, one
generally finds gentle birds and domesticated animals. To the
tragic vision belong more violent animals such as 'beasts and
birds of prey'.[8] A major function of Green's animals is to reflect
various characters' attitudes by their reaction to these animals.
The pig, the goose and the cat are treated by Rock as domesticated
farm animals. Yet, they are seen by Edge as 'serpents' in her
garden, because their natural instincts represent a powerful force
which resists complete domestication. Edge fears Rock and
everything connected with the forest, the to-her dark abyss of
lust and disintegration. She is in terror of the goose: '"A blow
from one of its great wings", and her voice rose ... "one blow,
in one of its savage tempers, and the miserable bird could smash
a leg"' (p.106). She protests against Rock's cat: 'and who is
there can stop a cat making free with the Grounds?' (p.107).
Precisely the animals' instinctual self-sufficiency is of great
significance for a full understanding of *Concluding*. Rock's animals
have a strong will of their own, they act on their own impulses,
and they thereby represent a certain set of values of their own
accord. In central montage contexts, they embody a comic
suggestion.

The rotten, muddy lake is as deep and mystical as the forest
surrounding it. Here Rock takes Daisy, his pig, to help him
search for the disappeared Mary, for, he believes, 'pigs ...
possessed a sense of smell which might come in handy amongst
thick reeds'. Daisy's manner of confronting darkness answers to
the ideal as communicated in *Concluding*. What is an activity
burdened with sinister undertones – Daisy burying her snout in

black earth and rotten leaves – Daisy turns into pure delight:

> now that they had moved once more under the beeches, she
> kept turning last year's leaves with her snout, also the ground
> beneath, but so slowly and with such loud delight that they
> hardly progressed forward; and the ends of sticks of sunlight,
> pointed down from high trees, moved across his pig's flanks
> like pink and cream snails, then over his own face in little
> balls of warmth. . . .
>   – He would never get her home, he knew. She would have
> to be left to make her own way back at meal time.   (p.146)

In a conflict of masses, in which prodding 'sticks of sunlight'
collide with the dark, decaying ground, Green creates an intense
visual experience of time stopped, 'moments when Daisy actually
knelt, and all was still'.

The competitiveness of life and death necessitates Daisy's
affirmative response. Rock reveals his affinity with the animal
by possessing the same perceptual power. He sees the surface of
the lake, now in full sunlight, as

> a white mirror almost to the level of his eyes, and out of which
> grew rushes, pink and green, with willows and other smaller
> gray bushes everlastingly leant over their several likenesses in a
> faint lakeside, sunlit smell of rotting, for perhaps all of three
> times seventy years.   (p.147)

The shining 'white mirror', adorned with vivid, sunlit pinks and
greens, creates an intense present moment. Rock's perception of
instant beauty counteracts disintegrating forces. 'Everlastingly'
bending 'gray bushes' in the lakeside and a 'smell of rotting'
form a contrasting atmosphere of decay. Furthermore, by suggesting that the process of decay has been going on for a period of
'three times seventy years', Green (besides emphasizing the
significance of number three) makes a clear reference to Rock,
who is in his mid seventies.

Green's visualization in his montage scenes of man's tragic
predicament only enhances the vital necessity for countering
powers with which Rock's pig is communing. Daisy possesses
the capacity to conquer darkness, a capacity visualized through
conflicts of graphic directions and audio-visual counterpoint: at

the scent of rotting from the lake, Daisy 'in her startled whiteness'

> suddenly trotted forward, burst through a little undergrowth with a great amount of noise . . . halted at the brink, nose up, ears folded forwards over violet eyes, and with deeply heaving flanks, by which Mr Rock assumed she must wish to challenge. . . .   (Ibid.)

The montage conflicts produce the sensory impact of a filmic close-up. Dynamic intensity absorbs the reader's senses into the very life of the scene so as to render the impression of time being transcended. Thus, with Daisy standing heaving at the brink of the lake, 'All was still, not a bird moved, but the sun was already turning edges of green leaves red, and soon it would be time for russet pheasants roosting' (ibid.). When Green suddenly turns his attention back to the passage of time, a sense of affective distance between reader and scene results, a transition which functions as a conflict between close and long shots. This conflict intensifies the values of the present moment, offering a sensuous fulfilment despite the cyclic reassertion of darkness.

As a result of the way in which montage brings the vital human aspects into prominence, Rock's search for Mary is put into a metaphysical perspective. Mary will never be found; the lake is too deep and impenetrable to reveal what it might hide. The essential point made by Green is that the answer Rock is seeking can be found not in the ultimate attainment of his goal – the recovery of Mary – but in the actual *process* of turning darkness into sensuous delight. Into this realm of values, Daisy, in all her unself-conscious but self-assertive sensuality, is the key. In the world of the dark woods, rational 'eyesight' is an insufficient guide, a lesson Rock has partly learnt after a long life. Rock 'reminded himself that he should not come out from the shelter of the trees, must not be seen. Daisy would be his eyes' (ibid.).

Ted, Rock's goose, serves the same structural function and points to the same values as does Daisy. In fact, along with Daisy, Rock, in his search for Mary, also makes use of Ted's instinctual powers. 'Ted, his goose, covered a deal of ground each day' (ibid.). Daisy and Ted also possess the same intuitive judgement as to who are their enemies. When Daisy suddenly

rushes forward as if to 'challenge' the rotting lake, there is also
some intimation that she has sensed another threat that she
wants to challenge, 'someone on the further bank to whom, in
her startled whiteness, she might seem his [Rock's] goose' (ibid.).
On the other bank are Baker and a representative of another
'regiment', a police sergeant come to look into the mystery of
the disappeared Mary. Green's direct association of the rotting
lake and the official suggests his alliance with life-negating forces.

On the other side of the lake, there is Ted to face the enemy
Daisy cannot reach. Rock has just caught sight of the police
sergeant. 'The blue uniform gave Mr Rock a jolt.'

> The old man's cottage stood, like the hub of a wheel, on a
> spot at which several rides met. As he watched the policeman
> he saw, out of the corner of an eye, his goose come in a rush,
> absurd sight, its neck outstretched, wings violently beating to
> help cover the ground it had never left. Sun now made the
> bird a blaze of white. (p.72)

The visual counterpoint between the policeman's 'blue uniform'
and Ted – a 'blaze of white' in the sun – heightens the dynamic
conflict of graphic directions between the policeman and Ted,
who comes in a rush to confront the enemy. A conflict of planes
deepens the opposition between the two, for 'as Ted came up
hissing, the policeman walked round his bike to put this between
the goose and himself'.

Green's attention to the position of Rock's cottage, 'like the
hub of a wheel' at the centre of a crossroads, brings associations
of the grinding of time. Into the wheel's mechanical rotation
(suggestive of the decaying lake) all the divergent 'rides' of life
eventually meet. However, Green here equates Rock's values
with the counteracting powers of Ted. Rock explains to the
policeman, 'Well, if you live on a place you take part in the day
to day affairs.' To what values Rock, or Green, is referring is
immediately made evident by a rapid shift in point of view: 'The
goose, having finished what there had been, made off, wagging
its tail.' ' "You come to feel part of it", Mr Rock corrected.
"Still missing, eh?" ' The sergeant, in his rational officialdom,
misinterprets Rock's incoherent talk. He thinks that Rock's
confession that he feels 'part of it' refers directly to Rock's own
oppressive preoccupation with the void left by the missing girl.

What Green intends to convey is the necessity of man's active commitment to life due to its precariousness. The policeman's alienation from the goose, and from Rock, is visualized in the image of the policeman's bike, which Green significantly terms a 'machine'. 'He left the machine where it lay on the ground. Mr Rock noticed, with a dreadful reluctance, that its uppermost pedal still revolved' (p.74). The revolving pedal suggests a mechanical rotation, a counterpart to the grinding 'wheel' and the decaying lake.

The preceding montage scenes enforce Green's distinction between objective world and non-rational subjective perception. The revolving pedal (with related images) does not encompass the material world and all sustaining powers and human endeavours in a tragic vision. Tone is produced in the image of contradiction, in the polarity of the cyclic and human sensibilities. 'To feel part of it' attains another significance than mere surrender to flux, to the continuum. Hence, Daisy and Ted are not portrayed as mere beasts, representing pure animalism (they have human names), but are part of a more complex sensibility which implies spiritual commitment to life. Sensuous delight is directed towards the particular and has therefore the capacity to crystallize moments amidst life's cyclic flux. Green emphasizes this point in the scene in which Rock, introducing himself as 'the swill man', identifying himself with the natural susceptibilities of his animals, enters the kitchen of the Institute early one morning. Rock sees

> a great shaft of early sunlight which, as it entered one of the windows, shone so loud already that it bisected the kitchen, to show him air on the rise in its dust, like soda-water through transparent milk. It hid the line of girls beyond, fetching their own breakfasts at the other cooker. They were no more to him than light blue shadows, and their low voices, to his deafness, just a female murmuring, a susurration of feathers. . . .
>
> The girl [Marion, who has fetched Rock a cup of tea] and the old man came together over this, in the megaphone of light. . . .
>
> 'You didn't catch sight of Mary and Merode?' (p.21)

Though the girls are no more than indistinct shadows, this picture is not a sinister one. The principle of montage implies that the girls, even if they stand in darkness, are not necessarily

- consigned to dark, destructive forces; all characters in *Concluding* exist in darkness. Again, it should be pointed out that in montage it is not the sum of elements that provides the meaning, but the 'product'. The meaning of the scene is illuminated by Coleridge's idea of montage (referred to by Eisenstein in the epigraph to *The Film Sense*): 'Give Coleridge one vivid word from an old narrative; let him mix it with two in his thought; and then (translating terms of music into terms of words) "out of three sounds he [will] frame, not a fourth sound, but a star".' What is emphasized, in other words, is the actual collision of images whereby a third meaning is produced in terms of the graphic totality of the picture. The collision of masses is so powerful, the passage so filled with sexual imagery, that it generates the impact of darkness being raped by sunlight. Like the sun in a Turner painting, Green's sun 'bisects' the darkness so that the whole 'picture' comes alive with particles of light, to reveal 'air on the rise in its dust'. In the graphic totality of the picture, then, 'female murmuring' does not function as an antagonistic force; rather, it functions, together with the 'loud' sunlight, as an audio-visual counterpoint, to intensify the sensuous impact produced by the colliding, vibrant sunlight. The girls are not individuated, because they are important not as characters in themselves, but as images which emphasize the vitality of Rock's presence.

This interpretation is supported by Green's association of the 'female murmuring' with a 'susurration of feathers', the image of birds suggesting a comic vision and freedom of flight. A transition which has the effect of a conflict of close and long shots further supports this interpretation. The dynamic intensity of the quoted passage is so high that sexual as well as audible images are needed to convey the pervasive insistence of the scene. As a result, the whole passage renders the sensory impact of a filmic close-up. As Rock and Marion 'came together' in the 'megaphone of light', there is an abrupt dispersal of sensual intimacy. Marion's mentioning of the missing girls, and the dark overtones that evokes, brings the narrative back to the intriguing topic concerning them all. In terms of montage, however, the sense of disparity produced by this transition heightens the values of the preceding scene.

The interpretation of the kitchen scene as signifying a penetration of darkness by forces allied with the sun is reinforced by the close connection of this scene with qualities characterizing Rock's animals. Outside Rock's window, on the first page of *Concluding*,

> the goose posed staring, head to one side, with a single eye, straight past the house, up into the fog bank which had made all daylight deaf beneath, and beyond which, at some clear height, Mr Rock knew now there must be a flight of birds fast winging – Ted knows where, he thought.   (p.5)

Ted pierces the thick fog with his single-eyed stare in the same way that the 'shaft' of sunlight 'bisects' the dark kitchen. Just as Rock senses a 'susurration of feathers', so Ted is in some mystic, instinctual communion with 'birds fast winging'. Ted's powerful stare penetrates the 'deafening' fog (suggestive of confinement) to the 'clear height' of 'winging' freedom above. This is an implicit suggestion of Ted's affinity with other birds that fluctuate through Green's fiction. Correspondingly, the schoolgirls, in *Concluding*, are repeatedly attributed qualities of birds. As Edge and Baker enter the refectory, the girls 'with a rustle of a thousand birds rising from willows about a warm lagoon ... stood in silence to mark the entrance'. They sit down again 'with another outburst of talk as of starlings moving between clumps of reeds to roost' (p.99). Green chooses the image of 'birds fast winging' as a metaphor for a natural vitality, and the embodiment of a comic suggestion. Reality, then, is determined by point of view, and truth depends on the subjective, perceptual state of mind. Ted's natural integrity has not been ossified by institutional mandates; he possesses an independent perceptual vitality and potentiality which have not been blurred by institutional limitations.

Ted's perceptual self-reliance becomes a pervasive model for the human world. When Miss Marchbanks momentarily recovers from her official 'farsightedness', Moira sheds the less appealing aspects of her personality.

> Extremely shortsighted, she had taken off her spectacles and put these on Miss Edge's desk as though, in the crisis, at a time when she had been left in charge, she wished to look inwards, to *draw on hid reserves*, and thus to meet the drain on her resolution which the absence of the two girls had opened

like an ulcer high under the ribs, where it fluttered, a blood stained dove with tearing claws. (Emphasis added)

Taking off her spectacles of officialdom, the girl's sensual vitality wells in on her:

> So that when Moira entered, and did not shut the door but stood leant against it, half in, half out of the room, dressed in pink overall . . . her bare legs a gold haze to Miss Marchbanks's weak eyes, her figure, as the older woman thought, a rounded mass softly merged into the exaggeration of a grown woman's, her neck and face the colour of ripening apricots from sun with strong eyes that were an alive blue, shapeless to Miss Marchbanks's dull poached eggs of vision, but a child so alive, at some trick of summer light outside, that the older woman marvelled again how it could ever be that the State should send these girls, who were really women, to be treated like children. (pp.47–8)

The sensual youthfulness of the girl, expressed in florid images of colour and light, impinges on Miss Marchbanks's senses, wants to encompass her. Her rationalism, however, pulls her away from this blooming vitality, which begins to irritate her, because competing with her instinctual self-assertion is her need to solve the more pressing problem: what has happened to Mary and Merode? When Moira refuses to answer, because the question cannot be answered, Miss Marchbanks resorts to official detachment. Moira's youth suddenly dwindles out of the range of sensuous nearness to where it can only be empirically observed through official lenses. Putting on her spectacles again, 'Miss Marchbanks no longer approved, and was even half irritated with the creature's blankness. . . . "You've a smut on your nose, child", she said' (p.50).

Green's demonstration that reality is largely determined by the projection of subjective states significantly affects his narrative technique when dealing with experiences that invigorate the deeper recesses of the mind. These scenes are often given a surreal, dreamlike quality that heightens the sense of their being the product of a subjective, symbol-making imagination. Since Green employs imagery as an emblem for consciousness, one should be cautious in seeking a direct correspondence between the meaning of the imagery and an ulterior, empirical reality. Green's portrayal of Merode in her bath is an illustrative example of his surreal technique. The girl lies

> stretched out under electric light and water, like the roots of a gross water lily which had flowered to her floating head and hands. This green transparency was so just right, so matched the temperature of the hidden blood, that she half closed her eyes in a satisfied contemplation of a chalk white body. She felt it seemed to sway as to light winds, as though she were bathing by floodlight in the night steaming lake, beech shadowed, mystically warmed ... her hair ... in this light, was dark honey coloured.   (pp.63–4)

To the literal mind, Merode's resting figure may seem at one with an element of decomposition, a sinister image with overtones of drowning or of complicity with deadly forces. A more valid interpretation is one which incorporates the images as metaphors of her subjective mind, which stem from Merode's (and Green's) 'satisfied contemplation' of her body. As elements of style, the juxtaposition of the flowering vividness of a floating water lily and the darker aspects contained under water primarily serves to enhance the mysticism of the experience, thereby heightening its deeply sensual impact. In effect, a synthesis expressing intense sensual fulfilment and harmony is produced.

The possibility that Merode, in her bath, might reflect the empirically observable movement of the world towards dissolution, and that the scene might represent an element of decomposition, is indirectly contradicted. In a later scene, Green likens 'Merode's hair in her bath' with a 'mass of bloom' which 'trumpeted the sun', 'a slope of deep golden honey with its sweet heavy scent and a great buzz of bees about' (p.95). Green associates these two compared images with life, not death. The vitality of golden flowers bathed in 'full sunlight' in the one passage has its parallel in the other, in the image of Merode's golden hair 'under electric light', or as bathed 'by floodlight in the night steaming lake'. Green's portrayal of Merode in her bath is not a statement concerning the organic unable to support life; it is a paean to organic life.

Green provides further examples that contradict suspicions

that female instincts might have been perverted into league with destructive forces.

> Moira came out of a ride into the small open space before Mr Rock's cottage. Its hideous mauve and yellow brick was swamped in shade, marked out by sunlight, for the beech trees were tall but not thick together hereabouts.
> Sun lit up blue smoke, spiralling out of the chimney for two full yards in this stillness. (p.81)

Dark shade and blue smoke serve as background in order to enhance, in a conflict of masses, the visual impact of sunlight which creates a vibrant moment of stillness. Into this picture, Moira enters, seemingly uniting herself with the life-giving sun. Moira is coming to see Mr Rock, who is chopping wood. ' "Why don't you use the tree Mr Birt found Merode under?", she asked. "Not dead enough", he said ... while he examined her youth.' Rock's remark is significant in so far as it offers a striking counterpoint to her youthful vitality. His remark naturally leads up to and sheds light on the meaning of the following passage – a love scene at the fallen beech under which Merode is found.

> A great beech had fallen a night or two earlier, in full leaf, lay now with its green leaves turned to pale gold, as though by the sea. It had brought more vast limbs down along with it, so, in the bright morning, at the thickest of the wood, colourless sky was suddenly opened to Elizabeth and Sebastian above a cliff of green. The wreckage beneath standing beeches was lit at this place by a glare of sunlight concerted on flat, dying leaves which hung on to life by what was broken off, the small branches joining those larger that met the arms, which in their turn grew from the fallen column of the beech, all now an expiring gold of faded green. A world through which the young man and his girl had been meandering, in dreaming shade through which sticks of sunlight slanted to spill upon the ground, had at this point been struck to a blaze, and where their way had been dim, on a sea bed past grave trunks, was now this dying, brilliant mass which lay exposed, a hidden world of spiders working on its gold, the webs these made a field of wheels and spokes of wet silver. The sudden sunlight on Elizabeth and Sebastian as, arms about one

another's waists, they halted to wonder and surmise, was a
load, a great cloak to clothe them, like a depth of warm water
that turned the man's brown city outfit to a drowned man's
clothes, the sun was so heavy, so encompassing betimes.
    'It will be hot', she said, as though stroking him.
    'I love you', he said. She pretended to ignore it.
    'I wonder what brought her down', she said. She might,
from the tone, have had in mind a middle aged woman he'd
seduced.
    'Oh Liz, I do love you, and love you', he replied. . . .
    [She] turned with a smile which was for him alone to let
him take her, and helped his heart find hers by fastening her
mouth on his as though she were an octopus that had lost its
arms to the propellers of a tug, and had only its mouth now
with which, in a world of the hunted, to hang onto wrecked
spars.
    'Darling', she said in a satisfied voice, coming up to
breathe.   (pp.54–6)

This is not a sinister picture of organic nature succumbing to
dissolution in a mystical sea world. It is precisely the bizarre
quality of the image world which suggests Green's concern with
creating an imaginary, aesthetic form. This implies that, although
form can scarcely be a self-sufficient artifact, Green's emphasis
extends beyond a narrow correspondence with the objectively
observable cyclic world. The nature of the images must be
examined in terms of their correspondence to the artistic form,
rather than in terms of their inherent, denotative meanings.
    Intimations of death fill the first part of the passage. The
fallen beech with fading leaves is personified with 'vast limbs'
and 'arms' 'which hung on to life by what was broken off'.
Mysticism and magic pervade this world, distinguishing the
account from realistic representation. It is a world transformed
in the subjective renditions of the wanderers. This impression is
strongly suggested by the occurrence of a conflict of masses, a
montage conflict providing a highly important clue to a full
understanding of the scene. It provides a separation between a
mood of darkness and decay, an imaginary world through which
'the young man and his girl had been meandering, in *dreaming
shade*', and a 'blaze' of sunlight which suddenly makes them halt
to 'wonder and surmise' among golden 'wheels and spokes of

wet silver' (emphasis added). Shining wheels of reflected sunlight
have previously been identified as the visualization of a life-
giving instant moment separated from the onward cyclic rotation
of the external world. Thus, the conflict of masses most
significantly creates a conflict between 'then' and 'now'.

In providing a framework of correspondence, or synthesis,
between 'then' and 'now', Green suggests a romantic vision
which reintegrates the alienated observer with life, physically as
well as spiritually. Through sensuous contemplation of the
particular, Green transcends naturalistic pessimism by the recognition that

> No waste so vacant, but may well employ
> Each faculty of sense, and keep the heart
> Awake to Love and Beauty![9]

These lines from Coleridge's 'This Lime-Tree Bower my Prison'
may well be said to communicate the same essential sensibility
as does Green's passage. Coleridge's juxtaposition of darkness
and light produces a perceptual polarity between objectivity
and subjectivity. The synthesis of opposing worlds provides a
framework of counterpoint in which the underlying sordidness
of the dell brings into relief the import of love and beauty. The
first part of the poem, like the passage from *Concluding*, conveys
the darkened solipsistic mood of the author who sits brooding
in his bower. Imaginatively accompanying his friends who are
walking in the hills, he imposes his dejection onto the scenery
through which he imagines they wander:

> The roaring dell, o'erwooded, narrow, deep,
> And only speckled by the mid-day sun;
> Where its slim trunk the ash from rock to rock
> Flings arching like a bridge; – that branchless ash,
> Unsunn'd and damp, whose few poor yellow leaves
> Ne'er tremble in the gale, yet tremble still.

As in the world of 'dreaming shade' through which Liz and
Sebastian have been wandering, the scenery which Coleridge
here envisages is filled with a surreal, dreamlike quality. However,
as he imagines his friends emerging from the 'dark green file of
long lank weeds', there 'all at once' appears to him 'a most

fantastic sight'. By a transition which renders the sensory impact
of a conflict between close and long shots, the poem emerges
from the more distant dream world of the author's drifting mind
to a confrontation with the concrete, visual instant present. The
transition also involves a conflict of masses and of scales.

> *Now*, my friends emerge
> Beneath the wide, wide Heaven – and view again
> The many-steepled tract magnificent
> Of hilly fields and meadows, and the sea.
>   (Emphasis added)

This panoramic experience is remarkably similar to the way in
which 'at the thickest of the wood', 'on a sea bed past grave
trunks', 'colourless sky was suddenly opened to Elizabeth and
Sebastian above a cliff of green'. To both Coleridge and Green
the contemplation of the particular is unifying.

> Silent with *swimming* sense; yea, gazing round
> On the wide landscape, gaze till all doth seem
> Less gross than bodily; and of such hues
> As veil the Almighty Spirit.
>   (Emphasis added)

Similarly, as Liz and Sebastian halt to 'wonder and surmise',
they are 'clothed' by a 'cloak' of 'sudden sunlight', a unifying,
life-giving image, made the more so because the cloak of sunlight
is like a 'depth of warm water' which blurs the outlines of
Sebastian's 'brown city outfit' into unity with the world of
perception. Green expresses the same longing as does Coleridge –
that of someone having 'hunger'd after Nature, many a year, /
In the great City pent'.

  The idea underlying Coleridge's montage technique, a vision
analogous to Green's, is finally formulated in his contemplation
of an old walnut-tree bathed in sunlight:

> a deep radiance lay
> Full on the ancient ivy, which usurps
> Those fronting elms, and now, with blackest mass
> Makes their dark branches gleam a lighter hue.

Juxtaposition of light and darkness is not meant as a mere contrast between the positive and the negative, but should, in terms of montage conflict, produce a synthesis in which the dark intensifies the values of light in spatial collision. With regard to the vision of *Concluding*, the extension of this idea would be that one must recognize the presence of darkness in order to strongly perceive the vital aspects of nature, or of life. This process is clarified by Green's previously cited statement in *Pack my Bag*: that 'there must be a threat to one's skin' to awaken vital images, and that these we should 'take with us like a bar of gold'. It is thus with a strong awareness of decay that Sebastian, towards the end of Green's passage, urged by Liz's concern with the fallen beech, exclaims, 'Oh Liz, I do love you, and love you.' This vital connection of 'darkness' and 'light' is not made through senseless immersion into flux, but by commitment to the sacred, vibrant moment, when

> *now* the bat
> *Wheels* silent by, and not a swallow twitters,
> Yet still the solitary humble-bee
> Sings in the bean-flower!

> (Emphasis added)

The images used here by Coleridge are all recurrent in Green's most poetic passages. They signify momentary transcendence of darkness; the sensuous appreciation of Love and Beauty.

Throughout *Concluding*, scenes which depict love and beauty incorporate darker aspects of reality in order to heighten dynamic tension, thus intensifying the reader's participation in a scene. Commitment to nature, then, implies commitment to both the positive and negative aspects of it, for it is only in the private imagination that disparate sense impressions may form a montage or synthesis of a higher order. In the extension of this attitude there are suggestions that surrender to the particular must take place to the exclusion of disturbing impressions from the world at large. It is on this level that the power of the will becomes a necessary instrument by which to defend human integrity. With this aim, Rock has retired from his life as a scientist and now refuses to open mail, especially 'official' mail. His attitude links him to some extent with the Eameses in *Living*, who are unwilling to allow intrigue to quench the growth of their

garden. Their selective self-sufficiency is bound up with fears of
disintegration. Green, however, allows his characters these fears
(from which most of them suffer) if only they do not quench
their humanness which is of vital importance since 'the sequence
here is light then darkness', and the 'glare of morning' is 'to be
lost at last, when the usual cloud drifts over the full moon'
(*Concluding*, p.109). Perhaps the girls in *Concluding* are the only
ones who do not let Mary's disappearance seriously disturb
them. If her disappearance is viewed as an integral part of
Concluding's sequential structure, the girls' disaffectedness is not
meant to reveal inhumane negligence of a fellow human being.
Rather, the girls' attitudes are intended to highlight how their
youthfulness preserves its vitality in face of an inexplicable dark
void.

The impression that Green is seriously concerned with the
necessity of excluding oppressive forces from the mind is strengthened by two parallel scenes. In the first, the two lovers are
seen obliviously asleep in one another's arms:

> Meantime the lovers, Sebastian and Elizabeth, were asleep
> in that same corner of a fallen beech found by Merode, and to
> which they had returned. They lay under lace of gold, through
> the hush of an afternoon's fine heat, at rest in one another's
> added warmth, in a peace of sleep.... Then she sat straight
> with a jerk.
>
> He lay on his back, wore a sulky expression.
>
> 'Good heavens', she went on, 'Here we've been snoring,
> isn't it awful, and all the while that poor girl's lord knows
> where, dear. What d'you think? Isn't it awful?'
>
> He gently said, 'Don't fuss.'   (p.110)

A 'hush' of warm, sunlit stillness unites the two lovers in a
blissful intimacy enhanced by the presence of the 'fallen beech'.
The abrupt way in which this intimacy is shattered by the
disturbing element of Mary's disappearance produces the sensory
impact of a sudden filmic close-up. The effect is partly to awaken
a sense of guilt in Liz; but much more significantly, the dark
undertones enhance the intense beauty of Liz's and Birt's
oblivious sleep, suggesting the vital importance of 'Living' in face
of existential uncertainty.

This scene sheds light on the meaning of the one, involving

Miss Edge, parallel to and immediately preceding Green's portrayal of the oblivious lovers. That Green is seriously concerned with the necessity that life must go on in the midst of an encompassing uncertainty is suggested by the emphasis he gives to these scenes. Like Liz and Sebastian, Edge has been drifting into sleep in the warm afternoon, but is awakened at the noise of the buzzers. 'Then she sat up straight. How could she have dropped off, she asked herself, with Mary missing yet?' Despite the fear and uncertainty which has gripped her, she is nevertheless determined to carry out her plans of arranging an evening dance; 'the coming entertainment', she rationalizes, 'could not be cancelled at the whim of a single student' (p.110). James Hall takes Green's attitude towards Edge's undauntedness to be favourable because, he says,

> though Miss Edge's determination to keep organized fun going is grimly comic, it also comes through as real. Better grim fun in the face of the disturbing than not carrying on at all – and her determination to go on with the dance even when she has near-hallucinations about Mary's body concealed in the floral decorations is one of Green's memorable scenes.[10]

The arrangement of the evening dance represents the climax of *Concluding*. It brings to a peak the various levels of conflict in the novel – that between organization and the individual, between the individual and metaphysical uncertainty, and most essentially, between life and death. On a symbolic level, the centrifugal dance might be seen as the culminating motion into darkness, a collective feast of drowning, since it is replete with autumn, sea and water images. True, life and death are in a constant competitive relation throughout the dance, a fact which is of course reflected in Green's use of imagery. However, images in *Concluding* may produce different meanings, and tone, depending on the context in which they occur. This is very much the case in Green's depiction of the dance.

The following passage demonstrates the manner in which montage calls attention to thematic conflicts which alter the function of the autumn and water images.

> The music was a torrent, to spread out, to be lost in the great space of this mansion, to die when it reached the staff

room to a double beat, the water wheel turned by a rustling rush of leaf thick water. It was so dispersed and Winstanley, seated alongside Sebastian, could, for the conversation of her fellow teachers, hear no breath, neither the whispering in the joists from a distant slither of three hundred pairs of shoes, nor the cold hum of violins in sharp, moonstruck window glass. She did not know until Sebastian, who could not tell why, other than that he was restless, got up to open a door, when at once she realized the house had come to *life*.

(p.199, emphasis added)

The music, streaming through the 'great space' of the mansion, in this context clearly suggestive of a great metaphysical void, dies 'to a double beat' in a conflict of graphic directions as it collides with the walls of the staff room. It is as a comment on this lethal collision that Green includes the deadly image of the rotating water wheel which carries away dying leaves. The meaning becomes quite clear in an audio-visual counterpoint (Sebastian opens a door so that the distant music suddenly becomes insistent) which thus signals another montage conflict, of planes, between the staff room in the Institution and the music and dancing outside which are identified with 'life'.

Green's inclusion of bird imagery, and its relation to Rock's goose, Ted, contradicts a narrow interpretation of the dance as a contribution to death. The bird imagery is used as metaphor to reflect individual feelings. Green thereby stresses his vital distinction between subjective experience of the dance and an objective cyclic world represented by the rotating water wheel. To the women who rise and 'make haste' to the dance, the music 'called as air, beaten through stretched feathers, might have spoken to the old man's goose, that long migratory flight unseen' (ibid.). The appeal of the music correlates with that of 'birds fast winging', with which Ted communes through the thick fog. Green's association contains a comic suggestion of freedom and flight, not the confinement of death.

It seems then, that Green, on one level, views all that the Institution stands for, embodied by the staff as a group, as alienated from, even opposed to, life, as represented by the violins. The very *arrangement* of the dance, when viewed on the level of individual freedom in relation to institutionalization, is certainly treated as something negative. 'They must and shall enjoy themselves', says Edge, and she 'will not be bothered tonight with individuals' (p.213). When Green, at times, adopts the encompassing view of a detached observer, Edge's idea of organizing the human spirit in the celebration of the Founder's Day is charged with grim irony. At the opening of the dance, the lonely figures of Miss Edge and Miss Baker, 'oblivious, inside their long black dresses ... lovingly swayed in one another's bony grip, on the room's *exact centre* ... at spinsterish rest in movement, barely violable, *alone*' (p.195, emphasis added). Around the two spinsters circle 'one hundred and fifty pairs in white' in a 'soft ritual'. The organized pattern becomes a mechanically revolving universe with an *exact* number of turning pairs and with two spinsters isolated by their blackness at its axis.

Green's suggestion that the mechanical patterns of organization are life-denying and leave the individual alienated in an empty universe is emphasized by a cinematic technique of gradually widening long shots. Starting from the 'exact centre' of the dance floor, Green switches his focus to the lonely figure of Merode, who is being kept in custody after her night walk. 'Above, locked safe into a sick bay, curtains close drawn against the moon, Merode's infant breathing told she was asleep. Still farther off, in their retiring room, unaware that the dance had opened, the staff sat to make scant conversation.' In this remote room, Sebastian Birt is being isolated by the others who, 'out of sympathy, perhaps, for the lovesick Winstanley, had chosen to pretend, by ignoring him, that Birt, who seemed most ill at ease, was not present in fat flesh amongst them'. The whole mansion has an atmosphere of alienated isolation. 'All over the Institute hardly a word more was now spoken.... Then, suddenly at a doorway, there loomed unheralded the figures of Elizabeth and the old man. Both were dressed as black as those two Principals' (ibid.). The fact that Rock and Liz are dressed in black does not have any obvious thematic significance. Their blackness does not set them off from the two Principals; in fact, Green stresses that the two newcomers are 'as black as' they. Moreover, there is in this scene no major opposition between Rock and the girls in white, for, although he has on a black suit, 'His great white head nodded to rapt, dancing students' (p.196). Only if viewed in terms of montage does Green's cinematic technique in the preceding scene become clarified. Focusing first on the two lonely spinsters turning on the dance floor's 'exact centre', Green gradually widens the scope of the camera to reveal the sordid state of affairs in various corners of the Institute building: alienated, subdued human beings in increasing distance from the centre. On this note, Green suddenly presents a close-up of two black, 'looming' figures. The function of the sudden close-up is to create a sense of incongruity in the mind of the reader and thereby accentuate the sombre atmosphere of isolation which hovers about the mechanically rotating dance room. In this way, Edge's insistence on pattern is brought into a deeply ironic perspective.

In focusing on the theme of alienation and loneliness, Green's cinematic technique in the preceding scene strongly suggests the essential values and contrary forces with which the dance in all its aspects is concerned. It has been argued that Edge's manner of fitting dancing girls into an organized pattern is treated ironically by Green. It is also possible to show that on a different level – in the relation between individuals and a metaphysical void – the actual dancing, as experienced by the students, represents a communal vitality and ritual. Audio-visual counterpoints illuminate different aspects of *Concluding*'s central values. In the following passage, some students are involved in a disturbing dispute concerning Rock's old age, how his death will most probably mean the death of what he stands for, and how Edge and Liz are to be blamed for the threat they pose to everyone. 'Honestly I've got now so that I loathe my own cloth, I hate all women', one of them exclaims. Another calls Liz a 'viper'.

'You're all of you crazy', Moira said.

At this precise moment, and out of sight of these girls, Miss Inglefield, without warning, started the gramophone just once more to see if it would work. The loud speaker was full on so they could even hear the conductor, dead these many years, tap his stick at a desk some thirty summers back, and the music, with a roll of drums, swayed, swelled into a waltz. The girls, each one, gave a small sigh, moved, *as one*, each to her long promised partner, took her by the hand; they held hands as women but in couples, what had been formless became a group, by music, merged to a line of white in pairs, white faces, to the flowers and lighted ballroom, each pair of *lips*

open to the spiralling dance. Then it stopped sharp into silence. . . .
At once these students broke away disappointed, years younger
once again.
'False alarm', someone commented severely.

(pp.186–7, emphasis added)

The way in which the crash of music abruptly interrupts the
girls' intriguing conversation indicates that the music represents
conflicting values intended to disrupt the girls' animosity and
preoccupation with disintegration. Formlessness dissolves by the
patterned forms of the music, accordingly instilling a collective
pattern. The dancing pairs of girls do not thus testify to the
triumph of a superimposed, crippling institutional structure. The
scene expresses deep longings in the girls, a need for affection
and togetherness. Nor does the dancing become just a senseless
rotation towards death; it counteracts death; it is not a disintegrating experience, but an expanding one; the music 'swells' into a
motion of girls who sensuously open their lips to the spiralling
sensation. Such sensations are prohibited by the protocol of
the Institute. The disruption of the music leaves the girls
'disappointed, years younger once again'. This comment refers
to the Institute's denial of the girls' feminine maturity. When
Miss Marchbanks recognizes Moira's fecundity without her
'official' lenses, she 'marvelled again how it could ever be that
the State should send these girls, who were really women, to be
treated like children' (p.48).

Green emphasizes the meaning and significance of the music
and the dancing by also letting it be experienced from outside
in the dark.

A single pigeon, black in thickening sky, flew swift and on
past the Park.

It was dusk.

Light from wide open windows increased by strides, prim-
rose yellow over a dark that bled from blue.

With a swoop an owl came down across and hooted while
Mr Rock and his granddaughter crept up the last stone flight
when, unheralded, unannounced, and they could not see inside
for the windows were yet too high above their heads, the
gramophone crashed out once more, so loud now the old man

halted entranced by the first bars of another great valse of drums and strings. (p.187)

The solitary pigeon in darkening sky seems to function as a metaphor that mirrors the moods of Rock and his granddaughter. This image is made all the more sinister by a 'dark that bled from blue' and by the image of two dark figures 'creeping', as if they were reptiles, up the stone steps. There is a significant difference in function between the hooting of the owl and the sudden crashing out of the gramophone. The former serves as an audio-visual counterpoint to heighten the sinister atmosphere of lurking dark forces, as well as to increase the dynamic tension in the conflict of masses produced by the opposing light streaming from the window. The latter audio-visual counterpoint, on the other hand, is so forceful that it 'entrances' Mr Rock and halts the encroachment of dark forces. Green makes this a significant point, because, when the music is suddenly cut off, Rock immediately regresses to an implacable 'attack on Edge for not keeping the instrument in proper order'. Then again, however,

> he was silenced, made mute, because through his deafness, he had caught the last echoes of this music sent back by the beeches, where each starling's agate eye lay folded safe beneath a wing.
>   'We've started well', he then contented himself by suggesting. (ibid.)

These montage conflicts are clearly a technique by which Green communicates human values to the reader. They function as an urgent appeal to Rock, as well as to the reader, consciously to turn darkness into light, animosity into life-giving feelings of sympathy.

Inside, in the light, the eyes of the dancing girls are like precious gems as the girls swirl out of their solitude into one another's embrace.

> Quite soon, girls began to cut in. While Inglefield kept the instrument hard at it, the original partners began to break up, to step back over the wax mirror floor out of one another's arms, moving sideways by such as would not be parted yet, each to tap a second favourite on a bare, quiet shoulder. Then

the girl so chosen would give a little start, open those great shut eyes, much greater than jewels, as she circled and, circling yet, would dip into these fresh limbs which moved already in the dance, disengaging thus to leave her first choice to slip sideways in turn past established, whirling partners until she found another *who was loved and yet alone*.

(p.198, emphasis added)

The swirling dance absorbs the girls into a community of good feeling and intimacy. As the music starts working on their senses, the original partners, who have been revolving in orderly formation around the room's 'exact centre', break up. The mechanical rotation of ordained repetition is dispersed; so is flux. New affections are nourished in expanding circles over the dazzled floor; the movements are steered not by programmed dancing-routines, but by the beating of human emotion. Only the two Principals revolve unaffected at the geometrical centre of events. 'One after the other they would be tapped on a hard, black garmented back. But, as was traditional on these occasions, they lingered in one another's orbit, until at last Edge had had enough' (ibid.). The authority of the two spinsters is not strong enough to restrain the natural rhythm of human emotion. In oblivious intimacy, Liz is seen to

give herself over, dance as one with Sebastian, deep in his arms. They moved as though their limbs had mutual, secret knowledge, were long acquainted cheek to cheek; the front of their thighs kissed through clothes; an unconscious couple which fired burning arrows through gasping music at her. (p.201)

The dancing may, of course, be an anaesthesia, as Miss March-banks suggests: 'People plunging into the hurly-burly to forget their miserable condition, their worries' (ibid.). Yet on the other hand, the dancing comes through as something deeply valuable. In its centrifugal dynamism, it elicits basic sides of human nature that give room for hope. Most important, dancing is movement away from spiritual death. Mrs Blain, the cook, 'pushed that spiralling orderly away at arm's length until, she felt, the girl revolved about her like a wisp of kitchen paper.

"Lost?" she yelled', referring to the missing Mary, 'but it was drowned by music' (p.197).

As exemplified by this last passage, imagery of water and of drowning are used by Green not necessarily to render an atmosphere of dying, but, on the contrary, in order to provide a strong contrast which intensifies the meaningfulness of 'living', of dancing. Thus, in response to her own exclamation, 'Lost?', the cook 'folded the child to an enormous bosom. Upon which both gave their two selves over, entire. As they saw themselves from shut eyes, they endlessly danced on, like horns of paper, across warm, rustling fields of autumn fallen leaves' (p.198). The dance of the two women is not a death dance, not a destructive self-immersion into a dying vegetative world. Their dance is a surrender to 'warm', 'rustling', benevolent human feelings which carry them above and across an external world of decay.

Once it becomes clear that the theme of metaphysical loneliness versus life-giving exchange of love and sympathy is one of *Concluding*'s major themes, one also notices how autumnal imagery is recurrently used not simply to describe empirical reality, but in order to bring human values into relief. Thus, when Rock, offended after a strange encounter with a group of girls in an underground room, suddenly decides to leave the dance and thrusts past 'a white bunch of children', they 'fell open to let him through like a huge dropped flower losing petals on a path'. When in a commanding voice he makes Liz and Sebastian follow, the dancing children again 'parted as another vast bloom might that, torn by a wind in summer, lies collectedly dying on crushed fallen leaves' (pp.230–1). A sudden shift to a succinct statement (which gains emphasized meaning by the omission of the definite article modifying the noun, a rarity in *Concluding*) explains why these deadly images occur: 'The three left music.' The images are meant not as a contribution to a dominant mood in *Concluding*, but as a value comment on Rock's determination to leave the music. It suggests something precious and 'living' destroyed by a callously proceeding force. The precise tone is revealed by an audio-visual counterpoint, so powerful that it functions as a conflict of graphic directions. When Rock 'shamble[s] off uglily' towards the dancers in order to command the two lovers to leave with him, precious flowers falling apart in his wake, 'then the thunderous, swinging room

met him smack in his thick lenses' (p.230). Mental 'farsightedness', failure, due to thick lenses, to see what is valuable and
alive, is a recurrent motif in *Concluding*, and accounts for the
ironic tone of this passage.

Since montage only creates tone in relation to specific scenes,
Green does not imply that Rock's decision to leave the dance
reveals basic traits in his personality. Throughout most of the
novel, Rock is presented as a vital force. In fact, when he sits
overlooking the dazzling dance floor, he thinks it is a 'grand
sight' (p.200). It is after Rock's integrity has been seriously
challenged by experiences in an underground room that he
denies his generally affirmative attitude to life. The preceding
montage conflict between the dance music and Rock's negation
of it significantly extends tone back to Green's portrayal of
Rock's reactions in the cellar.

The cellar into which Rock is enticed by Moira is the secret
meeting-place for girls who rebel against the conformity of
Institute life. Entrance into the dark cellar signifies descent into
a void of 'blinding silence'. This is where Green makes Moira take
Rock in order 'to leave him alone' (p.204). ' "What foolishness is
this?" he pettishly demanded aloud of his solitude.' Still, old
Rock, despite his misgivings, has confidence in the dark; he
ventures into it because he lets himself be led by instinctual
impulses rather than by reason or eyesight; 'this was like the
pretty child that led the blind', he thinks on his way down.
When Moira startles him by letting her 'soft lips' brush 'his
that were dry as old bone' (ibid.), Rock is not really shocked; it
is what he has subconsciously wanted, perhaps even expected.
He even agrees to entering the cellar a second time. So, when
Melissa 'laid a cheek against him, then rolled it over until her
lips brushed his', Rock steps back, but having half wanted, half
expected it to happen, 'not so far that he got whitewash on his
clothes this time' (pp.224–5). In fact, while down in the cellar,
'he began to have a gross feeling of immoderate amusement,
such as had not come his way in years' (p.226).

Rock's real motive for entering the cellar with the young girls
is suggested earlier in the novel, in the scene where Rock is
chopping wood, and Moira comes and invites him to the dance.
'Because, if you did, I might even give you a kiss', she teases.

The chopping stopped. But he did not look up.

'There's an absurd idea', he said loudly. 'If you want to
know I've completely forgotten about it.'
  'I mean what I promise', she insisted.
  'All I intended to convey', he said, frightened and embar-
rassed, 'was, thank God, I've reached an age when I've long
since forgotten everything to do with all such nonsense. Now
do you understand?'
  'No', she answered.
  'Then why not?'
  'Because I bet you haven't really', she said. He went on
with his work rather fast.   (pp.85–6)

Moira is right. Rock retains his juices of youth. The girls do
not offend him with their tantalizing sensualism. He must
consequently have other reasons for escaping from the cellar.
  It is not until Moira mentions Liz's and Sebastian's engage-
ment that Rock is offended and leaves. Rock's jealousy of Seb,
mixed with insecurity and dread for the future if Liz is to share
her devotion for himself with someone else, is what upsets him:
to his mind, 'she could not have them both' (p.174). Despite his
basically affirmative response to life, Rock is also in need of
permanence. In his self-pity, he unjustly evokes his granddaughter's feeling of guilt and becomes a restraining force against her
happiness. Green here links Rock with Craigan in *Living*, who for
similar reasons restrains Lily's search for fulfilment. Furthermore, Green's acknowledgement of the vitalness of Liz's and
Sebastian's love, from Liz's point of view, indicates criticism
of Rock's negative response in the cellar. Sebastian is a
contradictory, elusive character. His flaws obviously correlate
with his official position as a representative of state rationalism,
virtues against which Rock rebels. Green repeatedly points out
that Sebastian's officialdom competes with his real, natural
self. However, it is also hinted that Rock's anti-statism and
possessiveness of Liz blind him to Sebastian's worth. Sebastian's
care for Liz is revealed in small gestures: ' "Don't you fuss, my
dear", Mr Birt said in his natural voice, which Winstanley heard
so seldom that she was not sure to recognize it' (p.97). There
are suggestions that only Liz knows the 'natural' Sebastian: 'But
he's true, Gapa, you must believe. Because, naturally, I realize
you don't like him. But I do know what you don't, that you will
in time, you'll come round, there's no one in the world who

wouldn't, once they'd seen the real person underneath the skin'
(p.176). Green (for example in the love scene at the fallen beech)
does reveal Sebastian's poetic capacity to 'wonder and surmise'.
Rock's jealous distrust of him is countered by Sebastian's own
sense of attachment to Rock, by 'the chance which bound
him to these two strange people by the love he had for the
granddaughter, the love, he thought, of his life' (p.38). In
accordance with the comic elements in *Concluding*'s design, Green
seems to give Sebastian the benefit of the doubt. Green's reminder
that 'all's well that ends well' essentially refers to man's capacity
to perceive the positive in the negative.[11]

Green, then, is basically optimistic with regard to humanly
sustaining powers. The girls certainly cause much intrigue; they
may be petulant and inconsiderate, even malicious at times, but
they are not basically corrupt or destructive. The negative sides
of the various characters do not alter the value pattern which is
discernible in *Concluding*, nor the tone concerning Rock's
behaviour in the cellar. Green, by means of montage, draws
attention to those aspects of his narrative which he wants
emphasized. It is in accordance with this technique that the
scene in the cellar does not portray a confrontation with insidious
forces, but functions rather as a test of Rock's ability to face
existential darkness, and to turn it into something 'living'.

It is significant that when Rock, together with his granddaughter, first arrives outside the mansion before entering the dance,
he approaches 'sure of himself, from the dark' (p.190). 'Never
try to duck when you're in the open', he advises Liz and Sebastian
(ibid.). When nearing the sunset scene earlier that evening, he
had also given this advice: '"Don't be afraid of life, Liz", he
said. "Everything settles itself in the end. I've lived long enough
to know that"' (p.176). Thus, when first arriving at the mansion,
Rock is prepared to courageously confront the darkness surrounding the house; he is ready 'to enter and be lost, as if by magic,
in a cube of impenetrable shade', and in order to gain access to
the dance, to recover 'his dead hand' from the dark 'to stab the
bell' (p.190). Significantly, Rock, at that moment, is still under
the encouraging influence of '*music* sent back by the beeches,
where each starling's agate eye lay folded safe beneath a wing'
(p.187, emphasis added). On leaving the music to go home,
however, he is unresponsive to its message. As he faces 'the pitch
black between trees at night, which they were yet to meet in the

ride leading to their cottage', he turns round 'to view the hated mansion', and exclaims the name, 'Petra' (pp.244–5). The word, which means 'rock', brings associations of hardness or tenacity, but it also suggests, in light of its biblical connotations, denial (allusion to Simon Peter's denial of Christ). Certainly, a strong individual integrity, as exhibited by Rock throughout most of the novel, is essential in order to fight the crippling influence of conformity. Green, however, stresses that resistance against conformity must not quench sympathy and tolerance for other individuals. The reason for this is that the preservation of individual integrity in a metaphysical perspective implies fighting against spiritual death. Life depends on positive response to good feelings as expressed in the dance. This seems to be the message to be drawn from Rock's last meeting with Edge before finally leaving the house. For a moment, he finds that 'he no longer seemed to hate the woman' (p.235). However, mutual misunderstanding intervenes, and Rock leaves the mansion as defiant as ever.

By means of a series of montage conflicts, Green brings central values into relief and reveals Rock's irreconcilable mood during his nocturnal walk through the woods to be life-negating. Rock

> cautiously lifted boots one after the other in an attempt to avoid cold lit veins of quartz in flagstones underfoot because these appeared to him like sunlight that catches in sharp glass beneath an incoming tide, where the ocean foams ringing an Atlantic.
>
> So much so, that when he came to the first flight of stone steps Mr Rock turned completely round and went down backwards.
>
> Upon which a faint cry came from those beechwoods he had been facing.... 'Mar ... eee', the gabled front returned.
>
> He was halted by it between two steps.   (p.245)

Throughout *Concluding*, the girls' eyes are recurrently referred to as jewels. They contain the brilliance and vitality to which the individual must respond if he wants to create something which is alive. The same motif recurs in Green's description of Rock's walk through the dark woods, where he treads over ground covered with brilliant quartz. The function of this image may be accounted for by reference to 'Ariel's Song' in *The Tempest*:

Full fadom five thy father lies;
Of his bones are coral made;
Those are pearls that were his eyes:
Nothing of him that doth fade,
But doth suffer a sea-change
Into something rich and strange.

These lines reflect the spirit of *Concluding*. Shakespeare presents a grand vision of poetic order in nature. It requires only a transformation of perception to recognize precious 'coral' and 'pearls' in a world of cyclic flux. The sea is seen to be not merely at the service of disorder; it is an aspect of a natural force that is both threatening and beneficent. Through a dialectical process of the imagination, the sea regenerates the world 'into something rich and strange'. Man's capacity for wonder turns reality into something magic and precious. Similarly, in Green's passage, jewels are hidden 'where the ocean foams ringing an Atlantic'. Failure to enchant their raw potentiality implies the binding of the human spirit to solid rock and flux.

In the scene from *Concluding*, Rock attempts to 'avoid' the jewels under his feet, jewels which, to his darkened mind, appear 'cold' and dangerous. When at last he turns his back on them, fearing them, he is suddenly interrupted by the cry for Mary. The cry, with its associations of a dark void into which Mary has been lost, serves as an audio-visual counterpoint to accentuate the irony of Rock's attitude. Explication of this passage in terms of Shakespeare's vision in 'Ariel's Song' is made even more relevant when it is viewed in relation to its juxtaposed passage. Green provides a contrary glimpse of the vitality Liz experiences along the same path: 'she walked as someone will who, in a dream, can find herself on frozen wastes where the frost is bright then black, but will still keep warm with the warmth of bed, although that imagined world outside stayed cold, dead cold' (p.245).

The cry comes three times, increasingly louder and more insistent, suggesting the threefold denial of 'life' by Simon Peter, the 'rock'. When these have no profound effect on him, Green leads him on to a confrontation with two of his three animals in the dark forest. Rock's life-denying alienation makes him dependent on his torch in order to find his way, for even if 'every

twenty yards or so there was a separate marsh of moonlight . . .
the way looked lonely to him'.

> When he had the thing on, he shone around him. Immedi-
> ately there came a string of startled grunts. He shuddered,
> then waved the small megaphone of light here and there
> through a black shadow of trees till he lit on his pig. Daisy
> was caught looking full in their direction, until she turned,
> began to make off, squealing.   (p.251)

The conflict of masses is intensified by Daisy's squealing, which
creates an audio-visual counterpoint and is a direct negative
reaction to Rock's ironic attempt to illuminate the darkness.
Rock increases Daisy's uneasiness so that when 'he gradually
turned his wrist to bring his dunce's cap of moonlight on all of
Daisy, she grunted crescendo. . . . Till he saw a slipper in white
satin had been tied round her white neck.' Significantly, when
Rock switches off his light again, Daisy is quiet. The slipper may
be plural in significance. It reinforces the magic atmosphere of
Shakespeare's fairy-haunted woods. The fact that the pig carries
a satin slipper may signify its alliance with the fairies who play
tricks on mortals, perhaps as a warning to Rock. It also heightens
the sense of a menacing forest, and serves as a metaphor of
Rock's fears. The slipper, which may be Mary's, serves the same
purpose as the recurrent calls in the woods: it functions as if it
were an exclamation, 'Lost!' In this way, the image of the slipper
deepens the irony of Rock's persistent attempt to illuminate
darkness to provide eyesight. In contrast, Daisy relies on her
intuitive senses.

It is, of course, natural to raise the question of who is
responsible for tying the slipper round the pig's neck. Both Liz
and Rock think that it has been done by schoolgirls who prowl
the forest at night playing all sorts of mean tricks on them.
However, there is no sign of the girls anywhere. Not even in his
next traumatic encounter, this time with his goose, does Rock
find an answer. 'He listened, intent for giggles. He heard no hint
of such' (p.252). At the end of the novel, Rock concludes about
his experiences that night: 'We shall never know the truth'
(p.253). This statement seems to cover all the mystic experiences
in *Concluding*; they are not meant to be explained. Rock's

encounters with his animals in the forest must rather be seen as part of a montage structure intended to convey tone.

Hence when Rock, still 'oppressed by the dark', fearing the worst, enters

> the second pool of moonlight which was let through by a break in trees, and Daisy skirted this, keeping to black shade, Mr Rock heard Ted, his goose, burst into sharp cries of alarm not sixty yards in front. He halted dead.

Rock's anxious resort to light is checked by his terror at Ted's screaming, which marks his position with symbolic irony. The tone is deepened through an ensuing conflict of graphic directions.

> Next there was a rush out there towards him, a rising string of honks like an old fashioned bicycle, and the goose, which had never flown before, came noisily by at speed six foot off the ground, while Daisy grunted. The granddaughter stepped to one side. But the old man knelt, trembling.
> He feared a collision.
> Then Ted was gone.   (p.252)

'She came straight for my spectacles', Rock cries. Rational bias, through spectacles, is in direct opposition to instinctual self-assertion as represented by Ted. The image of spectacles (a recurrent motif stressed by Green) points back to Miss March-banks's disapproval of Moira's fair person through 'official' lenses and to Rock's denial of the dancing girls who then 'met him smack in his thick lenses'. Rock's mistrust now is evident by his previous reliance on Daisy (down by the rotting lake) and Moira (in the dark cellar) to be 'his eyes'. In Ted's wake, old Rock is left in a pitiable position, trembling on his knees, wondering what is 'at the bottom of this'.

The ending of *Concluding* is ironic as well. Rock is surprised to find that all his animals – the goose, the pig and the cat – have found their way home on their own. Once Rock is home, he almost forgets his fears. 'How many times have I to tell you I am never nervous', he grumbles to his granddaughter. 'It's only my eyes, can't you understand' (p.253). When he finally falls asleep, 'on the whole ... well satisfied with his day', it is after

having experienced the truth of his own statement made earlier
in the evening, and lastly by Liz: 'All's well that ends well.'

Although Rock, however, is satisfied with his day, he is finally,
and ironically, not quite able to respond positively and creatively to darkness. His last significant act is to tear the slipper
from Daisy's neck and hurl it away, as if to emphatically defy
the night. 'Once it was no longer in moonlight it disappeared,
the thing might have flown. He did not, of course, hear it fall'
(p.254). Rock hurls the white satin fairy slipper into a magic
void so unfathomable that it does not send back a single sound –
'Upon which he realized he still had Elizabeth's shoes in the
despatch case.'

Green's direct association of the bottomless void and dancing
(Liz's shoes are, significantly, dancing-shoes) creates a symbolic
counterpoint between the two. At the same time, it makes Rock's
act of throwing away the slipper, associated with Liz's dancing-
shoes, deeply ironic. He wonders if he should call Liz back to
give her her shoes, knowing that she cannot enter the dance floor
in her rubber boots. However, he decides against it for selfish
reasons. 'Gum boots would not help Birt, he considered, not
realizing they would force her to take the young man outside'
(ibid.). The final irony of Rock's position is that darkness cannot
be obliterated; therefore he should respond positively to it. This
is what Liz does at the end of the novel. Once she has seen her
grandfather safe home, she dives into the darkness again, full of
love and hope. Her last words to him 'the young woman sang
over a shoulder, stepped out of moonlight, and disappeared'
(p.253).

Concluding is primarily a metaphysical, not a political, novel.
This means that Green advocates individual freedom in relation
to society in terms of what contributes to life. Political issues as
to the organization of society are bypassed in ambiguous, general
terms. Green is obviously antagonistic towards a political
arrangement which breeds conformity, as represented by the
new state directive that the Institute should be provided with a
pig farm, the expression of a desire to institutionalize natural
instincts. Sebastian accounts for this plan:

'A mass feeding of swine should not be haphazard. The surplus

of a hundred thousand State factories must be made up into balanced pig foods.'
'And what if the pigs don't like?'
'They will. That is the purpose of the State', he said. (p.207)

The whole novel, with all its individual vitality, runs counter to this plan. On the other hand, Green never takes a clear standpoint as to the positive and negative effects of complete political freedom for the individual. The state's view on this matter is also formulated by Sebastian:

'But an incautious movement towards the centre', he went on *with an effort*, 'towards the shaft upon which our little world revolves, that is to say upon the State which employs us at our main function, that of spinning like tops on our own axis', and here he gave one of his *cracked laughs to point the jest*, 'can only fracture the spinning golden bowl, the whole unit, and bring the lot to nought, in other words, reduce us to the lowest, the unemployable'. (p.118, emphasis added)

Sebastian, when making a dogmatic political statement, tends to assume a pompous, mocking style as if he does not sincerely believe what he is saying is true (this supports the assumption that he may possess redeeming 'natural' qualities). Green repeatedly stresses that Sebastian 'fell back on the voice of the sort of lecturer he was not' (p.117). In fact, there is no sign in *Concluding* that the centrifugal motion of the dancers, which leaves the two Principals isolated at the centre, signifies the collapse of the state. In terms of political statements, there is no intimation that 'the centre cannot hold', to quote Yeats's 'The Second Coming', or that 'anarchy is loosed upon the world'. Nowhere in the novel does Green anticipate fundamental political changes, mainly because this is not his central concern.

The centrifugal motion of dancing girls, upsetting a repetitively revolving pattern, is applauded by Green because it is not a political statement. Rather, it expresses the girls' sensuously fulfilling commitment to the present moment. Green is concerned not so much with social and political institutions as with individual attitudes to life. Rebellion against order is justifiable to the extent that it defeats spiritual death. Thus, when Rock, after his traumatic experience in the cellar, has a misanthropic fit, he tells Edge that 'there must be limits, after all'. However, at Edge's question, 'Where would you draw them?', Rock falters. '"Where would I draw the line?" he echoed, but without conviction. Then he pulled himself together. "Yet there must be human decency"' (p.237). In the world of *Concluding*, human decency is not a faculty of the state. This point, therefore, does not interfere with the basic tone of *Concluding*.

In the final analysis, it is not Rock that is the principal projector of values, but Green, the author and narrator. It is Green that arranges and perceives the world in relation to his characters' sensibilities. This world eludes symbolic meaning or illumination of the rational faculties. Green's poetic conception of intelligibility is inherent in his spatial composition of discordant qualities. Images of contradiction enact moments of human significance. Their tone is a projection of a cohesive, evaluating artistic sensibility. *Concluding*'s providential design reflects the author's commitment to basic human values which provide hope of reintegration. The vision that 'all's well that ends well' applies to the human capacity that subordinates empiricism to the effect of wonder. *Concluding*'s magic, enchanted atmosphere ultimately represents Green's comment on the relation between art and life. It is a place through which the reader passes in order to renew and strengthen his sense of reality.

6 *Party Going* (1939), *Nothing* (1950) and *Doting* (1952)

PARTY GOING (1939)

From a technical point of view, *Party Going* differs considerably from *Nothing* and *Doting*. In his last two novels Green aims to consummate his theory of the abstract, non-representational work of art. His authorial detachment from his characters is complete; their motives, attitudes or values are merely intimated through direct speech and appearances. The reader must fill in the rest. *Party Going*, published a decade previous to *Nothing* and *Doting*, only partly conforms to Green's Modernist idea of depersonalization in art. Stokes notes that *Party Going* is

> the most omniscient of all Green's novels.... We have an almost constant double view of the characters, which is almost indecent, for it is as if these members of the *beau monde* were all sitting about naked, without knowing it. Not only do we hear what they say, but simultaneously we are told what are their motives for saying it, what they hope to get out of their present attitude, what, in fact, their game is at the moment.[1]

Notwithstanding the great technical differences between these three novels, there are substantial thematic reasons for examining them in relation to one another. They present the same Mayfair set of frustrated, shallow party goers – beautiful, self-gratifying, spoilt, cunning, deceitful, intriguing and bored. It is primarily the lack of vital values in these three novels that sets them apart from novels such as *Living, Caught, Back, Loving* and *Concluding*. A second important reason for stressing parallels between *Party*

Going, *Nothing* and *Doting* is that the obviously satirically or ironically presented themes in *Party Going* thereby aid the interpretation of similar aspects of *Nothing* and *Doting*, novels which are far more oblique. Finally, such comparison, aided by a montage approach, will support the argument that Green fails to make his two last novels 'as diffuse and variously interpretable as life itself', and that they do reveal the orderings of an evaluative author.

Party Going is a novel in which practically nothing happens at all. A group of young socialites destined for a holiday in France are delayed by a heavy fog and have to wait in a fashionable hotel at the railway terminus. They kill time with gossip, drinking and chasing. Max, the playboy host of the party, and the richest of them all, is the cause of much intrigue and jealousy among the women who compete to capture him. An operator seeking his own gratification, his job is also to cater to the whims and needs of his fellow travellers, which means an endless ordering of drinks and extra rooms.

Unlike those in Green's other novels, the party goers' (the characters of *Nothing* and *Doting* included) suppression of vital perceptual powers makes synthetic techniques, as defined by Coleridge, redundant. Rather, their activities and preoccupations form a monotonous pattern, revealing the author's satire and irony on the demerits of its triviality and absurdity. As in *Back*, as long as Green focuses on his characters' minds and behaviour (Charley's confusion; the party goers' static self-centredness), he presents a claustrophobic atmosphere which precludes synthetic dynamization. On the other hand, Green is far more emotionally estranged from the party goers' consciousnesses than from Charley Summers's. In *Party Going*, his detachment enables him to interrupt his characters' diversions through juxtaposition of contrasting scenes, focused outside the travellers' immediate sphere. These cinematographic devices bring the characters' ironic position into relief. Two major recurrent images serve as components of *Party Going*'s most significant montage effects: the window image, which deepens the party goers' separation from the crowd outside, and the image of Miss Fellowes with the dead pigeon, counteracting the party goers' mindless triviality. As in *Back*, Green begins *Party Going* with a montage that sets the tone of the ensuing narrative. In fact, the opening passage encapsulates the central themes in the novel:

Fog was so dense, bird that had been disturbed went flat into a balustrade and slowly fell, dead, at her feet. There it lay and Miss Fellowes looked up to where that pall of fog was twenty foot above and out of which it had fallen, turning over once. She bent down and took a wing then entered a tunnel in front of her, and this had DEPARTURES lit up over it, carrying her dead pigeon.

No one paid attention, all were intent and everyone hurried, nobody looked back.   (p.384, emphasis added)

The essential irony of this passage stems from the party goers' total negligence of the bird. They are all blindly hurrying to their trains, which are to carry them away to the insouciance of an exotic setting – indicative of escape, in the context of this novel. (Amabel envisages 'that smiling country their journey together would open in their hearts as she hoped, the promised land' – p.510). Miss Fellowes is the only person to care. She carries the dead pigeon with her and washes it conscientiously in the ladies' room and then wraps it in brown paper. Her name connotes fellow feeling, although her personality is too obscure, her behaviour too peculiar, to make her a moral centre in the novel. Her main function is to create a counterpoint to the party goers, thereby highlighting the significant conflicts. A complex interaction of montage conflicts specifies and accentuates the important themes. As in the introduction to *Back*, where the cackle of panic-stricken geese warns Charley against continuing his absurd quest for Rose, so, in *Party Going*, the pigeon, falling at Miss Fellowes's feet, creates a conflict of graphic directions that warns her against pursuing the mindless course of the travellers. Birds usually represent vivacity in Green's fiction. It is therefore significant that the bird which suddenly disturbs Miss Fellowes, and which she afterwards carries into the tunnel, is dead. The tunnel into which they all proceed forms a conflict of scales against the outer world, producing a sense of enclosure and confinement (enhanced by associations of a flying pigeon now dead). The main conflict of the passage is obviously related to the symbolic connection of the dead bird and the entering into the tunnel. This message is intensified by a shift of focus from the bird in the direction they are all heading, a close-up of a luminous sign with prominent capital letters: 'DEPARTURES'.

Green's visual technique highlights the party goers' estrangement
from vital concerns.

Somehow the pigeon and Miss Fellowes are symbolically
connected. After solemnly cleansing it in the lavatory, she feels
ill and wonders whether she will fall downstairs, like the bird.
Frank Kermode provides an interesting commentary on the
symbolic relations by placing them within a myth structure. He
compares the station to a 'death's dream kingdom ... the place
of departures'. The ceremonious cleansing of the dead bird by
Miss Fellowes, 'who may be dying', is in 'some secondary world
of magic and ritual' the manifestation of 'a satisfying spiritual
order'.[2] This possibility deepens the discrepancy between ideal
and reality in the opening scene, though the mystery of the lady's
dead pigeon can never be fully paraphrased. On another plane,
however, the image of the bird is associated with closely related
images throughout the novel for the purpose of bringing the
travellers' actions and preoccupations into ironic relief, through
montage. Their departure is a symptom of their mindless
inhumanity. In a Green novel, the urge to depart for exotic
settings admittedly suggests deep underlying needs for sexual
and spiritual fulfilment. However, the tone enveloping the party
goers' venture is not, specifically for this reason, identical with
the tone enveloping Lily's similar yearnings in *Living*. Close
inspection reveals that, in *Party Going*, Green focuses on his
characters' self-centred obliviousness of pressing existential
human concerns.

The moral to which Green relates his network of montage is
indicated by Alex, one of the travellers, who is pondering how
these 'clean-shaven port drinkers' all have 'lace curtains to guard
them in from fog and how many naked bodies on sentry go
underneath adequately, inadequately dressed'.

> Here he pointed his moral. That is what it is to be rich, he
> thought, if you are held up, if you have to wait then you can
> do it after a bath in your dressing-gown and if you have to
> die then not as any bird tumbling dead from its branch down
> for the foxes, light and stiff, but here in bed, here inside, with
> doctors to tell you it is all right ... no worry since it did not
> matter if one went or stayed.   (p.493)

From the point of view of Green's existentialist preoccupation, the impenetrable pall of fog is a reflection of the pervasive cosmic uncertainty in the novel. To Julia, the walk to the station seems frightening:

> As a path she was following turned this way and that round bushes and shrubs that *hid from her what she would find* she felt she would next come upon this fog dropped suddenly down to the ground, when she would be *lost* ... it was so strange and dreadful to be walking here in darkness when it was only half-past four.   (pp.389–90, emphasis added)

The travellers avoid direct confrontation with uncertainty, which might incite growth, instead escaping from it. Their anxiety is evident in their obsession with comfort and triviality. They all nervously await the arrival of Max, on whom their escape depends. Without him, they are trapped and rendered impotent in this tedious station. Julia is worried because she forgot to bring her charms: a little wooden pistol, an egg with tiny elephants in it, and a painted top. These charms represent some sort of magic by which she can protect herself. They belong to the security of the past, of her childhood, from which she cannot liberate herself. Julia's charms belong in the category of the 'hobby-horses', extensively discussed in the chapter on *Loving*. Significantly, the party goers' egocentrism cramps the growth of their human instincts. Claire Hignam asks her husband 'if he had seen that Edward Cumberland was dead, so young. He paid no attention for he was thinking of something he had forgotten' (*Party Going*, p.391). The recurrent intimations of death, in *Party Going*, are in some mystical way connected with the dead pigeon, and with the characters' negligence of its significance. Miss Fellowes meditates, 'There was that poor boy Cumberland ... what had he died of so young? One did not seem to expect it when one was cooped up in London and then to fall like that dead at her feet' (p.394). The series of montage arrangements involving Miss Fellowes and the travellers highlights the disparity of their respective experiences. Miss Fellowes immerses herself in storms of darkness and death – antecedent to a symbolic resurrection, whereas the others are oblivious of her ordeal and remain entangled in gossip, petty intrigues and trifles. Julia worries about her luggage and asks Robert to call the station master (who is attending to far more pressing matters at the

moment) so that he may send someone out to look for her
servant, Thomson, who again is to go and see her porter does
not put her luggage in the cloakroom. The porter has been
instructed not to put it in the cloakroom, 'Whatever happened',
because she does not trust those places.

> 'But I say, Julia, you know that station master must be a
> pretty busy man, what with the fog and everything. What do
> you think?'
> 'He'll be glad to do it because of my uncle. It would be ever
> so sweet of you, my dear.'
> Miss Fellowes, in her room, felt she was on a shore wedged
> between two rocks, soft and hard. Out beyond a grey sea with,
> above, a darker sky, she would notice small clouds where sea
> joined sky. . . . As this cumulus advanced the sea below would
> rise, most menacing and capped with foam, and as it came
> nearer she could hear the shrieking wind in throbbing through
> her ears. . . . Each time this scene was repeated she felt so
> frightened, and then it was menacing and she throbbed
> unbearably, it was all forced into her head; it was so menacing
> she thought each time the pressure was such her eyes would
> be forced out of her head to let her blood out. And then when
> she thought she must be overwhelmed, or break, this storm
> would go back and those waters and her blood recede, that
> moon would go out above her head, and a sweet tide washed
> down from scalp to toes and she could rest.   (p.423)

The sudden shift of focus from Julia's conversation with Robert
to Miss Fellowes's struggle with a menacing darkness does not
merely provide two contiguous impressions of disparate realities.
The images are calculatingly juxtaposed in a montage fashion
to produce incongruity, and in this resulting perspective expose
Julia's shallowness and self-deception. In contrast, Miss Fellowes
encounters the ultimate darkness and isolation from which she
cannot escape, and which admits of but one solution: a strong
determination to live. Like Charley Summers on the night of Mr
Grant's death, Miss Fellowes does exhibit the strength to oppose
desolation. Green states that 'she was fighting. Lying inanimate
where they had laid her she waged war with storms of darkness
which rolled up over her in a series, like tides summoned by a
moon' (p.421).

The following passage demonstrates even more obviously how Green employs montage to negate the party goers' outlooks. Julia stands by her hotel window, observing the masses of people in the station below, in her estrangement feeling like a queen condescending to her subjects. She imagines 'how wonderful it would be when they had arrived'.

> Alex came up and said what they saw now was like a view from the gibbet and she exclaimed against that. And Miss Fellowes wearily faced another tide of illness. . . . But now with a roll of drums and then a most frightful crash lightning came out of that cloud and played upon the sea, and this was repeated, and then again, each time nearer till she knew she was worse than she had ever been. One last crash which she knew to be unbearable and she burst and exploded into complete insensibility. She vomited.
> 'Come away for a minute', Max said to Julia. As they went off and passed that door it opened and Claire came out with Evelyn. Both of them were smiling and said she would do better now, now she had done what the doctor said.   (p.430)

Alex appears as a cynical, disillusioned observer aware of the hollowness of their lives, and, for this reason, a joyless character. He is Dick Dupret's counterpart. On another occasion, Green watches him as he, exactly like Dick, 'picked up a newspaper and behind it picked his nose' (p.495). The presentation of Julia, on the other hand, stresses her naïve evasion of the deeper existential vision propounded by Green. Claire's and Evelyn's confident comment on Miss Fellowes's health betrays their complete lack of understanding for the real nature of her trauma. Green emphasizes the irony of the passage by next focusing on Max's and Julia's escapism: 'As she walked down that corridor with Max . . . all the while she was telling him about her charms, her mood softening and made expansive by his having taken her away' (p.431).

As is demonstrated by one more example, the manner in which Green repeatedly employs montage to oppose Miss Fellows to the rest of the group forms a clear pattern which points towards a single moral. Alex is now telling Angela about previous travels with Max:

'I'm not saying that one isn't exceedingly comfortable, but it's definitely wearing.' ...
'Have you ever been to Barshottie?'
'No', she said, 'why do you ask?'
Miss Fellowes was better. She was having a perfectly serene dream that she was riding home, on an evening after hunting, on an antelope between rows of giant cabbages. Earth and sky were inverted, her ceiling was an indeterminate ridge and furrow barely lit by crescent moons in the azure sky she rode on.
In the sitting-room next to where she lay dreaming watched by those two nannies, Claire and Evelyn discussed Angela's looks, which they admired, and her clothes, of which they did not think so much. (p.440)

As indicated by a double shift of focus, Miss Fellowes's profound trial is surrounded by tedium and superficiality, by people who are killing time. Whereas Miss Fellowes wrestles for life and is now improving, the other characters' condition is static and powerless. While Alex and Angela discuss their endless travelling, Miss Fellowes is 'riding home'. It is also significant that Miss Fellowes's 'ride' is endowed with a serene, magic vision which transcends the prosaic realities of the party people. At the end of the novel, when the trains resume running, Julia ecstatically rushes about to relay the good news. Believing Miss Fellowes still to be unconscious, she has a shock when she hears Miss Fellowes's voice. Miss Fellowes, now sitting up in bed, thinks they have finally come to remove her from the confinement of the hotel. '"My dear", she said, "I'm very glad to hear it, I feel I've been here long enough"' (p.522). She counters their protests, 'But I feel quite well now, Claire, quite well.' They implore her not to fuss.

She was about to say she was in no fuss ... when she realized it would be better to let them think they were having their own way like Daisy had when they put her in that asylum. She had kept on telling them how glad she was to be there until they had pronounced her sane and let her go.

Miss Fellowes equates the hotel, inhabited by party goers, with an asylum. Her situation suggests a parallel between the travellers' uncomprehending judgement of her state of mind and the doctors' and officials' insensitive treatment of Pye's sister in *Caught*. The ending of *Party Going* reveals Miss Fellowes's disengagement from Max's companions. 'She looked as if she had been travelling.' She has indeed been travelling, not on the surface of life, but into the 'Heart of Darkness'. In fact, Miss Fellowes never intended to join the party to the south of France. She only came to wave goodbye to her niece, Claire (p.385). Now recovering, she only wants to be left alone and 'to be allowed to get better in the comforts of her home' (p.522).

The kind of magical imagery imbuing Miss Fellowes's profound experiences does occur in other contexts in the novel, but somehow does not surface in conjunction with the characters' acute encounter with an immediate reality. It is in a sense merely vaguely contemplated by them, or experienced by a detached author, beyond the characters' own sensibilities. Despite elements of poetry and wonder, the characters' estrangement from a palpable reality, and the author's disaffection with them, account for the novel's lack of 'vital', 'synthetic' montage as defined by Coleridge. An examination of poetic images in *Party Going* illuminates this clearly. There is, for example, the passage comparing Angela and Robin to 'two lilies in a pond, romantically part of it but *infinitely remote*, surrounded, supported, floating in it if you will, but projected by being different on to another plane' (p.395, emphasis added). Amabel's beauty is compared to 'ground so high, so *remote* it had never been broken' (p.463, emphasis added).[3] Images of fragile sublimity testify to Amabel's physical beauty, but the presentation generates no sensual or spiritual intimacy; the experience is merely one of contemplated beauty, an abstraction. Similarly, moments of strong spiritual fulfilment tend to belong to a present now merely distantly remembered. Max recalls that

> When he opened his eyes close beside her [Amabel] in the flat she had blotted out the light, only where her eye would be he could see dazzle, all the rest of her mountain face had been that dark acreage against him. He had lain in the shadow of it under softly beaten wings of her breathing, and his thoughts, hatching up out of sleep, had bundled back into the other darkness of her plumes. So being *entirely delivered over* he had

lain still, he *remembered*, because he had been told by that dazzle
her eyelids were not down so that she lay still awake.

(p.482, emphasis added)

Amabel, in the preceding passage, is associated with a bird.
Significantly, birds in *Party Going* – otherwise symbols of life and
flight – tend to be obscurely connected with the past by the
characters, consequently failing to convince as conveyers of
vitality (in terms of the novel's tone). On her way to the station,
Julia crosses a bridge under which seagulls fly: 'Then three
seagulls flew through that span on which she stood and that is
what had happened one of the times she first met him [Max],
doves had flown under a bridge where she had been standing
when she had stayed away last summer' (p.391). Julia repeatedly
returns to the memory of her first meeting with Max. For her,
the significance of birds refers to that moment in the past:
'everything she felt now would come right between them if only
it was not hurried, and that promise of the birds which had
flown under the arch she stood on would be fulfilled if only, as
seemed likely, she could see sea-gulls that night on their crossing'
(p.467). Later, she again 'remembered those two birds which
had flown under the arch she had been on when she had started,
and now she forgot they were sea-gulls and thought they had
been doves and so was comforted' (p.473). Julia imbues birds,
as she imbues her charms, with some kind of magic which can
provide protection by invoking the reassurance of the past.

Images of life do exist in *Party Going*, but it is significant that
they do not really vitalize the characters' immediate present;
they tend to recede into some contemplated intangibility. For
this reason, Green's alert poetic eye for beauty in unexpected
places cannot succeed in counterbalancing the impression of
desolation and aridity. His imagery of vitality and wonder does
not exist in complete textural freedom, segregated from a
determining context. Tone, when applicable, must be viewed as
a product of the interaction between imagery and context. On
this level, *Party Going* creates a consistent pattern of significations.
The following example, involving Amabel and Max, demonstrates the validity of this argument:

> She lay on his shoulder in this ugly room, folded up with
> almost imperceptible breathing like seagulls settled on the

water cock over gentle waves.... Lying in his arms ... her hands drifted to rest like white doves drowned on peat water, he marvelled again he should ever dream of leaving her who seemed to him then his reason for living as he made himself breathe with her breathing as he always did when she was in his arms to try and be more with her ... and dropped off on those outspread wings into her sleep with his, like two soft evenings meeting.

They slept and then a huge wild roar broke from the crowd outside.   (pp.511–12)

The audio-visual counterpoint, created by the great roar, punctures the luxuriant stillness of their apparent communion. What is more, the disturbing sound effects a reaction disclosing that, in reality, theirs is no true rapport. Max's feelings are superficial and self-centred. At one moment believing Amabel to be 'his reason for living', he in the next 'wondered what it would be like to have Julia here in his arms to sleep on his shoulder.... His sleep had made him forget the urgency of what Amabel had been' (p.512). This passage demonstrates that tone is signalled through montage despite the ambiguity created by poetic metaphors; in other words, this imagery does not counterbalance the dominant ironic tone in the novel.

Green's persistent theme concerning his characters' remoteness from life, their lack of vital sensibility, is emphasized by his constant use of the window image. 'Through those lidded windows, the curtains so thick and heavy they seemed made of plaster on stage sets', the individuals in the station outside are 'dimmed into anxious Roman numerals' (pp.466, 482). Frank Kermode wonders 'why, when among the rich in the hotel there is only a prurient, timid, low-toned sexuality, do we find among the proletarians in the concourse a capacity for sexual joy?' He notes that 'The drop from the lowest hotel window into the concourse is measured thus: a man standing on another man's shoulders can just kiss a maid leaning out.' And the servant Thomson, standing outside guarding the luggage, suddenly receives a beautiful spontaneous kiss from a girl, a complete stranger who, he says happily, 'came up out of the bloody ground' to kiss him. We clearly have to do with boundaries here. In keeping with his mythical approach, Kermode suggests that Hermes, 'as patron of travellers' and with 'the marks of his proletarian origins' 'may preside over any railway station; as god of boundaries and messenger between worlds.... Are we here under the rule of some phallic caduceus, on a boundary marked by some phallic herm?'[4] The following conflict of planes nevertheless suggests the party goers' anxious withdrawal from the boundary, and from vital perceptual experience.

> Looking down then on thousands of Smiths, thousands of Alberts, hundreds of Marys ... lightening the dark mass with their pale lozenged faces; observing how this design moved and was alive ... leaning out then, so secure, from their window up above and left by their argument on terms of companionship unalloyed, Julia and Max could not but feel infinitely remote.   (pp.466–7)

In Green's survey of the railway station, there is an obvious analogy between the 'pale lozenged faces' seen against the 'dark mass' and Ezra Pound's vision in his famed poem 'In a Station of the Metro'. The faces in the crowd appear to Pound as 'Petals on a wet, black bough.' Their technique, montage of masses, is pure Imagism, a concentrated juxtaposition of diverse elements intended to evoke a strong visual response in the reader or spectator. However, secure behind their window high above, Julia and Max feel 'infinitely remote' from this 'design', which seems 'alive'.

Emotionally inadequate, Max and Julia can only imagine what instead they would need truly to experience – 'companionship unalloyed'. '"Have you ever been in a great crowd?" she said, because she had this feeling she must exchange and share with him' (p.468). It is important to note that Green's values are not exclusively aesthetic, nor simply concerned with human 'companionship'. These two qualities are not separate, but inextricably interdependent. Acute perceptual awareness of one's surroundings is a quality responsive to both beauty and human sympathy. It has to do with the capacity and need to penetrate into the vital essence behind and beyond appearances. Such a connection is accentuated in the following scene.

> Upstairs Max and Julia had finished their tea and, in an interval of silence, she had gone over to the window and was looking down on that crowd below ... she seemed to hear a

continuous murmur coming from it. When she noticed heads everywhere turned towards that section just below she flung her window up. Max said: 'Don't go and let all that in.' . . . Also that raw air came in, harsh with fog and from somewhere a smell of cooking, there was a shriek from somewhere in the crowd, it was all on a vast scale and not far above her was that vault of glass which was blue now instead of green, now that she was closer to it. She had forgotten what it was to be outside, what it smelled and felt like, and she had not realized what this crowd was, just seeing it through glass . . . their faces so much lighter than their dark hats, lozenges, lozenges, lozenges . . .

'It's terrifying', Julia said, 'I didn't know there were so many people in the world.'

'Do shut the window, Julia.'   (pp.436–7)

Smells, sounds, the vaporous quality of the air, visual impressions of colours, forms and people, 'all on a vast scale', intrude upon Julia's repressed senses. She realizes that her sensations possess some vital significance, and, in an attempt to get closer, she opens the window. Her yearning to participate is not solely directed towards the crowd of people on the platform. The scene displayed before her represents the amorphous quality of existence on a 'vast scale'. Julia reveals a fundamental human need for a full sensuous and spiritual response to her own natural being, a desire directed towards a self-expanding communion with the dynamic essence of 'Living'. The audio-visual counter-point produced by the crowd's unison chanting, 'WE WANT TRAINS, WE WANT TRAINS . . . WE WANT TRAINS, WE WANT TRAINS', interspersed in the scene, is accompanied by Julia's visual impressions, 'lozenges, lozenges, lozenges'. These powerful repeated images provide the sensory impact of filmic close-ups, acting as projected intensifications of Julia's repressed excitement. Her projection of sensual impulses into the scene is evident in her perception of the people as 'corpuscles in blood, for here and there a narrow stream of people shoved and moved in lines three deep and where they did this they were like veins'. Her susceptibility to beauty finds expression in her envisaging the electric lighting in the station as 'November sun striking through mist rising off water' (p. 430).

Despite images of vitality and wonder, however, it is the

conflict of planes that sets the basic tone of the passage. The
window is a recurrent motif in Green's fiction. It is the shield
behind which Miss Edge, in *Concluding*, retreats from the vivid
display of prismatic colours in her garden, and from her own
natural needs. It separates Lily, in *Living*, from the vitality of
swarming pigeons prior to her abortive escape, and Lily's and
Bert's constant opening, leaning out of, and shutting the window
in their train compartment suggest their longing for fulfilment
as well as beginning withdrawal. In *Loving*, before Raunce's
falling in love with Edith, Raunce is frequently referred to as being
at the 'wrong side of the window' (*Loving*, p.34). Significantly,
the party goers' repression of their perceptual awareness also
estranges them from the reality of human beings. Standing by
the same hotel window, having been implored by Max to shut
the window, Julia retorts,

> 'But why? Max, there's a poor woman down there where
> that end of the crowd's swaying. Did you hear her call?
> Couldn't you do something about it?' ... 'After all', she said,
> 'one must not hear too many cries for help in this world.' ...
> It was extraordinary how quiet their room became once that
> window was shut.   (pp.437–8)

Max's and Julia's decision to ignore that poor woman's cry for
help draws attention to Miss Fellowes's plight, and the party
goers' negligence of her. In terms of *Party Going*'s basic themes
and structure, all elements in some way relate to the central
significance of Miss Fellowes – and the dead pigeon. ' "My dear,
what are we to do with her?" ... Claire went on. "I don't care",
she said, "she must get well, it's too absurd her being ill here." '
Claire is more worried about Max who is to take them travelling.
' "But it's unfair to him if she doesn't get well soon or get over
it, whichever it is, or both", she said' (p.470). In accordance
with Green's use of montage in *Party Going*, a conflict of planes
contrasts the disparate images of Amabel 'pink with warmth
and wrapped round with steam so comfortable', and, in the
adjacent room, of Miss Fellowes under 'mists which wrapped
her round not sweet and warm' (pp.469–70). The party goers
will continue their endless travelling, oblivious of the message
of the dead pigeon and Miss Fellowes. As Julia's servant,
Thomson, ironically remarks, 'And if she did die why you'd

never be the same, none of them would, not for three days at all events' (p.500).

NOTHING (1950), *DOTING* (1952)

The crucial question with regard to *Nothing* and *Doting* is whether their abstract designs preclude a reliable assessment of tone. Donald S. Taylor, who has probably conducted the most thorough study of the two novels, argues that 'evaluative tendencies are countered in *Doting* by the textural innovations'.[5] Taylor's assertion coincides with Green's idea that neither dialogue nor a character's behaviour, in *Nothing* and *Doting*, should have a reliable meaning in itself. Green states that 'we should use combinations of words with the widest possible range of meaning in dialogue. That is, dialogue should not be capable of only one meaning, or mood.'[6] What is left of description (which is largely effaced in favour of dialogue) is mainly Green's directions to the reader about surface action.

Green's 'textural innovations' imply that especially the nature of the characters' motives is kept at an elusive distance from the reader. Ryf outlines perfectly the web of contra-indications surrounding the motives of Jane Weatherby in *Nothing*.

The figure which emerges in central focus in all this is that of Jane Weatherby, and the central mystery is her motivation. She presides over the novel, manoeuvring to separate John from Liz and Philip from Mary. She wins John for herself again after all these years, even proposing to him, and when he accepts she claims it's his idea. She is adept at putting words in other people's mouths, and at the end, if anyone can be said to have won out, it is she.

However, 'the question remains of her', states Ryf, 'is she a well-meaning matron or a manipulative monster?'[7] Apparently charitable traits are countered by her selfish outmanoeuvring of her surroundings with the aim of marrying John Pomfret. Finally reunited, they decide that their children will have to take care of their own problems from now on. Mr Pomfret casually remarks that their parents 'can't do everything for them' (p.167). Penelope, like the other children, is manipulated out of the way

to boarding school. Although Mr Pomfret's and Mrs Weatherby's
motives are ambiguous, their achievement is obvious: they have
won each other for themselves. At the end of the novel, the
couple lapse into lazy luxurious complacency. ' "And is there
anything at all you want my own?" "Nothing ... nothing", he
replied in so low a voice she could barely have heard and then
seemed to fall deep asleep at last' (p.168).

The ending is predictably equivocal. The question is whether
Mr Pomfret's profession of contentment coincides with the tone
of *Nothing*. It could be that the couple's self-centred machinations
leave them in a spiritual vacuum – 'nothing'. A crucial related
question is whether *Nothing*, as a whole, evades value assessment
principally as a consequence of Jane Weatherby's enigmatic
moral consciousness. A more functional approach is to simply
acknowledge the obscurity of her motives as a realistic manifestation of the impossibility to know the full truth, neither about
oneself, nor about others. One could argue that the obscurity of
her disposition is a value statement in itself; her behaviour is
not sufficiently convincing to term her a 'well-meaning matron'.
It seems that, like Charles Addinsell in *Doting*, she can 'love no
one too much' (*Doting*, p.266).

Tone cannot be determined on the basis of Green's 'textural
innovations' alone. It is necessary to look for a larger structural
and thematic perspective in which the entire worlds of *Nothing*
and *Doting* are presented. Only with Green's underlying existential vision detected can the characters' dialogues and actions be
brought into ethical relief, and a pattern of montage conflicts,
conductive to a dominant tone, confirmed. One incident,
especially, suggests the imminent threat of death: on the first
page of *Doting*, as in *Party Going*, appears the image of a dead
bird carried by the Middletons's son, Peter. 'So they were three
in full evening dress apart from Peter's tailored pin stripe suit
in which, several weeks later, he was to carry a white goose
under one arm, its dead beak almost trailing the platform, to
catch the last train back to yet another term' (*Doting*, p.171). As
in *Party Going*, travelling by train seems to be associated with
monotony – 'yet another term'. Like the travellers in *Party Going*,
Charles Addinsell, a friend of the Middletons, recoils from
'loving' because he fears death. 'No, what I have against living,
is the dirty tricks fate has in store', he tells the young Annabel
Paynton, his new object of interest (*Doting*, p.263).

'And so what has anyone to live for?'

'Blessed if I know.' ...

'Yet ... would you really warn a woman against looking forward to her own children?'

'They can always die, too.' ...

'Then am I not to love anyone because, like all of us, they've got to die some time?'

'Don't know.'

'But, please, you do truly love your Joe, don't you?'

'Certainly.' ...

'Then are you going to love him less for that?'

'I am. You see, Ann, on account of if he died.... My point is, love no one too much, in case they do.'   (pp.265–6)

Despite the textural ambiguities of *Nothing* and *Doting*, there is strong evidence that the effete Mayfair set is mocked for their lack of an affirmative commitment to 'living'. Their inadequacy is recompensed by sex, lunching out, partying and 'doting'. The dead bird in *Doting* does not have a structural function as in *Party Going*, where it is associated with Miss Fellowes and so recurs in montage conflicts throughout the novel. Several other incidents, however, bear witness to the characters' escapism. In one of the very few descriptive passages in *Nothing* – the picturing of the dining-room decorated for the celebration of Philip's (Mrs Weatherby's son's) twenty-first birthday – appearances are close to perfection. Not insignificantly, the reserved private room is located in the same fashionable hotel where they hold their habitual luncheons. Tall mirrors suggest that the ornamented dining-room may be a reflection of the quality of the characters' lives. Mirrors repeat the image of the ostentatious chandeliers 'to a thousand thousand profiles to be lost in olive grey depths'. In this great room, 'prepared, empty, curtained, shuttered', '*time stood still for Jane*, even in wine bottles over to one side holding the single movement, and that unseen of bubbles rising just as the air, similarly *trapped* even if conditioned, watched unseen across itself in a superb but not indifferent *pause of mirrors*' (p.61, emphasis added). Like Mrs Tennant in *Loving*, Jane Weatherby 'fingered daffodils here and there ... not to disarrange these but almost as though to reassure herself that all were true'. 'But it is perfect!', she exclaims (p.63). It seems that these flowers have fulfilled their function as such perfect ornaments that they are divested of natural life and vitality. They belong to a world of appearances, reflecting the party goers' empty rituals. A newly arrived couple 'came up to go through *the shrill ritual of delighted cries* at Jane's appearance ... and at the blossoming, the to them so they said incredible conjuring up out of these *perfect flowers*' (p.66, emphasis added). The party comes through as deeply ironic. Philip discovers a place card with a name, Mr William Smith, which is not mentioned on the seating list. There is obviously some mistake, because Mr William Smith is long dead, and his card is all yellow. Mrs Weatherby despairs, ' "How odd and sad", she tore the thing up into very small bits.... "How dreadful", she murmured. "Philip you didn't do this to me?" ' And then she adds, 'I never like to look the other side of anything in hotels' (p.64). At closer inspection, Mrs Weatherby's 'full cream of flesh' reveals eyes 'red veined as leaves' (p.62).

To Russell's question 'whether Green has despaired of humane values, and resorted to the emotional consolations of abstract art', the answer is, no.[8] Not Green, but Mrs Weatherby and her companions attempt to escape their private fears by resorting to the consolations of an artificial pattern of appearances, as demonstrated in the ornamented dining-room scene. Their pretensions are ironically undermined. If the existentialist perspective of *Nothing* and *Doting* is recognized (notably the necessity of imposing human values into a meaningless void), Green's repudiation of his characters is not difficult to detect. His creation of incongruity between characters' talk and their behaviour afterwards serves the same function as cross-montage. It exposes their escape from the threat of death to a life of triviality. There is old Arthur Morris in *Nothing* who is having his leg amputated bit by bit due to blood-poisoning. When Mr Pomfret, Miss Jennings (his present lady-friend) and Mrs Weatherby (his lady-friend-to-be) first talk about it in their usual restaurant, they giggle hysterically because of Mr Pomfret's solemn face at announcing it. Later, they are a little more serious: ' "Poor Arthur isn't it bad luck?" she said. "Frightful", he agreed. "Now what are you proposing to have now? Cheese or sweet or both?" ' (p.38). Green stresses Mr Pomfret's insincerity – the manner in which he pretends to care, while his behaviour reveals the opposite. ' "Why", he protested, "it's the most frightful thing I ever heard in all my life! Poor old fellow. No knowing where these things'll stop either. And the bill too if you don't mind, waiter"' (p.39). Green deliberately creates ambiguity as to how much the characters really care about poor Arthur Morris. When Jane Weatherby is told of his death, tears stream down her face. Green remarks, 'She might have been able to cry at will or it could be that she dreadfully minded' (p.142).

Critics might argue that, behind these characters' evasion of death, there is commitment to life. Green might be suggesting comedy as a cure for the moralistic, the sentimental and the banal. Pomfret utters something towards this effect when, after having finished laughing over Arthur Morris's misfortune, he remarks to Miss Jennings, 'If I lay in bed about to be amputated ... I wouldn't expect you to laugh of course my dear and naturally Mary couldn't, but I'd lose a certain amount of resistance if I thought our acquaintances weren't roaring their beastly heads off!' (p.13). Green's fiction testifies to his belief that comedy should conquer tragedy, that tragedy should be met with an affirmative smile. However, the characters of *Nothing* and *Doting* are incapable of such a positive encounter. Instead, they escape death, their inhumane disregard of their 'friend's' death being a sign of their fear. This argument is supported by parallels between *Nothing, Doting* and other Green novels. Arthur Morris is a counterpart to Charley Summers in *Back*, who loses his leg in the war. They represent loss in a metaphysical sense, a loss which can only be remedied by a full commitment to life through 'living' and 'loving'. Similarly, Miss Fellowes represents encounter with a void of darkness and uncertainty, from which the party goers ensconce themselves in the hotel. From the point of view of the novels' existentialist preoccupation, the characters' half-hearted responsiveness to 'living' in general leaves them in a spiritually impoverished world of 'doting' and triviality. It is true that sensuality is not absent from the middle-aged couple's world, but whether sex in itself is enough to make their lives fruitful is a different matter.

The following scene encapsulates the dominant tone of both *Nothing* and *Doting*. John Pomfret has just countered Mrs Weatherby's complaint about their children's failure to live up to their parents' life-style by intimating that their own lives have been a mess. 'Now darling you're not to speak so of what is still absolutely sacred to me. How delicious this lobster is!' (*Nothing*, p.126). The irony is produced by the *non sequitur*. It highlights the possibility that what Mrs Weatherby pronounces as 'absolutely sacred' implies a superficial dependence on appearances and a life of luxurious pleasure-seeking.

With regard to tone, in *Nothing* and *Doting* obscurity resides mainly in the dubious nature of people's motives, the reality of which equals the ambiguity of linguistic meaning. In the larger metaphysical perspective, however, these textural ambiguities cannot conceal the authorial irony. The characters' lives appear monotonous and futile. Rarely do *Nothing* and *Doting* present experience that transcends the prose logic of the linguistic medium to produce what may be termed poetry. Green justifies his abstract style by explaining that a writer 'has to create or inspire a conscious act of imagination in the reader ... the reader of a novel somehow or other must be encouraged by the writer to extend his imagination over the whole of all the questions that have been asked in life and can never be answered'.[9] If *Nothing* and *Doting* are meant to kindle the reader's imagination to all aspects of life's mystery, one may argue that ethical, spiritual and poetic values are so well disguised that the central mystery is reduced to the question of whether they exist at all.

The lack of values *actually present* in the works explains the absence of 'vital' montage. Green asserts that the reader's imagination is to be fired by 'the magic which has to be created between writer and reader'[10] If there is magic in *Nothing* and *Doting*, it is due to Green's creation of a value void, whose specific characteristics insist upon and direct the reader's own evaluative faculties. The vacuity energizes the reader's disdain so that moral quality emerges between reader and work rather than between specific elements within it. Yet contrasts do exist within the works. As in the descriptive opening passage of *Nothing*, however, dynamism is dulled, not so much, perhaps, by any failure of Green's artistic powers as by the characters' lack of vital sensibility. John Pomfret is out lunching with his mistress, Liz Jennings, to whom he professes his love:

> He did not look at the girl and seemed nervous as he described his tea the previous Sunday when Liz had to visit her mother ill with flu so that he had been free to call on Jane Weatherby.... It was wet then, did she remember he was saying, so unlike this he said, and turned his face to the *dazzle* of window, it had been dark with *sad tears* on the panes and streets of blue canals as he sat by her fire ... while outside a

single street lamp was yellow, reflected over a thousand raindrops on the glass, the fire was rose.

(p.9, emphasis added)

There is a sense of unreality in the passage which renders the impression of something contemplated rather than vivaciously perceived. The conflict of planes, indicated by the 'great window that opened on the Park', clarifies the underlying tension. It accentuates Pomfret's separation from the 'dazzle' outside, making him a spiritual shadow. Evading this 'dazzle', as he also evades looking at his woman, he lapses into memories of the previous week, the vivacious images of which (the reflection of 'a thousand raindrops on the glass' and 'sparkling points of rose') fail to convince, because only sadly, distantly remembered. It is the image of 'dark with sad tears on the panes and streets' that sets the mood of the passage. It echoes Green's comment on the guests who, at Philip's twenty-first birthday party, admire the perfect ornamentations of flowers, 'of a spring lost once more for yet another year to the sad denizens of London in rain fog mist and cold' (p.66). The sadness and terror of the surrounding existential void seem to be the underlying motivational forces behind their endless lunches, gossip, affairs, intrigues, and their way of making 'mountains out of molehills' (a favourite expression by which they characterize one another's pastimes). They lack vital imagination, commitment to the present moment, required in order to impose human meaning upon existential nothingness. Despite John Pomfret's and Jane Weatherby's seeming fulfilment after their reunion in front of the rosy fire, the ending of *Nothing* is replete with lazy, somnolent yawning, suggestive of spiritual stasis. In light of *Nothing*'s and *Doting*'s almost identical structures of appearances and endless triviality, it is likely that the meaning of their endings would converge – that John Pomfret's satisfied, 'Nothing ... nothing', translates 'The next day they all went on very much the same' (*Doting*, p.337).

The preceding discussion of characters and linguistic particulars needs to be outlined against the larger structural patterns of *Nothing* and *Doting*. The ambiguity of specific contexts and passages is diminished once the close connection existing between structure and content is recognized. Green's concentration on dialogue, with a minimal degree of commentary, naturally presupposes a scenic structure. Paradoxically enough, tone is produced not in spite, but as a result, of Green's abstracting montage method. Life is confined into a structural pattern, a reflection of the author's evaluations. Melchiori compares it with that of the Cubist painters, a 'complete abstraction – a pattern of rigid geometrical figures creating abstract emotions through the intellect rather than the heart'.[11] Like the Cubists, Green does present simultaneous impressions of life's different facets. However, everything redundant to the characters' trivial preoccupations is almost eliminated from the world of these novels. Montage is scarce in the sense that life's complexity is reduced to a diagram of monotonous scenes which exclude a multiplicity of contrasting impulses. Montage, restricted within the individual scenes because of their claustrophobic quality, exists between the scenes, in the transitions between the different couples entering the arena. This composition conforms to Eisenstein's ideas on the creation of tone in film, which again echo Green's statement that the arrangement and superimposition of 'one scene on another, or the telescoping of two scenes into one' give the novel 'substance and depth'. The monotonous juxtapositions of different but constantly repeated settings, of alternating couples endlessly gossiping about the same trivial things behind one another's backs, are what produce the spiritually impoverished atmosphere of *Nothing* and *Doting*.

The disparity between what the other novels achieve, and what *Nothing* and *Doting* fail to achieve, illuminates the nature of Green's values. *Nothing* and *Doting* fail to stretch the reader's imagination to all the questions which life asks. Incantatory visualization, colours, swarming birds and natural imagery do not intrude adequately in order to infuse the prosaic with an imaginative dimension. The spiritual void may stimulate the reader's compensatory private imagination, but one could not possibly have imagined the magically enchanted world of *Concluding* without its visual immediacy. In *Nothing* and *Doting*, however, it may happen that Green invokes an artistic vision. Although his attempt fails to achieve true spontaneity, it at least highlights the vacuous sensibilities of the indifferent spectators. It is highly significant that *Doting* both opens and closes with a show of artists – a structural device to contrast the non-artistic lives of the characters. The first paragraph of the book portrays Annabel and the Middletons watching a performance of snake dancers and jugglers. ' "Pretty squalid play all round, I thought!" His son only grunted back at him, face vacant, mouth half open, in London, in 1949.' A juggler, to whom they react with bored indifference, reappears in the nightclub at the end of the novel. The window motif recurs as a device to enhance the sense of distance between the distracted audience and the arena. It is also worth noting that, as in *Party Going*, leaning out of the window, towards a more palpable reality, instils fear. 'Ann and Claire were leaning out of an open window on the dancing side. "No Charles, or I shall feel quite sick", Diana implored the man, plainly nervous at the sight' (p.325). When the same conjuror they had watched at the beginning appears at the end, Peter says, 'Oh God!', the party breaks up, and the novel terminates. While, at the beginning, they focus their attentions on the restaurant bill,

> they altogether ignored . . . miracles of skill spun out a few feet beneath – no less than the balancing of a billiard ivory ball on the juggler's chin, then a pint beer mug on top of that ball at the exact angle needed to cheat gravity, and at last the second ivory sphere which this man placed from a stick, or cue, to top all on the mug's handle – the ball supporting a pint pot, then the pint pot a second ball until, unnoticed by our party, the man removed his chin and these separate objects fell, balls of ivory each to a hand, and the jug to a toe of his patent leather shoe where he let it hang and shine to a faint look of surprise, the artist.   (pp.175–6)

The conjuror may be Green himself, the juggler-artist conjuror who dexterously juggles words, phrases and characters as if they were billiard balls and beer mugs. If it is indeed Green, his juggling-act is not convincing; it does not quite come alive because it is too precise and controlled. No incantatory prose conveys the true quality of this miraculous artistic performance. The reason, probably, is an echo of the protagonists' unimaginative minds, which 'altogether ignored' the act. And what they completely fail to appreciate is the beauty of the instant moment; they fail to stretch their imaginations to the 'magic' of artistry. *Nothing* and *Doting* fail to attain 'a life of their own' because they lack, unlike most of Green's other novels, the dynamic interaction of stasis and dynamism; order and disorder; prose and poetry; tragedy and comedy: the dynamic vitality of montage.

7 Conclusion

Green's successive experiments in creating an autonomous, non-representational novel, culminating in *Nothing* and *Doting*, evince certain characteristics of the *nouveau roman*. Robbe-Grillet (the French novelist) contends that external surfaces and appearances alone have validity. Any authorial attribution of human significance to the factual world distorts reality. What traditionally is termed 'meaning', he maintains, is only due to man's fictitious arrangement of reality into patterns that suit his needs. Robbe-Grillet, deriding contrived 'truths' in a work of art, aims at duplicating life's non-coherent nature. This, he believes, is achieved through 'scientific', neutral observation of characters and events.[1]

Robbe-Grillet's theory of art and reality resembles Green's in important respects. It coincides with Green's idea that the novel should be ambiguous and have a life of its own, so as to enable the reader to construct his own meaning. Green's characters are simply there without any obvious psychological or explanatory past. Their condition reflects the peculiar uncertainties and contradictions of living in an age of social and cultural disorder. The lack of traditional plots in Green's novels, and the inconclusiveness of their endings, mirror the modern dubiousness about goals and identity. Instead, Green's artistic world is composed of gestures, images, situations and heterogeneous items.

Robbe-Grillet, as well as Green, employs montage to provoke a true sensation of reality. However, Robbe-Grillet's attempt to convey an authentic image of the factual world involves a subjective interpretation of non-coherent data. His use of montage is finally incompatible with his ambition to maintain objectivity and neutrality. The very choice of montage as a literary technique – its principle being 'emotional intensification' – seems to reflect the author's private needs. The following passage from *The Voyeur* demonstrates this point.

It suggests interesting correspondences between Green's and Robbe-Grillet's technique and vision.

It was as if *no one had heard*. The whistle blew again – *a shrill, prolonged noise* followed by three short blasts of ear-splitting violence: a violence without purpose that remained without effect. . . .
A *motionless* and parallel series of *strained*, almost anxious stares crossed – tried to cross – *struggled* against the narrowing space that still separated them from their goal. . . . A last *puff* of *heavy, noiseless* steam formed a great plume in the air above them, and vanished as soon as it had appeared.[2]

(Emphasis added)

In a montage fashion, Robbe-Grillet juxtaposes incongruous words within the sentences. A static image, 'motionless', counterpoints stares which 'strained' and 'struggled'; 'heavy noiseless' contradicts 'puff'. Montage compresses opposites into simultaneity, into a conceptual synthesis whose equivalent Eisenstein would call 'graphically undepictable'. The above juxtaposition between visual and auditory images creates a tension between stasis and 'violence' which is strongly dynamic. Its dynamism possesses the potential power to conjoin fragments and contradictions by evoking a sense of perceptual immediacy between the reader and the depicted scene. Robbe-Grillet's disengaged, factual description seeks to avoid the projection of human needs into the scene. However, his attempt to create perceptual immediacy without compromising his emotional disengagement fails to reflect the author's complete 'scientific' objectivity.[3] In his portrayal of his alienated travellers, Robbe-Grillet does betray a secret impulse towards reconciliation with an ulterior reality. His depiction echoes the human need behind Julia's and Max's alienated perceptions from the hotel window in *Party Going*. Robbe-Grillet's technique of humanizing reality through montage aligns him not only with Green, but also with Pound, Joyce, Faulkner and D. H. Lawrence, who all employ montage to effect a dynamic sense of integration with perceptual phenomena.
The comparison of Green's and Robbe-Grillet's montage methods does not imply a full correspondence. Essentially, there is a level of value commitment in both authors' use of montage. Montage animates an otherwise disconnected world of things.

For both Robbe-Grillet and Green it is the imagination that invents meaning. Thus, there is no fundamental divergence in Robbe-Grillet's and Green's conceptions of the relation between montage and reality; fresh, unexpected, concrete juxtapositions violate conceptualization, creating reality anew through unprejudiced senses. Green, however, reveals a far greater conviction than Robbe-Grillet in colouring the world with human significance. Their difference is due to Green's abundant use of metaphor, which Robbe-Grillet rejects on the grounds that it would humanize the universe by being an extension of man's soul. Robbe-Grillet's depictions 'will renounce their pseudo-mystery, that suspect interiority which Roland Barthes has called "the romantic heart of things"'.[4] Green's metaphors evade symbolic signification, thereby denying the world logical intelligibility. However, they do create a third dimension of mystery and wonder which is absent in Robbe-Grillet's work. Green's impulse towards integrating man and universe through spiritual unification is what makes him an essentially Romantic writer.

To restore some harmony between reality and reader by sensitizing him to the particular in life is one of Green's main motivations. His creation of a sensual intimacy in his portrayals of man and nature links him with Lawrence. Green also stresses the spiritual side of the momentary experience. Such values, one may argue, are essentially Romantic. Green's technique generates an almost paradisal identity of self with the universe of perception, of experience, of imagination and of process. At one moment, swirling light revives 'the fallen world'; in the next, swarming birds and shades of red and gold counteract a 'dying world', uniting 'sky' and 'sea'.

Green's experience of sublime beauty in the contradictory quality of reality aligns him with Keats. Keats's sensitivity to the visual moment incites an impression of sensual and spiritual encompassment, as in his depiction, in 'The Eve of St Agnes', of Porphyro waking in Madeline's bedroom:

Thus whispering, his *warm*, unnerved arm
Sank in her pillow. Shaded was her dream
By the *dusk curtains*; 'twas a midnight charm
Impossible to melt as *iced stream*.
The *lustrous* salvers in the moonlight gleam,
Broad *golden fringe* upon the carpet lies.

It seemed he never, never could redeem
From such a steadfast *spell* his lady's eyes.[5]

(Emphasis added)

Dissonant images – of warmth and cold, energy and calm, vividness and stasis, light and dark – create a visual polarity. It is enhanced by an accented rhythm which, in filmic terms, produces sensory close-ups, attracting the reader's senses to the immediacy of the vision. The visual intensity of the scene creates a synthesis between objective details and the poet's subjectively projected passion. Keats's exaltation is bound up with his sense of life's total presence, an image which, to use Coleridge's expression, strikes him as a reconciliation of discordant qualities. Keats's vision is basically equivalent to the effect gained by Green's use of montage in his oft-referred-to depiction of the reclining Merode (*Concluding*), or in the final picture of Edith and the birds (*Loving*). Images of vitality are juxtaposed with the darker aspects of reality to produce an encompassing moment of beauty.

Robbe-Grillet's montage of static and dynamic images has traits in common with Keats's and Green's techniques, but his depiction lacks emotive force. Robbe-Grillet aims at objectivity in presentation, but projects a subjective disposition. Keats's and Green's energetic visualization, on the other hand, transcends the terms 'subjective' and 'objective' in a process of poetic unification. Coleridge's preoccupation with the two terms indicates how Green, while being a Modernist writer, is fundamentally a Romantic. According to Abrams, Coleridge regards Milton's three adjectives 'simple, sensuous, and passionate' as the main components of poetry. Coleridge suggests that '"the second condition, sensuousness, ensures that framework of objectivity, that definiteness and articulation of imagery", without which poetry evaporates into day-dreaming'. At the same time, 'the third condition, passion, provides that neither thought nor imagery shall be simply objective, but that the *passio vera* of humanity shall warm and animate both'.[6] Green's incantatory prose contains all the three elements required to make a fragmentary, unintelligible world poetic.

For a further elucidation of Green's methods and value commitments, a comparison with similar, though different, techniques is useful. Henry James's experimentation with visual dramatization has certainly had a strong influence on twentieth-century novelists. A most vivid example of James's visualization occurs in the latter part of *The Ambassadors*. Strether, the central character of the novel, has gradually come to a full realization of the constrictions and deprivations of his former conventionalized existence. As he travels deeper into the French countryside, the freedom of a new world strikes upon his senses. The village he comes to affects him 'as a thing of whiteness, blueness, and crookedness, set in coppery green, and that had the river flowing behind or before it'. Down by the stream,

> the confidence that had so gathered for him deepened with the lap of the water, the ripple of the surface, the rustle of the reeds on the opposite bank, the faint diffused coolness and the slight rock of a couple of small boats.... The valley on the farther side was all coppery-green level and glazed pearly sky, a sky hatched across with screens of trimmed trees.... [Mme de Vionnet's parasol made] a pink point in the shining scene.[7]

'Coppery-green', 'pearly' white, 'pink', and 'screens' of green reflect a 'shining' light over the scene, with the 'lap of the water', the 'ripple of the surface', the 'rustle of the reeds'. James's sensitivity to natural motion, to sound, and to the play of light places the emphasis on the subjective visual impression rather than on the thing itself. The total sensory effect, however, is not identical to the one created by Green. James freezes motion into pictorial details, as if in a painting: the 'lap' of water, the 'rock' of boats. Whereas Green's active, mimetic phrases have a kinetic impact, James's verbs have been made into nouns which stimulate the reader's visual imagination rather than his immediate sensual involvement. In reference to Coleridge's three conditions of poetry, James's passage lacks a 'vital' polarity between 'sensuousness' and 'passion'. It is predominantly impressionistic, a function which may be attributed to the faculty of mind Coleridge terms 'Fancy'. In contrast, Green's 'Imagination' is able to 'create'; an animating human sensibility synthesizes a hard external surface into a dynamic interdependence of discordant qualities.

Romantic conflict between human values and an industrialized world pervades Green's fiction. The term 'pastoral', closely associated with Romanticism, applies to basic streams in his work. William Empson associates the term with a work of art which contrasts good, simple life and complicated, less natural ways.[8] Other applications of 'pastoral' refer to individuals' withdrawal from a complex civilization to an enlightening reconciliation with the elemental rhythms of nature. Some pastoralists equate the term with 'shepherd' (*pastor* is Latin for 'shepherd').[9] Mr Rock, in *Concluding*, is a 'shepherd', watching over his three animals. The Christian allusions embodied by Rock, the 'shepherd' (whose name, in addition, means Peter), are reinforced by the idyll of the Eameses' 'Garden of Eden' in *Living*.

Man's sensual and spiritual communion with his own natural being, the qualities implied in 'living' and 'loving', is Green's ideal. The fulfilment of the ideal is facilitated through a simple life in natural surroundings, the main reason why the different definitions of 'pastoral' emerge as central values in Green's novels. The term 'pastoral', however, does not apply to their entire structure. The forest in which Rock seeks refuge is not the Forest of Arden in Shakespeare's romantic comedy *As You Like It*, or the fairy-haunted wood of *A Midsummer Night's Dream*, in which all complications are resolved, enmities reconciled, and true love cultivated.[10] The forest of *Concluding* is haunted by ghosts as much as by fairies. There is love among the characters, but hostility and suspicion prevail between Rock and Adams, the forester. Amorous love exists, not between two inhabitants of the forest, but, significantly, between Rock's granddaughter and Sebastian, an official of the State Institute. Hence, the forest, in *Concluding*, does not function as a *symbol* of Arcadian innocence. Rather, pastoral qualities are employed to express a sense of mystery, wonder and natural fulfilment despite the presence of disintegrating forces. The 'green world', in *Concluding*, possesses values of growth and fertility, not by virtue of being a refuge, but as a reflection of man's soul. Northrop Frye illuminates the value of Green's forest by assessing its similar function in Shakespeare's comedies: the 'Shakespearean comedy illustrates, as clearly as any *mythos* we have, the archetypal function of literature in visualizing the world of desire, not as an escape from "reality", but as the genuine form of the world that human life tries to imitate'.[11]

'Reconciliation' with nature, in Green's world, does not imply the value of abandoning the self to the continuum. Green is a predominantly Modernist writer, whose recognition of fragmentation is all-pervasive. In accordance with his existentialist orientation, the diurnal processes represent a threat to humanity, and to 'living'. Critics tend to ignore the full implications of the manner in which different levels of reality operate in a Green novel. The significance of characters' confrontation with darkness exceeds a symbolic, representational meaning. There is a poetic level, in Green's world, consisting of dynamic polarity between projected human values and an immanent, inorganic reality. Coleridge's poetic technique matches Green's vision; meaning is basically a spiritual and sensual interaction between human impulses and objective reality. Its principle of unity resides within the imagination.

Green's focus on the vital balance of opposites makes him rather unique among British novelists. Lawrence's novels reveal a deep conviction of the value of immersing the ego in the impersonal (perhaps divine) flow of nature. A merging with empirical reality provides a reconciliation with metaphysical reality, and a vital expansion of the self. Lawrence's attitudes, although to a large extent shared by Green, become difficult or dangerous in a Green novel. Whereas Lawrence tries to ignore the modern, industrialized and fragmented world, Green has to live with it. The factory in *Living*, also employing the Eameses, may clearly be seen as a symbol for the modern world in which man is trapped. Opposition between material necessity, the need to survive as an individual in face of disintegration, and the need for fulfilment, seems to be the dilemma of the modern world as Green portrays it. It may be seen in many aspects of life – in Green's perceptions of the relationship between man and nature; in the relationship between the sexes; and in man's relation to social institutions. 'Living', in Green's work, seems to depend on an ability to avoid coercive forces, exclude distracting impressions, and to assimilate opposites into a perceptual unity. It requires active participation in life, an invigoration of human sympathetic powers. What makes Green's method poetic is the fact that his visual scenes and images do not have a primarily logical, symbolic significance. They are components of an artistic form, an artistic medium intended to arouse the reader's full response to the life (i.e. its contradictory quality) of the novel.

This study has argued that aspects of Green's method of organization resemble principles characteristic of moden poetry –

the kind of poetic technique that may be traced back to Whitman. In his *Leaves of Grass*, values are not communicated by a subjective rhetorical voice through a regular metrical rhythm. The form is visual – an irregular, accented unit, arousing the reader's perceptual awareness to the particular rather than the abstract. Akin to Whitman's practice are the ideas propounded by the New Criticism movement. The work of art should be a self-sufficient artifact providing its own, essentially aesthetic, frame of reference. It should not primarily signify, but basically *be*.

A reading of Green's novels in keeping with the ideas of modern poetry and the school of New Criticism elucidates intent and effects in Green's poetic scenes. His poetic passages catch a moment demanding the reader's active response. Principles of poetic montage also clarify the nature of Green's conception of a non-coherent reality, and his belief in the value of stimulating the unification of montage fragments within the reader's imagination. However, crucial aspects of Green's technique also diverge from that of most modern poetry. A poem not only conjoins a series of images, but is a concentrated unit or image in itself. It primarily insists that the reader see the picture. Values are not referential; they basically *are* that terse order of visual images. The basic difference between an Imagist poem and prose fiction implies that Green can juxtapose, not only single images, but scenes containing human beings and events. Since human beings generally dominate the novel, its total form cannot achieve complete self-sufficiency. Although Green's images do not represent specific characters or human qualities, their selection and position in relation to individual characters and events give them a referential structural function. This is why the tone of Green's novels can only be fully assessed through a combination of a poetic and filmic montage approach. Just as a poem forms one complete image in itself, so Green creates a formal sense of coherence and promise through repeated poetic scenes and by means of recurrent motifs, such as birds and water imagery. These and other images, however, are assimilated into a humanized sense of order only when viewed in relation to certain internal qualities in the characters. Robert Richardson elucidates a central difference between poetry and film. 'Modern poetry', he argues,

has tended rather strongly towards the abstract and the

philosophical. But the film, though it shares some of the ideas and some of the techniques of modern poetry, is not, as a medium, well adapted to expressing abstract ideas or carrying on philosophical dialogue. Thus it has been virtually forced to embody its ideas in specific human figures.[12]

The tone of Green's novels thus emanates principally from various characters' responses in relation to different contexts and events.

A special interpretative problem is presented by *Nothing* and *Doting*. In them, Green's attention to structural pattern preponderates over his interest in embodying vital responses in his characters. One possible approach to the problem is to view these two works as articulations of abstract art. Nathalie Sarraute suggests that 'Books about nothing, almost devoid of subject, rid of characters, plots and all the old accessories, reduced to pure movement, which brings them into proximity with abstract art, are these not the goals towards which the modern novel tends?'[13] Although Green does not eradicate characters, only impersonal appearances remain. From the point of view of abstract art, *Nothing* and *Doting* might be said to reflect the sense of nothingness, of void, typical of man's spiritual condition in the twentieth century. Viewed in the same perspective, Green's construction of an artistic pattern of scenes might therefore suggest his recourse from human confusion and imperfection to an abstract, aesthetic order.[14] However, viewed in terms of filmic montage, *Nothing* and *Doting* do not attain such a degree of abstraction as to fail to define individuals. A more vital dimension of poetic and artistic wonder is intimated in a few scenes (which fail to incite the characters' responses). These poetic and artistic glimpses are sufficient sign that existence, from the author's point of view, is not complete nothingness. Moreover, repeated montage conflicts between characters' utterances and contradictory behaviour indicate Green's concern with the individual attitudes of a certain group of people. Accordingly, the endless series of juxtaposed scenes does not primarily reflect Green's tragic vision and recourse to an abstract, inorganic pattern. It expresses the monotony of the individual characters' existences, brought into ironic relief.

In the final analysis, the sure communication of tone, in Green's work, depends on the interaction between texture and structure, between images or scenes and their context. Thus, the textural ambiguities in *Nothing* and *Doting* appear in the right ironic light when viewed against monotonously juxtaposed episodes. The clarity of Green's metaphors also depends on context. Frank Kermode points out that 'symbols, like signals, are meaningless outside some determining context, some accepted scale or structure of significations'. He maintains that 'Until we are disposed to detect these structures our eye or ear remains innocent'.[15] The relevance of Kermode's statement to Green's work may best be elucidated through citing a passage from Virginia Woolf:

The sparrows fluttering, rising, and falling in jagged fountains were part of the pattern; the white and blue, barred with black branches. Sounds made harmonies with premeditation; the spaces between them were as significant as the sounds.[16]

Our eye remains 'innocent' to the individual signification of Virginia Woolf's birds and colours. Individuality, contrasts and disparities yield to a coherent order. The design serves as frame of reference for its elements. It does not represent ulterior reality, but represents the apprehension of existence as a harmonious, organic interdependence. However, whereas Green's incantatory scenes focus on the animation of finite objects, Virginia Woolf's concentrates on pattern. Her order is an order of 'premeditation', of movement away from finite reality. Her proclivity to abstraction exposes her to F. R. Leavis's evaluative criteria for a 'great' novel: it should embody 'a responsibility involving, of its very nature, imaginative sympathy, moral discrimination, and judgement of relative human value'.[17] In order to meet all of Leavis's requirements, form and a reality of individualized characters need to interact closely.

Green's novels contain an abundance of 'free aesthetic life' (a term with which Leavis associates a narrative method detrimental to moral delineation), but do not, like Virginia Woolf's, evince a susceptibility towards formal orderings.[18] Admittedly, the image of birds circulating among the machinery in the factory (*Living*) imparts a sense of poetic unity. From another point of view, however, the birds contrast to the lives of the workers by their freedom and vivacity; or they may act as metaphorical embodiments of the workers' unfulfilled dreams. Green's central

images do possess certain general meanings, but their functions
are relative to particular contexts. Thus, Green basically culti-
vates 'innocence' of perception. Consistent intelligible connections and aesthetic orderings are deliberately broken up, disorder
maintained. Fragmentation of structure is the secret behind
Green's creation of tone. Poetic qualities permeate his novels,
but form and content interact dynamically. Accordingly, human
reality, in the manner of characters and events, constantly
intrudes into the poetic sequences. Furthermore, vital human
perceptions repeatedly animate an inorganic, empirical world;
or poetic images interrupt a character's life-reluctance. In the
juncture of heterogeneous elements arises a consistent code of
tonal qualities. This web of insinuations produces an affirmative
human order based on natural human impulses. Its frame of
reference is Green's ideal of full sympathetic participation in
life.[19]

Only a montage-based approach can provide the key to
understanding Green's novels. The fact that he is basically a
realistic writer facilitates the determination of tone through
montage. Green passes critical comment on certain attitudes and
events through their discordant juxtaposition with vital human
needs. Richardson suggests that the montage trope accommodates the fusion of conflicting qualities:

> One image plays against the next, the old can be pushed up
> against the new, the tender with the harsh, the lovely with the
> sordid ... [to achieve] that overpowering sense of the disparity
> between what life has been or could be, and what it actually
> is.[20]

Green also perceives a dimension of poetic illumination and
order in the midst of empirical disorder. Montage of prosaic
description and poetic evocation affects the reader as a conjunction of the matter-of-fact world and the author's regenerating
subjective imagination. Juxtaposition operates between scenes
as well as between characters and images within a scene. This
is why Green's dynamic values of 'living' and 'loving' are best
accounted for in terms of Coleridge's poetic practice and of
Eisenstein's idea of filmic montage. Coleridge's polarization of
'sensuousness' and 'passion' assimilates subjective qualities and
objective fragments into a perceptual synthesis. In a basically

similar fashion, Eisenstein's 'emotional intensification' of colliding elements in filmic montage stimulates the spectator's synthesizing imagination. Both Coleridge's and Eisenstein's techniques inspire the spectator's or reader's attention to the visual present moment. Green's incorporation of realistic representational aspects in his poetic vision prevents the invocation of the kind of poetic order which Coleridge would term 'day-dreaming'. The image of human order, in Green's world, resides in the image of contradiction.

Appendix: Examples of Montage

Conflict of graphic directions arises from the opposition of two or more 'lines' of direction. These 'lines' can be either static or dynamic. As an example of this kind of conflict Eisenstein depicts a human figure crawling down across the prominent horizontal lines (static) of a flight of stone steps. In Eisenstein's film *Potemkin*, the emotive quality of the massacre on the Odessa steps is heightened in the following way: 'the *break-neck* movement of the *mass* downward leaps over into a *slowly solemn* movement upward of the mother's *lone* figure, carrying her dead son'.

Conflict of scales involves collision of different spatial dimensions. To illustrate, Eisenstein pictures a wide, open yard viewed through the narrow space of an overhanging roof.

Conflict of volumes derives from opposition in size. Eisenstein's example presents a huge, fat woman juxtaposed with a slender one.

Conflict of masses is described by Eisenstein as conflict between 'volumes filled with various intensities of light'. This kind of conflict also includes the counterpoint of different shades of colour. In Eisenstein's film, *Alexander Nevsky*, the sense of conflict is heightened by the opposition of the black-clothed Russian troops and the white-clothed Teutons.

An example from *Living* demonstrates Green's use of conflict of masses. As Lily goes to meet Bert,

> Night was mauve about her, mauve and cold. She only felt warmer....

228

She came nearer street lamps and then stumbled a little. Looking up she saw them, light sticking out from them, and as she came nearer so night left, excitement effervescing in her she put coat straight, and felt cold. When she stepped into cone of light of this lamp, night was outside and it might not have been night-time.

She met Bert at corner. . . .

They walked from cone of light into darkness and then again into lamplight, nor, so their feeling lulled them, was light or dark, only their feeling of both of them which was one warmth, infinitely greater. (*Living*, p.293)

The passage is cinematic in its close attention to transitions between light and dark. However, it is not an example of detailed realistic description for the purpose of being exact. Nor do light and dark, in this context, reveal any decipherable symbolic meaning. The light and darkness effects reflect Green's preoccupation with a 'non-representational' form which is essentially imagistic. Juxtaposition of visual images evokes a dynamic tension in the scene. The polarity of light and dark is intended to create response in the reader and to enhance the sense of Lily's apprehension, expectation and excitement concerning her date with her lover.

Conflict of depths is created by the counterpoint of foreground and background. Conflict of depths intensifies the emotive impact of a scene, as in *Potemkin*,

where the 'good people of Odessa' . . . send yawls with provisions to the side of the mutinous battleship. This sending of greetings is constructed on a distinct cross-cutting of two themes.

1. The yawls speeding towards the battleship.
2. The people of Odessa watching and waving.

At the end the two themes are merged. The composition is basically in two planes: depth and foreground. Alternately, the themes take on a dominant position, advancing to the foreground, and thrusting each other by turns to the background.

Close shots and long shots: rapid transitions between close and long shots form 'antagonistic pairs of pieces'; the second shot acts as an 'impulse of intensification'. Eisenstein provides an example of the close-up (also conflict of depths) from *Paradise Lost*, where Milton depicts the approach of the 'Host of Satan':

> at last
> Farr in th' Horizon to the North appeer'd
> From skirt to skirt a fierie Region, stretcht
> In battailous aspect, and *neerer view*
> Bristl'd with upright beams innumerable
> Of rigid Spears and Helmets throng'd, and Shields
> Various, with boastful Argument portraid,
> The Banded Powers of *Satan* hasting on
> With furious expedition....
>
> (First emphasis added)

Close-ups and composition in depth may also intensify an image of beauty. Eisenstein pictures a lilac bough and a distant background, the perception of which becomes a 'process whereby, from the overall structure of a picture, one of its elements progressively advances into the foreground' to imprint itself in the mind of the spectator. [Quoted in Yon Barna, *Eisenstein* (London, 1973), p.26]

Eisenstein stresses another important function of the close-up: its ability to dynamize images into a surreal unity; objective reality becomes a vivid metaphorical reflection of a subjective perception. This effect corresponds to Green's 'sensually palpable' depiction of Merode's knee in *Concluding*, producing the sensory impact of a close-up, which counteracts naturalism and death. Eisenstein points out that

> A healthy, handsome woman's body may, actually, be heightened to *an image of a life-affirming beginning*, which is what Dovzhenko had to have, to clash with his montage of the funeral in *Earth*.
>
> A skilfully leading montage creation with *close-ups*, taken in the 'Rubens manner', isolated from naturalism and abstracted in the necessary direction, could well have been lifted to such a 'sensually palpable' image.
>
> But the whole structure of *Earth* was doomed to failure,

because in place of such montage material the director cut into the funeral *long shots* of the interior of the peasant hut, and the naked woman flinging herself about there. And the spectator could not possibly separate out of this concrete, lifelike woman that generalized sensation of blazing fertility, of sensual life-affirmation, which the director wished to convey of all nature, as a pantheistic contrast to the theme of death and the funeral!

This was prevented by the ovens, pots, towels, benches, tablecloths – all those details of everyday life, from which the woman's body could easily have been freed by *the framing of the shot*, – so that *representational* naturalism would not interfere with the embodiment of the *conveyed metaphorical* task.

Conflict of planes is collision between graphic surfaces or areas. Eisenstein depicts the execution of a mother and her child by shooting. The ground on which the aiming soldiers stand is marked by horizontal lines that counter the vertical lines in the ground around the victims. Thus, the conflict of planes is fashioned by a conflict of graphic directions which deepens the sense of division between the executioners and the executed.

Conflict between matter and viewpoint, according to Eisenstein, is 'achieved by spatial distortion through camera-angle'. Eisenstein finds this conflict in the works of Picasso, 'where a face or a figure is presented from multiple viewpoints, and at varying stages of an action'. Furthermore,

the copperplate frontispiece to a seventeenth-century Spanish biography of St John of the Cross shows the saint at the moment he beholds the miraculous appearance of the crucifix. With striking effect, there is incorporated into the same plate a second view in perspective of the same crucifix – as seen from the saint's viewpoint.

Conflict between an event and its duration accentuates the importance of a certain content by highlighting the incongruence between the logical sequence of an event and its distortion by cinematic montage. The effect is 'achieved by *slow-motion* and *stop-motion*'.

Audio-visual counterpoint is produced by 'conflict between optical and acoustical experience'. Eisenstein says that Milton's *Paradise Lost*

> is a first-rate school in which to study montage and audio-visual relationships. . . . Studying the pages of his poem, and in each individual case analyzing the determining qualities and expressive effects of each example, we become extraordinarily enriched in experience of the audio-visual distribution of images in his sound-montage.

The movement of the 'Heavenly Hosts' produces these effects:

> Th' Imperial Ensign, which full high advanc't
> Shon like a Meteor streaming to the Wind,
> With Gemms and Golden lustre rich imblaz'd,
> Seraphic arms and Trophies: all the while
> Sonorous mettal blowing Martial sounds:
> At which the universal Host upsent
> A shout that tore Hells Concave, and beyond
> Frighted the Reign of *Chaos* and old Night.

Association montage. Eisenstein also presents a special form of montage which deals 'not only with the visible elements of the shots, but chiefly with chains of psychological association'. Association montage produces *emotional dynamization* giving birth to concepts. Eisenstein's first example is from his film *Strike*:

> the montage of the killing of the workers is actually a cross montage of this carnage with the butchering of a bull in an abattoir. Though the subjects are different, 'butchering' is the associative link. This made for a powerful emotional intensification of the scene.

A similar means of emotional dynamization is found in Pudovkin's film *Mother*. It shows 'the ice-break on the river, paralleled with the workers' demonstration'. In Eisenstein's *October*,

> the dramatic moment of the union of the Motorcycle Battalion with the Congress of Soviets was dynamized by shots of

abstractly spinning bicycle wheels, in association with the entrance of the new delegates. In this way the large-scale emotional content of the event was transformed into actual dynamics.

In another scene from *October*,

a trench crowded with soldiers appears to be crushed by an enormous gun-base that comes down inexorably. As an anti-militarist symbol seen from the viewpoint of subject alone, the effect is achieved by an apparent bringing together of an independently existing trench and an overwhelming military product, just as physically independent.

In *October*, association montage, used as symbolic montage, occurs

in the scene of Kornilov's *putsch*, which puts an end to Kerensky's Bonapartist dreams. Here one of Kornilov's tanks climbs up and crushes a plaster-of-Paris Napoleon standing on Kerensky's desk in the Winter Palace, a juxtaposition of purely symbolic significance.

'Cross-montage of dialogues' may also be included under the denomination of association montage. As Eisenstein points out, it is 'used with the same intention of expressive sharpening of idea'. Eisenstein quotes a passage from Flaubert's *Madame Bovary* in which the speech of a public orator interlaces the conversation of the two prospective lovers, Emma and Rodolphe.

Monsieur Derozerays got up, beginning another speech ... praise of the Government took up less space in it; religion and agriculture more. He showed in it the relations of these two, and how they had always contributed to civilization. Rodolphe with Madame Bovary was talking dreams, presentiments, magnetism. Going back to the cradle of society, the orator painted those fierce times when men lived on acorns in the heart of woods. Then they had left off the skins of beasts, had put on cloth, tilled the soil, planted the vine. Was this a good, and in this discovery was there not more of injury than gain? Monsieur Derozerays set himself this problem. From magnetism little by little Rodolphe had come to affinities, and while the president was citing Cincinnatus and his plough, Diocletian planting his cabbages, and the Emperors of China inaugurating the year by the sowing of seed, the young man was explaining to the young woman that these irresistible attractions find their cause in some previous state of experience.

'Thus we,' he said, 'why did we come to know one another? What chance willed it? It was because across the infinite, like two streams that flow but to unite, our special bents of mind had driven us towards each other.'

And he seized her hand; she did not withdraw it.

'For good farming generally!' cried the president.

'Just now, for example, when I went to your house'.

'To Monsieur Bizat of Quincampoix.'

'Did I know I should accompany you?'

'Seventy francs.'

'A hundred times I wished to go; and I followed you – I remained.'

'Manures!'

'And I shall remain to-night, to-morrow, all other days, all my life!' (*Madame Bovary*, tr. Eleanor Marx-Aveling (New York, 1929))

Eisenstein remarks that

this is an interweaving of two lines, thematically identical, equally trivial. The matter is sublimated to a monumental triviality, whose climax is reached through a continuation of this cross-cutting and word-play, with the significance always dependent on the juxtaposition of the two lines.

(Eisenstein citations from *Film Form*, pp.12–13, 57–9, 115–16, 170–1, 242; *Film Sense*, pp.54–5, 86]

Notes

CHAPTER ONE: INTRODUCTION

1. Mark Schorer, 'Introduction to Henry Green's World', *New York Times Book Review*, 9 Oct 1949, p. 1. Henry Green has been lavishly praised by a number of contemporary writers and critics. W. H. Auden has described him as 'the finest living English novelist'; John Updike considers his novels 'sufficiently unlike any others, sufficiently assured in their perilous, luminous fullness, to warrant the epithet incomparable' – Introduction to *Loving, Living, Party Going* (London, 1978). Walter Allen calls *Living* 'the best English novel of factory life' and awards Green a unique position in English literature in the 1930s: 'for any writer of the thirties to have been non-political, to have aimed at pure art, is in a way suspect; and Henry Green is very possibly the only pure artist of the thirties' – *Tradition and Dream: The English and American Novel from the Twenties to our Time* (London, 1964) p. 214, and 'An Artist of the Thirties', *Folios of New Writing*, 3 (1941) 143.
2. James Hall, 'The Fiction of Henry Green: Paradoxes of Pleasure-and-Pain', *Kenyon Review*, 19 (1957) p. 76.
3. Edward Stokes, *The Novels of Henry Green* (London, 1959) p. 7.
4. Henry Green, 'A Fire, a Flood, and the Price of Meat', *Listener*, 23 Aug 1951, p. 294.
5. Henry Green, 'A Novelist to his Readers', I, *Listener*, 9 Nov 1950, p. 506.
6. Henry Green, *Pack my Bag* (London, 1952) pp. 7–8.
7. In Terry Southern, 'Henry Green', *Writers at Work: The Paris Review Interviews*, 5 (Harmondsworth 1981) p. 104.
8. Henry Green, 'The English Novel of the Future', *Contact*, 1, no. 2 (1950) p. 22.
9. In Southern, 'Henry Green', *Writers at Work*, 5, p. 109.
10. Green, 'The English Novel of the Future', *Contact*, 1, no. 2, p. 23.
11. Wayne Booth, *The Rhetoric of Fiction* (Chicago, 1961) pp. 76, 149.
12. Frederick R. Karl, *A Reader's Guide to the Contemporary English Novel* (London, 1963) p. 186.
13. Green, 'A Novelist to his Readers', I, *Listener*, 9 Nov 1950, p. 506.
14. Green, 'The English Novel of the Future', *Contact*, 1, no. 2, p. 23.
15. In Southern, 'Henry Green', *Writers at Work*, 5, p. 110.
16. Henry Green, 'A Novelist to his Readers', II, *Listener*, 15 Mar 1951, p. 425.
17. In Southern, 'Henry Green', *Writers at Work*, 5, p. 103.
18. Green, 'A Novelist to his Readers', I, *Listener*, 9 Nov 1950, p. 506.

19. In Southern, 'Henry Green', *Writers at Work*, 5, p. 104.
20. Green, 'A Novelist to his Readers', I, *Listener*, 9 Nov 1950, p. 505.
21. Green, 'The English Novel of the Future', *Contact*, 1, no. 2, p. 21. In Alan Ross, 'Green, with Envy: Critical Reflections and an Interview', *London Magazine*, 6, no. 4 (1959) 22, Green also states that his central theme is love.
22. Green, 'The English Novel of the Future', *Contact*, 1, no. 2, p. 21.
23. Virginia Woolf, *The Voyage Out* (London, 1933) p. 416.
24. Virginia Woolf, *The Waves* (London, 1933) p. 119.
25. Virginia Woolf, *Mrs Dalloway* (London, 1933) pp. 35–6.
26. Quoted from Giorgio Melchiori, *The Tightrope Walkers: Studies of Mannerism in Modern English Literature* (London, 1956) p. 96. My discussion of Lawrence in relation to T. S. Eliot is indebted to Melchiori.
27. The lines from Lawrence and Eliot are quoted ibid., pp. 97–9. The references are to the American edition of Lawrence's *New Poems* (1920) and to the ending of 'Burnt Norton'.
28. Sergei Eisenstein, *Film Form: Essays in Film Theory*, ed. and tr. Jay Leyda (New York, 1968) p. 30.
29. Green's images escape classification by general literary or cultural conventions. Culler suggests that 'What is made intelligible by the conventions of genre is often less interesting than that which resists or escapes generic understanding, and so it should be no surprise that there arises, over and against the *vraisemblance* of genre, another level of *vraisemblance* whose fundamental device is to expose the artifice of generic conventions and expectations'. Due to the poetic form of Green's sunset scene, the reader 'must allow the dialectical opposition which the text presents to result in a synthesis at a higher level where the grounds of intelligibility are different' – Jonathan Culler, *Structuralist Poetics: Structuralism, Linguistics and the Study of Literature* (London, 1975) pp. 148, 151. For a definition of 'vraisemblance', see n. 35.
30. Green, *Pack my Bag*, p. 88.
31. Sergei Eisenstein, *The Film Sense*, ed. and tr. Jay Leyda (London, 1968) p. 24.
32. Green, *Pack my Bag*, p. 8.
33. In Southern, 'Henry Green', *Writers at Work*, 5, p. 102.
34. Roland Barthes, 'Criticism as Language', in *20th Century Literary Criticism*, ed. David Lodge (London, 1972) pp. 249–50.
35. One definition of 'vraisemblance' given by Tzvetan Todorov is that 'one can speak of the *vraisemblance* of a work in so far as it attempts to make us believe that it conforms to reality and not to its own laws. In other words, the *vraisemblable* is the mask which conceals the text's own laws and which we are supposed to take for a relation with reality' (quoted in Culler, *Structuralist Poetics*, p. 139). Culler suggests that the movement away from 'novelistic necessity' requires that generic terms of intelligibility 'are taken up in a higher *vraisemblance* or level of intelligibility, which is that of writing itself. The text finds its coherence by being interpreted as a narrator's exercise of language and production of meaning. To naturalize it at this level is to read it as a statement about the writing of novels, a critique of

mimetic fiction, an illustration of the production of a world by language' (pp. 149–50).
36. Green, 'The English Novel of the Future', *Contact*, 1, no. 2, p. 21.
37. Ibid.
38. Robert Richardson, *Literature and Film* (Bloomington, Ind., 1969) p. 67. Richardson writes that 'verbs are only one part of speech, to be sure, but they are crucial and one of the reasons why nearly everyone will concede the potential, if not the actual, power of the film may be its rich and varied range of ways to express action as verbs express it in writing'.
39. In 'The English Novel of the Future', *Contact*, 1, no. 2, p. 22, Green reveals his awareness of film's capacity to contract disparate elements of the narrative, to carry the novelist 'from one moment of action to another'. 'And while the cinema has had its influence, it is more than likely that in five years' time television will have a profound effect on novelists, and that narrative already split up into small scenes, will be split still further.'
40. Green, 'A Novelist to his Readers', I, *Listener*, 9 Nov 1950, pp. 505–6.
41. Eisenstein, *The Film Sense*, pp. 24, 37.
42. Sir Colin Anderson, quoted in Rod Mengham, *The Idiom of the Time: The Writings of Henry Green* (Cambridge, 1982) p. 15.
43. Green, *Pack my Bag*, pp. 198, 201.
44. Ibid., p. 211.
45. Quoted in Richardson, *Literature and Film*, p. 38.
46. Jonathan Culler, 'Structuralism and Literature' in *Contemporary Approaches to English Studies*, ed. Hilda Schiff (London, 1977) p. 63.
47. Green, 'A Novelist to his Readers', I, *Listener*, 9 Nov 1950, p. 506.
48. Booth, *The Rhetoric of Fiction*, p. 74.
49. I. A. Richards, *Practical Criticism: A Study of Literary Judgment* (London, 1954) p. 207.
50. Mario Praz, *Mnemosyne: The Parallel between Literature and the Visual Arts* (London, 1970) p. 214.
51. Henry Green, letter to Rosamond Lehmann, quoted in Lehmann, 'An Absolute Gift', *The Times Literary Supplement*, 6 Aug 1954, p. xli.
52. Green, 'A Novelist to his Readers', II, *Listener*, 15 Mar 1951, p. 425.
53. Ibid.
54. Eisenstein, *Film Form*, pp. 3–4.
55. Praz, *Mnemosyne*, pp. 214–15, and Melchiori, *The Tightrope Walkers*, pp. 204–6.
56. Praz, *Mnemosyne*, p. 29.
57. René Wellek, 'The Parellelism between Literature and Art', *English Institute Annual 1941* (New York, 1942) p. 62.
58. Jean Hagstrum, *The Sister Arts: The Tradition of Literary Pictorialism and English Poetry from Dryden to Gray* (Chicago, 1958) p. xxii.
59. Eisenstein, *Film Form*, p. 46.
60. Ibid.
61. Green, 'The English Novel of the Future', *Contact*, 1, no. 2, p. 23.
62. Eisenstein, *The Film Sense*, pp. 19, 33, 35.
63. Eisenstein, *Film Form*, pp. 150–1. The analogy between Eisenstein's and I. A. Richards's statements is suggested by James Allen Pearse, 'Montage

in Modern Fiction: A Cinematographic Approach to the Analysis of Ironic Tone in Joyce Cary's *The Horse's Mouth*' (unpublished doctoral dissertation, University of Arizona, 1973). Part of my work centres on basic montage principles also applied by Pearse to expose the irony of man's (notably Gulley Jimson's) struggle to impose form on an amorphous existence. However, whereas Pearse comments on the ironic irreconcilability of man and reality, Green is able to unify the two into images of sensual reciprocity. Green's comparison of 'tone' with the effect produced by colour in painting suggests that Green employs montage to give his fictional world 'a life of its own'. If a montage approach is to uncover expressive nuances in Green's three-dimensional world, the term must be applied and adapted to the examination of its multiform conflicts and values. It must identify that conceptual operation in which symbols and images, wonder and mysticism, become meaningful.

64. Sergei Eisenstein, *Film Essays with a Lecture*, ed. Jay Leyda (London, 1968) p. 83.
65. Eisenstein, *Film Form*, p. 47.
66. Cleanth Brooks, 'The Language of Paradox', in *20th Century Literary Criticism*, ed. Lodge, p. 296.
67. Eisenstein, *Film Form*, p. 47.
68. Melchiori, *The Tightrope Walkers*, p. 193.
69. Eisenstein, *Film Form*, pp. 249–50.
70. All of Eisenstein's montage conflicts introduced in this study are defined in the Appendix. They are listed in *Film Form*, pp. 39, 54–5.
71. Ibid., p. 50.
72. Ibid., pp. 37–8.
73. Ibid., p. 38.
74. Ibid., p. 30.
75. Ibid., p. 5.
76. 'Association montage' is also defined in the Appendix.
77. Eisenstein, *Film Form*, pp. 235–6.
78. In Southern, 'Henry Green', *Writers at Work*, 5, p. 102, Green confirms that *Blindness* and *Pack my Bag* 'are mostly autobiographical. But where they are about myself, they are not necessarily accurate as a portrait; they aren't photographs. After all, no one knows what he is like, he just tries to give some sort of picture of his time. Not like a cat to fight its image in the mirror.'
79. Green, *Pack my Bag*, p. 54.
80. Henry Green, *Blindness*, in *'Nothing', 'Doting', 'Blindness'* (London, 1979) p. 442.
81. Ibid., p. 375.
82. Ibid., p. 470.
83. Ibid., p. 443.
84. Green, *Pack my Bag*, p. 67.

CHAPTER TWO: 'LIVING'

1. Keith C. Odom, *Henry Green* (Boston, Mass., 1978) p. 49.

2. John Russell, *Henry Green: Nine Novels and an Unpacked Bag* (New Brunswick, 1960) p. 81.
3. In Ross, 'Green, with Envy', *London Magazine*, 6, no. 4, p. 22.
4. Russell comments on structural parallels between Craigan and Dupret (*Henry Green*, p. 79).
5. In Southern, 'Henry Green', *Writers at Work*, 5, p. 108, Green states that the omission of the article in *Living* is a device 'to make that book as taut and spare as possible, to fit the proletarian life I was then leading'. Besides, Green says, 'I suppose the more you leave out, the more you highlight what you leave in.'
6. W. B. Yeats, 'The Symbolism of Poetry', in *20th Century Literary Criticism*, ed. Lodge, p. 33.
7. Eisenstein, *Film Form*, pp. 237–8.
8. Stokes, *The Novels of Henry Green*, p. 135.
9. Melchiori, *The Tightrope Walkers*, p. 194.

CHAPTER THREE: 'CAUGHT' AND 'BACK'

1. Eisenstein, *Film Form*, p. 240.
2. A. Kingsley Weatherhead, *A Reading of Henry Green* (Seattle, 1961) p. 66.
3. This montage conflict is also defined in the Appendix.
4. Stokes, *The Novels of Henry Green*, p. 157.
5. Eisenstein, *The Film Sense*, pp. 100, 120.
6. Hans Kreitler and Shulamidt Kreitler, *Psychology of the Arts* (Durham, NC, 1972) pp. 94–101. Kreitler and Kreitler have studied the ways in which modern abstract painters create tension or conflict by juxtaposition of 'two or more dissimilar forms'. They discuss how triangles in different positions may in themselves be tension-laden. For example, 'A triangle with its apex down is experienced as less stable than a triangle with its apex up'. The image of Prudence standing at the apex of a vibrant triangle is likely to produce formal tension. On the other hand, a square or rectangle is a 'good gestalt'. Seen from the point of view of abstract art, Richard's withdrawal from the vibrant triangle towards a static rectangular form may suggest, ironically, his attempted escape from what disturbs the stasis of his dream-world.
7. Green, *Pack my Bag*, p. 54.
8. Joseph Conrad, *Youth: A Narrative* (London, 1967) p. 20.
9. Ibid., p. 30.
10. Ibid., p. 25.
11. Green, 'The English Novel of the Future', *Contact*, 1, no. 2, p. 21.
12. James Joyce, *A Portrait of the Artist as a Young Man* (London, 1950) p. 234.
13. Virginia Woolf, *To the Lighthouse* (London, 1927) pp. 311, 319–20.
14. Stokes, *The Novels of Henry Green*, p. 90.
15. M. H. Abrams, *A Glossary of Literary Terms*, 3rd edn (New York, 1957) p. 81.
16. Praz notes a 'faint echo' of Gertrude Stein in Green's work (*Mnemosyne*, p. 214).
17. Stokes, *The Novels of Henry Green*, p. 167.

CHAPTER FOUR: 'LOVING'

1. Stokes, *The Novels of Henry Green*, p. 75.
2. Lehmann, 'An Absolute Gift', *The Times Literary Supplement*, 6 Aug 1954, p. xli.
3. Green, 'The English Novel of the Future', *Contact*, 1, no. 2, p. 23.
4. Northrop Frye, *A Natural Perspective: The Development of Shakespearean Comedy and Romance* (London, 1965) pp. 48, 57.
5. Green, 'The English Novel of the Future', *Contact*, 1, no. 2, p. 23.
6. Dorothy Van Ghent, *The English Novel: Form and Function* (London, 1953) p. 93.
7. Ibid., pp. 94–5, 97.
8. Ibid., p. 98.
9. Coleridge, *Biographia Literaria*, p. 167.
10. Barbara Davidson, 'The World of Loving', *Wisconsin Studies in Contemporary Literature*, 2 (Winter 1961) 77.
11. In Ross, 'Green, with Envy', *London Magazine*, 6, no. 4 (1959) 22–3.
12. Ibid., p. 22.
13. Green indicates the central conflicts of *Loving* in Southern, 'Henry Green', *Writers at Work*, 5, pp. 110–11: 'The British servants in Eire while England is at war is Raunce's conflict, and one meant to be satirically funny. It is a crack at the absurd southern Irish and at the same time a swipe at the British servants, who yet remain human beings. But it is meant to torpedo that woman and her daughter-in-law, the employers.'
14. Davidson, 'The World of Loving', *Wisconsin Studies in Contemporary Literature*, 2, p. 77.
15. Earle Labor, 'Henry Green's Web of Loving', *Critique*, 4 (Autumn–Winter 1960–1) p. 31.
16. Although Green does not confirm the previously suggested correspondence of *Loving* with Elizabethan comedy, such a comparison reveals interesting similarities. As in *Loving*, *All's Well* opens with a reference to a funeral. The comic drive towards a festive conclusion involves defiance of 'laws ... preoccupied with trying to regulate the sexual drive, and so work counter to the wishes of the hero and the heroine'. Moreover, the suggestion that love releases Raunce from a certain mechanical behaviour and tyrannical whims points to Elizabethan comedy. 'Love conquers all, in general: it also conquers certain enemies of its own in particular. Of these, one of the most important is lust. Love is a specific relation between two people which individualizes them both; lust is an unspecified drive which cares nothing for its object' (Frye, *A Natural Perspective*, pp. 74, 86).
17. Hall, 'The Fiction of Henry Green', *Kenyon Review*, 19, p. 81.
18. Bruce Bassoff, *Toward Loving: The Poetics of the Novel and the Practice of Henry Green* (Columbia, SC, 1975) p. 153.

CHAPTER FIVE: 'CONCLUDING'

1. Stokes, *The Novels of Henry Green*, p. 170.

2. Green, 'A Novelist to his Readers', I, *Listener*, 9 Nov 1950, p. 506.
3. Frye, *A Natural Perspective*, p. 139.
4. Green, *Pack my Bag*, pp. 27–8.
5. Frye, *A Natural Perspective*, p. 122.
6. Northrop Frye, 'The Archetypes of Literature', in *20th Century Literary Criticism*, ed. Lodge, p. 432.
7. Frye, *A Natural Perspective*, p. 133.
8. Frye, 'The Archetypes of Literature', in *20th Century Literary Criticism*, ed. Lodge, p. 432.
9. Coleridge, 'This Lime-Tree Bower my Prison', *The Complete Poems of Samuel Taylor Coleridge*, ed. Morchard Bishop (London, 1954) pp. 158–60.
10. Hall, 'The Fiction of Henry Green', *Kenyon Review*, 19, p. 88.
11. *All's Well* and *Concluding* show similar thematic concerns, which support the previous interpretation. The King approves Helena's and Bertram's reunion, despite Bertram's dubious integrity. The King's geniality springs from his awareness that life, because competing with death, is best served by sympathy and tolerance. He forgives Bertram his rascality knowing that life is precious:

> Not one word more of the consumed time;
> Let's take the instant by the forward top;
> For we are old, and on our quick'st decrees
> Th'inaudible and noiseless foot of time
> Steals ere we can effect them.

Quoted from *All's Well that Ends Well*, ed. G. K. Hunter (London, 1967) pp. 131–2.

CHAPTER SIX: 'PARTY GOING', 'NOTHING' AND 'DOTING'

1. Stokes, *The Novels of Henry Green*, p. 86.
2. Frank Kermode, *The Genesis of Secrecy: On the Interpretation of Narrative* (London, 1979) pp. 8–10.
3. These images and scenes are also quoted by Stokes to illustrate the sense of remoteness (*The Novels of Henry Green*, pp. 204–5).
4. Kermode, *The Genesis of Secrecy*, pp. 8–9.
5. Donald S. Taylor, 'Catalytic Rhetoric: Henry Green's Theory of the Modern Novel', *Criticism*, 7 (1968) 92.
6. Green, 'A Novelist to his Readers', I, *Listener*, 9 Nov 1950, p. 505.
7. Robert S. Ryf, *Henry Green*, Columbia Essays on Modern Writers, 29 (New York, 1967) p. 38.
8. Russell, *Henry Green*, p. 203.
9. Green, 'The English Novel of the Future', *Contact*, 1, no. 2, p. 23.
10. Ibid.
11. Melchiori, *The Tightrope Walkers*, p. 209.

CHAPTER SEVEN: CONCLUSION

1. Alain Robbe-Grillet, 'A Future for the Novel', in *20th Century Literary Criticism*, ed. Lodge, pp. 467–72.
2. Alain Robbe-Grillet, *The Voyeur*, tr. Richard Howard (London, 1959) p. 3.
3. David Lodge argues that 'Robbe-Grillet succeeds as a novelist by violating the consistency of his theory' (*20th Century Literary Criticism*, p. 466).
4. Robbe-Grillet, 'A Future for the Novel', ibid., p. 470.
5. Keats, 'The Eve of St Agnes', *The Poems of John Keats*, ed. Miriam Allott (London, 1970) p. 472.
6. M. H. Abrams, *The Mirror and the Lamp: Romantic Theory and the Critical Tradition* (New York, 1953) p. 242.
7. Henry James, *The Ambassadors*, II (London, 1903) pp. 225, 228, 230.
8. William Empson, *Some Versions of Pastoral* (London, 1935) p. 14.
9. Northrop Frye, *Anatomy of Criticism: Four Essays* (Princeton, NJ, 1957) pp. 99, 144, 176.
10. Ibid., pp. 182–3. Frye suggests that some of Shakespeare's romantic comedies centre on 'the drama of the green world, its plot being assimilated to the ritual theme of the triumph of life and love over the waste land'. In terms of primitive myths, 'The green world charges the comedies with the symbolism of the victory of summer over winter.'
11. Ibid., p. 184.
12. Richardson, *Literature and Film*, p. 131.
13. Quoted from Praz, *Mnemosyne*, p. 235.
14. Melchiori, comparing Green's technique to Cubism, asserts that *Nothing* and *Doting* produce 'abstract emotions through the intellect rather than the heart'. He compares them to a Mozart opera and the work of Schoenberg in their 'perfect structure', their 'beautiful . . . delicate sequence of scenes, held together by a constant rhythm . . . a musical edifice made of elegant *nothings*' (*The Tightrope Walkers*, pp. 209, 211, emphasis added). Melchiori implies (his view is echoed by Praz, *Mnemosyne*, p. 215) that the abstract design is a device by which Green is desperately 'shoring fragments against his ruins'.
15. Frank Kermode, 'What is Art?', *New York Review of Books*, 20 Feb 1964, p. 1.
16. Woolf, *Mrs Dalloway*, p. 36.
17. F. R. Leavis, *The Great Tradition* (London, 1980) p. 41.
18. Ibid., p. 41. The expression 'absence of free aesthetic life' is one used by Henry James to characterize George Eliot's neat, symmetrical plots. He claims that her ' "figures and situations" are "not *seen* in the irresponsible plastic way" '.
19. There is no fundamental difference between Green's creation of tone through montage and what is associated by Wayne Booth's term 'implied author'. Booth dissociates himself from 'objective narration', which 'offers special temptations to the reader to go astray. Even when it presents characters whose conduct the author deeply deplores, it presents through the seductive medium of their own self-defending rhetoric'. However, the kind of objectivity involved in Green's montage technique – notably

that different realities are represented through visualization rather than explained by an intrusive author – is not indebted to Flaubert's model of dispassionate narration, a technique, Booth claims, which divorces form and content. Green's montage method serves as authorial commentary on the fictional landscape, a substitute for the rhetorical voice and moral sensibility of the narrator persona (Booth, *The Rhetoric of Fiction*, pp. 388, 399).

20. Richardson, *Literature and Film*, pp. 114–15.

Bibliography

PRIMARY SOURCES

Green, Henry, 'Apologia', *Folios of New Writing*, Autumn 1941, pp. 44–51.
——, *Back* (London, 1946).
——, 'Before the Great Fire', *London Magazine*, 7, no. 12 (Dec 1960) 12–27.
——, *Caught* (London, 1943).
——, *Concluding* (London, 1948).
——, 'The English Novel of the Future', *Contact*, 1, no. 2 (1950) 21–4.
——, 'A Fire, a Flood, and the Price of Meat,' *Listener*, 23 Aug 1951, pp. 293–4.
——, 'Firefighting', *Texas Quarterly*, 3, no. 4 (1960) 105–20.
——, *Loving* (1945), *Living* (1929), *Party Going* (1939) (London, 1978).
——, 'The Lull', *New Writing and Daylight*, Summer 1943, pp. 11–21.
——, 'Mr Jones', *Penguin New Writing*, 14 (July–Sep 1942) 15–20.
——, *Nothing* (1950), *Doting* (1952), *Blindness* (1926) (London, 1979).
——, 'A Novelist to his Readers', I, *Listener*, 9 Nov 1950, pp. 505–6.
——, 'A Novelist to his Readers', II, *Listener*, 15 Mar 1951, pp. 425–7.
——, *Pack my Bag* (London, 1952).
——, 'A Rescue', *Penguin New Writing*, 4 (Mar 1941) 88–93.
——, 'The Spoken Word as Written', review of *The Oxford Book of English Talk*, ed. James Sutherland, *Spectator*, 4 Sep 1953, p. 248.
——, 'An Unfinished Novel', *London Magazine*, 6, no. 4 (Apr 1959) 11–17.

SECONDARY SOURCES

(a) *Commentary on Green's work*

Allen, Walter, 'An Artist of the Thirties', *Folios of New Writing*, 3 (Spring 1941) 149–58.
——, 'Henry Green', *Penguin New Writing*, 25 (1945) 144–55.
——, *Tradition and Dream: The English and American Novel from the Twenties to our Time* (London, 1964).
Bassoff, Bruce, *Toward Loving: The Poetics of the Novel and the Practice of Henry Green* (Columbia, SC, 1975).
Breit, Harvey, 'Talk with Henry Green – And a P. S.', *New York Times Book Review*, 19 Feb 1950, p. 29.
Churchill, Thomas, '*Loving*: A Comic Novel', *Critique*, 4 (1961) 29–38.

244

Cosman, Max, 'The Elusive Henry Green', *Commonweal*, 72 (Sep 1960) 472–5.

Davidson, Barbara, 'The World of Loving', *Wisconsin Studies in Contemporary Literature*, 2 (Winter 1961) 65–78.

Dennis, Nigel, 'The Double Life of Henry Green', *Life*, 4 Aug 1952, pp. 83–94.

Hall, James, 'The Fiction of Henry Green: Paradoxes of Pleasure-and-Pain', *Kenyon Review*, 19 (Winter 1957) 85–97.

Johnson, Bruce, 'Loving: A Study of Henry Green' (unpublished doctoral dissertation, Northwestern University 1959).

Karl, Frederick R., *A Reader's Guide to the Contemporary English Novel* (London, 1963).

Kettle, Arnold, *An Introduction to the English Novel*, ii (London, 1953).

Labor, Earle, 'Henry Green's Web of Loving', *Critique*, 4 (Autumn–Winter 1960–1) 29–40.

Lehmann, Rosamond, 'An Absolute Gift', *The Times Literary Supplement*, 6 Aug 1954, p. xli.

Melchiori, Giorgio, *The Tightrope Walkers: Studies of Mannerism in Modern English Literature* (London, 1956).

Mengham, Rod, *The Idiom of the Time: The Writings of Henry Green* (Cambridge, 1982).

Odom, Keith C., *Henry Green* (Boston, Mass., 1978).

Phelps, Robert, 'The Vision of Henry Green', *Hudson Review*, 5 (Winter 1953) 614–20.

Powell, Anthony, *To Keep the Ball Rolling: The Memoirs of Anthony Powell*, i: *Infants of the Spring* (London, 1976); ii: *Messengers of Day* (London, 1978); iv: *The Strangers All Are Gone* (London, 1982).

Praz, Mario, *Mnemosyne: The Parallel between Literature and the Visual Arts* (London, 1970).

Quinton, Anthony, 'A French View of *Loving*', *London Magazine*, 6, no. 4 (1959) 25–35.

Ross, Alan, 'Green, with Envy: Critical Reflections and an Interview', *London Magazine*, 6, no. 4 (1959) 18–24.

Russell, John, *Henry Green: Nine Novels and an Unpacked Bag* (New Brunswick, NJ, 1960).

——, 'There it is', *Kenyon Review*, 26, no. 1 (Winter 1964) 433–65.

Ryf, Robert S., *Henry Green*, Columbia Essays on Modern Writers, 29 (New York, 1967).

Schorer, Mark, 'Introduction to Henry Green's World', *New York Times Book Review*, 9 Oct 1949, pp. 1, 22.

——, 'The Real and Unreal Worlds of Henry Green', *New York Herald Tribune Book Review*, 31 Dec 1950, p. 5.

Shapiro, Stephen A., 'Henry Green's *Back*: The Presence of the Past', *Critique*, 7 (1964) 87–96.

Southern, Terry, 'Henry Green', *Writers at Work: The Paris Review Interviews*, 5 (Harmondsworth, 1981) 97–111.

Stokes, Edward, *The Novels of Henry Green* (London, 1959).

Taylor, Donald S., 'Catalytic Rhetoric: Henry Green's Theory of the Modern Novel', *Criticism*, 7 (1968) 81–99.

Tindall, William, *The Literary Symbol* (New York, 1955).

Toynbee, Philip, 'The Novels of Henry Green', *Partisan Review*, 16 (May 1949) 487–97.

Turner, Myron, 'The Imagery of Wallace Stevens and Henry Green', *Wisconsin Studies in Contemporary Literature*, 8 (1967) 60–77.

Unterecker, John, 'Fiction at the Edge of Poetry: Durrell, Beckett, Green', *Forms of Modern British Fiction*, ed. Alan Warren Friedman (London, 1975).

Weatherhead, A. Kingsley, *A Reading of Henry Green* (Seattle, 1961).

——, 'Structure and Texture in Henry Green's Latest Novels', *Accent*, 19 (Spring 1959) pp. 111–22.

Welty, Eudora, 'Henry Green, a Novelist of the Imagination', *Texas Quarterly*, 4 (1961) 246–56.

(b) *A select list of other works*

Abrams, M. H., *A Glossary of Literary Terms*, 3rd edn (New York, 1957).

——, *The Mirror and the Lamp: Romantic Theory and the Critical Tradition* (New York, 1953).

Barna, Yon, *Eisenstein*, tr. Lise Hunter and ed. Oliver Stallybrass (London, 1973).

Booth, Wayne, *The Rhetoric of Fiction* (Chicago, 1961).

Coleridge, Samuel Taylor, *Complete Poems*, ed. Morchard Bishop (London, 1954).

——, *Biographia Literaria*, ed. George Watson (London, 1965).

Conrad, Joseph, *'Youth: A Narrative', 'Heart of Darkness', 'The End of the Tether'* (London, 1967).

Culler, Jonathan, *Structuralist Poetics: Structuralism, Linguistics and the Study of Literature* (London, 1975).

——, 'Structuralism and Literature' in *Contemporary Approaches to English Studies*, ed. Hilda Schiff (London, 1977).

Dickens, Charles, *Hard Times* (London, 1955).

Eisenstein, Sergei, *Film Essays with a Lecture*, ed. Jay Leyda (London, 1968).

——, *Film Form: Essays in Film Theory*, ed. and tr. Jay Leyda (New York, 1949).

——, *The Film Sense*, ed. and tr. Jay Leyda (London, 1968).

——, *Notes of a Film Director* (New York, 1978).

——, *Potemkin: A Shot by Shot Presentation*, ed. David Mayer (New York, 1972).

Eliot, T. S., *Collected Poems 1909–1962* (London, 1963).

Empson, William, *Some Versions of Pastoral* (London, 1935).

Frye, Northrop, *Anatomy of Criticism: Four Essays* (Princeton, NJ, 1957).

——, *A Natural Perspective: The Development of Shakespearean Comedy and Romance* (London, 1965).

Hagstrum, Jean, *The Sister Arts: The Tradition of Literary Pictorialism and English Poetry from Dryden to Gray* (Chicago, 1958).

James, Henry, *The Ambassadors* (London, 1903).

Joyce, James, *A Portrait of the Artist as a Young Man* (London, 1950).

Keats, John, *Poems*, ed. Miriam Allott (London 1970).

Kermode, Frank, *The Genesis of Secrecy: On the Interpretation of Narrative* (London, 1979).

——, 'What is Art?', *New York Review of Books*, 20 Feb 1964, pp. 1–2.

Kracauer, Siegfried, *Nature of Film: The Redemption of Physical Reality* (London, 1961).

Kreitler, Hans and Shulamidt, *Psychology of the Arts* (Durham, NC, 1972).

Leavis, F. R., *The Great Tradition* (London, 1980).

Lodge, David (ed.), *20th Century Literary Criticism* (London, 1972).

Muecke, D. C., *The Compass of Irony* (London, 1969).

Pearse, James A., 'Montage in Modern Fiction: A Cinematographic Approach to the Analysis of Ironic Tone in Joyce Cary's *The Horse's Mouth*' (unpublished doctoral dissertation, University of Arizona 1973).

Read, Herbert, 'The Poet and the Film' in *A Coat of Many Colours* (London, 1945).

Richards, I. A., *Practical Criticism: A Study of Literary Judgment* (London, 1954).

Richardson, Robert, *Literature and Film* (Bloomington, Ind., 1969).

Robbe-Grillet, Alain, *The Voyeur*, tr. Richard Howard (London, 1959).

Shakespeare, William, *All's Well That Ends Well*, ed. G. K. Hunter (London, 1967).

Stedman, Henry W., *Battle of the Flames* (London, 1942).

Sypher, Wylie, *Rococo to Cubism in Art and Literature* (New York, 1960).

Van Ghent, Dorothy, *The English Novel: Form and Function* (London, 1953).

Wellek, René, 'The Parallelism between Literature and Art', *English Institute Annual 1941* (New York, 1942) pp. 29–63.

——, *A History of Modern Criticism: 1750–1950: The Romantic Age* (London, 1955).

Woolf, Virginia, 'The Movies and Reality', *New Republic*, 4 Aug 1926.

——, *Mrs Dalloway* (London, 1933).

——, *To The Lighthouse* (London, 1927).

——, *The Voyage Out* (London, 1933).

——, *The Waves* (London, 1933).

Index